READING FOR THE DISADVANTAGED

Reading for the Disadvantaged

Problems of Linguistically Different Learners

edited by

THOMAS D. HORN

The University of Texas
at Austin

A PROJECT OF THE INTERNATIONAL READING ASSOCIATION

Harcourt, Brace & World, Inc.

NEW YORK / CHICAGO / SAN FRANCISCO / ATLANTA

ISBN: 0–15–575590–0 hardbound, 0–15–575591–9 paperbound

Library of Congress Catalog Card Number: 74–113708

Printed in the United States of America

Preface

In this decade, reading will be a more important part of the school curriculum than ever before as teachers seek to fulfill the mandate of the Commissioner of Education, James E. Allen, "that by the end of the 1970's the right to read shall be a reality for all." Attention will be paid particularly to the long neglected segment of the population variously known as the disadvantaged, the culturally different, the culturally deprived, and the culturally antagonized. This focus is the result of a nationwide re-examination of educational and social objectives, stimulated originally by the launching of Sputnik and the initiation of President Johnson's Great Society program, that has exposed the urgent need for inter-disciplinary cooperation in confronting the educational problems of the disadvantaged. It has become clear that students of education and in-service teachers need broader understanding of these pupils in order to find ways of treating their learning difficulties successfully.

Reading for the Disadvantaged, written by twenty-four reading specialists, linguists, sociologists, and psychologists, is interdisciplinary in approach. The book was conceived in early 1965 by Millard H. Black, then Elementary Reading Supervisor for the Los Angeles City School Districts, who proposed the project to Dorothy Kendell Bracken, 1964–65 President of the International Reading Association. A committee of IRA members, with Millard Black as chairman, was appointed to plan the book. Millard Black's assignment as Acting Administrator of Curriculum for the Los Angeles City School Districts eventually forced him to request relief from the chairman's duties, and I assumed the committee chairmanship in March, 1968. That the content and organization of

v

vi   *Preface*

Reading for the Disadvantaged are almost precisely those outlined in Millard
Black's proposal is a remarkable tribute to his creative thinking and organiza-
tional ability.

Parts I and II of the book, "Backgrounds" and "Language," provide the
social, economic, psychological, and linguistic settings for understanding the
reading problems of disadvantaged children. Chapters 2 and 7 contain discussions of the social patterns and the language characteristics of specific groups.
Part III, "Implications for Teachers," includes a series of recommendations for
teachers of all grade levels from preschool through high school that are based
on the observations made in the first two parts. A number of issues and divergent
views are in healthy evidence. There are no easy answers, but this book does
provide promising suggestions for making learning to read a more successful
and more personally meaningful experience.

Leo Fay, 1968–69 IRA President, and Ralph Staiger, Executive Secretary-
Treasurer of the IRA, read the complete manuscript and gave valuable counsel
and unfailing support throughout the project. The manuscript was also reviewed
by Altee Anderson, Sophie W. Aramburo, Charlotte K. Brooks, Mildred Freeman, Nick Garza, Florence Nelson, and Eugene Skinner. Althea Beery gave
valuable assistance during early planning of the book, when she served as a
member of the IRA Committee on Reading for the Disadvantaged. During the
phase of format development the 1968–69 committee members were extremely
helpful: Altee Anderson, Sophie W. Aramburo, Millard H. Black, Charlotte K.
Brooks, S. Alan Cohen, Leatrice Emeruwa, Mildred Freeman, Harvey Gold-
man, Anne Harris, Phillip Harris, and Gertrude Whipple. My thanks go also
to Mrs. Reeda Lee Anderson and Mrs. Jeannie Darling for their considerable
assistance during preparation of the manuscript, editing, and proofreading.

I would be remiss if I did not acknowledge the influence over the years of a
great teacher, a man whose nickname became my given name; this teacher was
also my father, the late Ernest Horn. Finally, I wish to express my appreciation
to my daughter Diane for bringing to my attention a bit of information on the
title page of my prized copy of Comenius (1673) that I sincerely hope is not a
prophecy for this book, "formerly translated by Tho. Horn: afterwards much
corrected and amended . . . ."

THOMAS D. HORN

Contributors

Alvin L. Bertrand
Departments of Sociology and Rural Sociology
Louisiana State University

Alberta M. Castaneda
Department of Curriculum and Instruction
The University of Texas at Austin

S. Alan Cohen
Reading and Language Arts Center
Ferkauf Graduate School
Yeshiva University

Dorothy Ebert
Austin (Texas) Independent School District

Joe L. Frost
Department of Curriculum and Instruction
The University of Texas at Austin

Frank J. Guszak
Department of Curriculum and Instruction
The University of Texas at Austin

William R. Harmer
Director, Learning Disabilities Center
The University of Texas at Austin

Robert J. Havighurst
Department of Education
University of Chicago

Contributors

Thomas D. Horn
Department of Curriculum and Instruction
The University of Texas at Austin

Kenneth R. Johnson
College of Education
University of Illinois at Chicago Circle

James L. Kinneavy
Departments of Curriculum
and Instruction and English
The University of Texas at Austin

William Labov
Department of Linguistics
Columbia University

Raven I. McDavid, Jr.
Departments of English and Linguistics
University of Chicago

Robert W. MacMillan
Department of Education
University of Rhode Island

William Madsen
Department of Anthropology
University of California, Santa Barbara

Clyde I. Martin
Department of Curriculum and Instruction
The University of Texas at Austin

Newton S. Metfessel
Department of Educational Psychology
University of Southern California

Albar A. Peña
Director, Bilingual Education Programs
Division of Plans and Supplementary Centers
Bureau of Elementary and Secondary Education
United States Office of Education
Washington, D. C.

William L. Rutherford
Department of Curriculum and Instruction
The University of Texas at Austin

Muriel R. Saville
Department of English
Texas A & M University

Mark W. Seng
Department of Curriculum and Instruction
The University of Texas at Austin

L. Jean York
Department of Curriculum and Instruction
The University of Texas at Austin

Robert W. Young
Area Tribal Operations Office
Bureau of Indian Affairs
Albuquerque, N. Mex.

Miles V. Zintz
Department of Elementary Education
University of New Mexico

Contents

READING FOR THE DISADVANTAGED

Introduction

Thomas D. Horn

IF OUR historic goals of individual opportunity and literacy are to be realized, contributions from all appropriate disciplines must be brought to focus in classroom language instruction, that is, in listening, speaking, reading, and writing. The organization and content of *Reading for the Disadvantaged: Problems of Linguistically Different Learners* reflect this interdisciplinary point of view. Listening-speaking abilities are considered of primary importance to beginning reading. Social, economic, psychological, and linguistic factors that will affect a child's probable success in learning to read and the profits he might gain from competent reading skills are clearly reflected in his language capabilities and conation level.

The various authors of this book have purposely excluded those handicaps that are typically handled by the field of special education and have utilized instead significant minority groups as points of focus. Concern for the mentally and physically handicapped has been manifested for years, but until relatively recently, however, very little concern has been evidenced for the linguistically different. In fact, over the years, Spanish-speaking and black children have erroneously been placed in special-education classes on the basis of tests that are invalid for children with linguistic differences. This represents one more item on the list of educational crimes committed against linguistically different learners.

Widespread confusion surrounds attempts to compensate for factors causing reading disability in so-called disadvantaged students. The assumption is often made that economic poverty alone is the prime cause of educational disadvantagedness; in fact, proper diagnosis of reading difficulties reveals a wide

1

range of causes. The source of the confusion is the absence of a commonly accepted working definition for the term "disadvantaged," that gives specific attention to such causal factors as intelligence, motivation, economic poverty, parental attitudes, physical characteristics, mental characteristics, personality, oral language, ethnicity, range of interests, work habits, values, self-concept, cultural context, as well as the specific nature of an individual's reading problem.

Webster's Third International Dictionary defines *disadvantaged* as "lacking in the basic resources or conditions (as standard housing, medical and educational facilities, civil rights) believed to be necessary for an equal position in society," and *disadvantage* as "the state or fact of being without advantage: an unfavorable, an inferior, or prejudicial condition . . . an unfavorable or prejudicial quality or circumstances: handicap." These definitions fail to suggest the wide range of kinds and causes of disadvantagedness or to reflect the scope of the term as it is used in this book.

Any individual may be disadvantaged socially, economically, psychologically, and/or linguistically, depending upon the particular social milieu in which he is attempting to function at a given time. Indeed, he may be completely oblivious to his disadvantaged condition and perceive others in the group as being disadvantaged rather than himself.

The state of disadvantagedness is a relative matter and may cover a wide range of situations. The mentally retarded son of a highly successful dentist is disadvantaged; a college-bound high school student attending a school too small to maintain an adequate academic program is disadvantaged; an urban family with a $3000 annual income is usually more disadvantaged than a rural family of the same size with the same income; a college professor's daughter who has not learned to read by the end of the second grade is disadvantaged; an individual who is turned down for a job because of language differences and/or skin color is disadvantaged; a deaf child is disadvantaged; a student who cannot afford school activities, supplies, or books is disadvantaged. Thus, any person may be described as disadvantaged who, for any reason or reasons, is unable to realize his potential fully or to enter the mainstream of life in his community. Although there is obvious emphasis in this book on socioeconomic factors as identifiers of the existence and extent of disadvantagedness, these factors alone are not sufficient to define the term adequately.

Definitions of the bases for being considered disadvantaged vary from situation to situation, from group to group, and from person to person, depending on personal values. A basic concern of this book is to explore possible solutions to educational problems—reading problems in particular—that arise from the differences in the values held by persons responsible for educational programs and by school patrons who evidence one or more of the characteristics that identify them as disadvantaged.

When this book was in the planning stages, it became apparent that the role of linguistic differences as a major contributing factor to reading disability was being generally misunderstood or overlooked entirely by both educators and laymen. As the subtitle, "Problems of Linguistically Different Learners," suggests, this book has two special aims: (1) to direct attention to the crucial part that linguistic differences play in the state of being disadvantaged; and (2) to highlight the need to meet the problems of linguistically different learners who, though not otherwise disadvantaged, are having serious language-based problems in reading.

When one speaks of a linguistically different learner, the question immediately arises, Different from whom or from what? Linguists are fond of pointing out that every person has, in effect, his own personal dialect (or idiolect) containing certain idiosyncrasies peculiar only to him. Likewise, certain ethnic groups have language characteristics peculiar to themselves; nevertheless, each individual identified as a member of a group uses language in a way that makes him unique.

It is probably redundant to state that language is what makes us human and that language makes each of us what we are. Evidence of narrow provincialism in people's perception of one another based upon language characteristics exists in every section of the United States and the world. A person's use of language often determines his success or failure, his acceptance or rejection. For example, the radio voice of Alfred Smith, former Governor of New York, contributed to no small extent to his losing the election for President of the United States. Other illustrations include a New Yorker's recent statement concerning taped language materials developed in Texas, "Nothing recorded in Texas could be any good"; the reaction of a personnel interviewer to a job applicant from New England, "I just can't trust anybody who has such an uppity accent"; and the reaction of a midwesterner to southern speech, "Southerners use lazy speech."

Almost every person regards his own speech as "standard" speech. Anyone deviating from this standard is regarded as linguistically different and as either something of an outlander or deliciously quaint. While accented English is a prime salable commodity for Charles Boyer, it is a block to employment for many Spanish-speakers and blacks.

If asked to define or describe standard language, in this case, American English, many people would reply, "In reality, there is no such thing as standard language. It is an imaginary form of language imputed to educated and cultivated speakers." Although many educators would agree that there is no standard language, this response provides no instructional goals for language learning. In addition, the problem of defining and identifying "educated and cultivated speakers" remains. Since it is a truism that language constitutes the main vehicle for instruction in our schools, a new focus on oral language and reading, particularly for disadvantaged populations, is long overdue.

In May, 1968, a group of educators and linguists vitally concerned with language development and individual opportunities met at the Center for Applied

Linguistics in Washington, D. C.[1] Having agreed to the position that competence in oral control of any language is a prerequisite to learning to read that language, the group further agreed that (1) describing "standard" American English sets a specific goal for language learning; (2) the instructional goal for language must be described in terms of easily available models; (3) learning a standard or nonstandard dialect, however defined, provides for versatility in language; and (4) by achieving a socially unmarked variety of American English, linguistically different groups would find social and economic mobility more easily possible.

One of the nettlesome tasks faced by the group was to evolve a working definition of standard American English. The committee drafted this definition: "A socially unmarked variety of spoken American-English used as a reference point in school language instruction to increase the individual's repertoire of important and useful ways of communicating. This variety of American-English is often heard on network radio and television newscasts."

None in the group was under any illusion that the definition would find universal acceptance. Instead, it was considered a necessary point of departure for establishing instructional goals and identifying eleven issues concerning oral language development for linguistically different learners. These issues are partially explored in this book, but most are desperately in need of more intensive research.

Questions About the Curriculum

1. To what extent and in what way are dialect- or other-language speakers linguistically different? Are they competent in their first language or dialect and deficient only in standard American English (in terms of curricular expectations); or are they deficient in both standard American English and the first language or dialect? To what extent should the curriculum be modified to compensate for language-concept deficiencies and provide for oral fluency in standard American English?

---

[1] Meeting participants: (1) Division of Compensatory Education, United States Office of Education (USOE): Bruce Gaarder; (2) English Educational Resources Information Center (ERIC): Roger Clark, Walter Wolfram; (3) International Reading Association: Thomas D. Horn (Chairman, Committee on Reading for the Disadvantaged); (4) Linguistics ERIC and Center for Applied Linguistics: Doris Gunderson (dyslexia), Alfred S. Hayes (Director of Educational Research Programs), A. Hood Roberts (Associate Director), Dorothy Pedtke (English for Speakers of Other Languages—ESOL), Roger Shuy (urban language), William Stewart (black dialects), and Adam Woyna; (5) New Orleans Educational Improvement Project: Altee Anderson and Sophie Aramburo (also members of the Committee on Reading for the Disadvantaged); (6) Operation Followthrough: Frieda Denenmark; (7) Reading ERIC: Roy Kress (also representing the International Reading Association and the National Conference on Research in English).

2. What are the nature, extent, and significance of interference of the native language or dialect in the acquisition of standard American English?

3. What is the optimum point (grade level) for beginning instruction in a second language or second dialect, that is, initially in school experience or when the native language or dialect has been developed more fully?

4. Are *structured* programs or *informal* oral language activities more desirable when learners bring to the learning environment inadequate listening-speaking vocabularies and immature and/or nonstandard sentence structures? Is listening alone enough to overcome language deficiencies? How pertinent to school demands are the experiences or backgrounds of linguistically different learners? Are informal learning experiences in school adequate for learners with nonstandard language, or must structured oral language instruction be provided, initially and/or subsequently?

5. Should the learner deal initially with content already familiar to him or should experiences needed for success in school be *provided* through environmental manipulation? How may the learner's experiences outside of school best be inventoried and utilized for instruction?

6. Should expository or literary content, or both, be used for developing language skills and self-concept? What roles should areas such as science, social studies, literature, and "emergency vocabulary" (communication concerning crucial physical needs) play in language and concept development?

7. Can English-as-a-second-language programs lacking in content and development of cognitive skills succeed; that is, should standard American English be taught as a subject or as a medium for concept development, or some combination of both? How can the point be determined at which pattern drills and other language practice may safely be diminished or modified?

8. To what extent are currently available measuring techniques useful for evaluating in linguistically different learners such characteristics as attention span, IQ, and language development? Are they helpful in planning instructional strategies? How might the learning potentialities of linguistically different learners be more accurately measured? What are the high-priority test needs?

9. What are the most promising techniques for developing fluency in standard oral American English. Is it necessary to provide different exercises for speakers of the various languages and dialects common to American school populations that have been found to interfere with learning through the language of instruction?

10. Under what conditions should initial experiences with printed symbols include stories in the child's own language—his first dialect or first language? Or, should initial reading instruction be delayed until sufficient command of standard American English is attained?

11. To what extent and in what ways should the learner's family be involved in school language programs?

Educational Goals
and Language Instruction

Issues involving educational goals that educators must resolve in designing programs for the disadvantaged include the following:

1. To what extent should school goals be stated in terms of the dominant culture, the minority culture, or some combination of the two?

2. Should aims be toward socioeconomic mobility or toward competence in and responsibility for solving the problems of disadvantaged groups—escaping from the ghetto or returning to serve?

3. Should goals be stated in terms of cultural assimilation or coexistence? For example, should standard American English *replace* or be *added* to a child's native language or nonstandard dialect?

4. Should goals be in terms of student behavioral changes, modification of educational programs, or a combination of the two? For example, how can school help a child establish a positive self-image in the face of culture conflicts between himself and the school?

5. What are realistic expectations for schools to meet the basic physical and emotional needs of pupils, such as food, clothing, medical care, and a positive self-image?

It has been said that "you can't teach a hungry child." The documentary produced by the Columbia Broadcasting System, "Hunger in America," telecast May 21 and June 22, 1968, while controversial, and possibly not entirely accurate, pointed up the widespread existence (surprising to many) of hunger in the richest country in the world. The possibilities for learning are also quite dubious for the child who is consistently deprived of sufficient sleep, of emotional support from parents and teachers, of adequate clothing and shelter, or of funds for school supplies and for experiential enrichment.

The paradox of poverty in the midst of plenty has had little impact on compensatory-education programs for teachers. Many existing compensatory-education programs do not give adequate attention to the overall broad spectrum of disadvantagedness and omit one or more crucial areas of consideration, especially that of linguistic differences.

The support of in-service teacher education by Title I funds provided by the 1965 Elementary and Secondary Education Act has met with mixed reactions, depending primarily upon the manner in which the funds were utilized and on differing political views. Articles about the Title I program such as that by Peter Milius (1969) entitled "Billion-a-Year Plan Termed Failure in Education of the Poor" highlight the continuing use of almost completely inappropriate instrumentation to assess achievement of disadvantaged populations. Despite criticisms of the use of currently available standardized tests with such populations, decisions are made concerning the effectiveness of programs for disadvantaged pupils based upon these very tests. Attempts to develop new tests have resulted in only partial and tentative success.

Instructional Implications

Only in recent years has the notion begun to occur to educators that the reading materials and methods utilized in American schools have constituted extremely effective built-in failure mechanisms for disadvantaged students. The school critics on the one hand and staunch defenders of American education on the other are both guilty of unrealistic expectations of what can be accomplished during a six-hour day for some 180 to 200 days out of the year. In addition to the limitations inherent in the nine-month school year, inappropriate tests, irregular attendance, lack of attention in class, and frequent lack of communication between teachers and pupils further reduce the effectiveness of instructional programs.

In addition to the health, social, economic, psychological, and linguistic problems that contribute to pupils' failure in reading and academic achievement, four other basic factors make failure or retardation inevitable or at least highly probable: (1) widespread ignorance on the part of practitioners concerning principles of language learning, for example, the erroneous belief that standard speech is attained by the memorization of rules of grammar; (2) frequent introduction of the decoding phase of initial reading instruction before adequate oral language development has occurred; (3) inadequate or nonexistent tests for assessing phonological and syntactical problems and oral language fluency in American English; and (4) teachers' inability or failure to diagnose and remedy oral language deviations that seriously inhibit learning to read in standard American English.

It is the conviction of this writer that the lack of valid oral language tests is a major block to effective reading instruction for the disadvantaged. In fact, the most frequent request made by educators concerned with disadvantaged populations is for valid oral language tests; less knowledgeable educators as well as some politicians tend to be concerned only with paper-and-pencil achievement tests, important as they are.

Few would disagree that the situation of disadvantaged pupils is critical. The authors of the various chapters in this book illustrate the growing movement to develop educational programs with materials and methods that are relevant to the specific needs of disadvantaged pupils, and the absolute necessity for attacking the *complete* spectrum of problems that prevent these pupils from enjoying the full benefits of living in the United States.

The writer and his colleagues[2] have identified through their research two major factors as prerequisites for success in meeting instructional goals for the disadvantaged: (1) a mandatory, adequate, and continuing language testing program; and (2) full use of technological developments, such as audio-visual cartridge tapes combined with appropriate programmed testing and instructional materials.

The success or failure of whatever enterprises are undertaken will, nevertheless, be primarily dependent upon those actually fighting "in the trenches." But teachers cannot do the job alone. Neither can psychologists, sociologists, anthropologists, linguists, nutritionists, supervisors of instruction, administrators, cafeteria managers, social workers, newsmen, or any other single group of persons concerned with the disadvantaged. The chapters that follow identify characteristics of disadvantaged populations and suggest ways various professionals and paraprofessionals can work together to meet the problems of disadvantaged pupils in learning to read as well as the many related problems that limit each child's realization of his potential.

[2] See the bibliography on page 247.

I
Backgrounds

1

Social Backgrounds:
Their Impact on Schoolchildren

Robert J. Havighurst

IN ALL OUR big cities, and in many smaller cities and rural counties, educators are trying to find better ways of teaching a group of children who are variously called culturally deprived, intellectually deprived, and socially disadvantaged. Another, perhaps more appropriate, term is "linguistically different." Whatever the descriptive terms for these pupils, however, this movement to teach them successfully is a major one, enlisting a large sum of money, the time of skilled teachers, and a considerable amount of research effort. There is consensus that this group of children and their families present a critical social problem, perhaps our greatest domestic one. It is important, then, to isolate those characteristics of the social backgrounds of these children that have particular relevance for their teachers.

Identifying the Disadvantaged

Disadvantaged children have been variously identified. The group is sometimes (and frequently enough to cause confusion in the minds of readers) defined as all children of manual workers. But few if any educators care to call this large working-class group, some two-thirds of the child population, socially disadvantaged. The great majority of working-class families give their children a fairly good start for life in an urban industrial democratic society. Their children are adequately fed and clothed, and they are loved and protected by their parents. The children learn to respect teachers and to like school, where they do average work or better.

Although working-class children as a group score slightly below children of white-collar families on intelligence tests, fall slightly below on tests of school achievement, and attain a somewhat lower level of formal education, it would not be reasonable to say that all working-class children are socially disadvantaged. The differences are relatively small, and they become even smaller when the socially disadvantaged children are removed from the group of working-class youth and those who remain are compared with children of white-collar families.

Some people consider the lower third or lower 30 percent of the child population disadvantaged. There is an infinite gradation of social advantage and disadvantage, and any figure for the percentage of children who are disadvantaged must therefore be a personal rather than a scientific judgment. The 30 percent estimate seems most reasonable of any proposed, however. This is approximately the percentage of boys and girls who drop out of school before graduation from high school. There are a few other dropouts, some with superior ability, who do not belong in this discussion, but they are only a small number.

As educators we are now committed to doing everything we can to give these disadvantaged young people an education that meets their needs and prepares them adequately for adult life as workers, parents, and citizens. The problems of finding suitable programs will be complicated if, as educators anticipate, education is made compulsory for students until they reach the age of eighteen. Educators will be forced to adapt programs for the group of young people from sixteen to eighteen who under the present system have dropped out of school.

Educational Retardation
Among Disadvantaged Children

About half the disadvantaged children in this country, or 15 percent of the total child population, are severely retarded in educational achievement. One basis for this figure is the proportion of unemployed, out-of-school youth between the ages of sixteen and twenty. These young people, the majority from poor families, have been unsuccessful both in school and in the labor market. There are more girls than boys in this group. Whereas many of the boys are clearly socially maladjusted, some of the girls are not; they are simply doing what girls have done for a long time, helping out at home while waiting to get married.

Since the poor tend to concentrate in the large cities, whereas upper-income families tend to move out of the cities to the suburbs, the proportion of socially disadvantaged and educationally retarded children in big cities is larger than 15 percent. Probably 30 percent of the children in such cities as New York, Chicago,

Philadelphia, Washington, Detroit, Cleveland, Baltimore, Atlanta, and Los Angeles fall into this category.

We shall distinguish between the two groups of disadvantaged children—those who are educationally retarded and those who are not—with the following examples.

DISADVANTAGED BUT NOT EDUCATIONALLY RETARDED

Michael is a ten-year-old boy in the fifth grade of a school in a working-class section of town. His father, who is a truck driver, makes a good income, but he must frequently be away for days at a time. Michael's mother stays at home and does her best to give her three children a good start in life. She looks after the children faithfully, and wishes her husband had enough money to rent a house in a "better" part of town where the neighbors have nicer children and there are not so many Saturday night fights and Monday morning hangovers.

When Michael was seven years old he was put into an experimental second-grade class consisting of eighteen children who had failed the first grade because they had not learned to read at the proper grade level. Instead of making them repeat the first grade, the principal put them all in one class with a teacher who volunteered to work with them. In addition, a social worker spent one day a week visiting the homes of the children. Michael, who had an IQ of 97, began to read by Thanksgiving of the second year and soon was reading at a second-grade level. He very much liked the trips his class took to the public library, where the children's librarian read to them and encouraged them to borrow books and take them home. Michael read about twenty children's books by the spring of the year. But he forgot to return his books on time, and one day his mother received a post card telling her that Michael owed a sixteen-cent fine for overdue books. She sent Michael to the library with the money, but told him, "Don't you ever go near that library again. They didn't have a right to fine you."

To Michael's mother a fine was bad, for she associated it with the punishment some of her neighbors received when they got into drunken fights at a nearby tavern and were arrested and fined for being drunk and disorderly. She was raising her children to avoid this kind of life, and besides she did not think Michael was guilty of a crime for keeping the library books too long.

Michael got along fairly well in school; his grades were average, and he behaved himself. One day, when he was in the fifth grade, he was playing after school and he saw the social worker who used to visit his home when he was in the experimental second grade. He greeted her and said, "Miss Jansen, please come to my house and see my books." He took her to his house and showed her a set of Britannica Junior books. "These are all mine," he said. "My dad pays five dollars a month for them." The social worker replied, "That's wonderful, Michael, and do your folks read to you from these books?" "Oh no, they don't like to read much, and besides, they said that these are my books, for me to read.

Of course, I can't understand everything, but I've been reading about the animals of the world."

Just then, Michael's mother came in and greeted the social worker warmly. "We'll never forget how much you helped us when Michael was in the second grade," she said, "and don't you think these books are wonderful?"

This case illustrates the point that parents may take very good care of their children in an emotional sense but still deprive them of a sound intellectual start in life. This mother and father simply did not *know* how to help their children do well in school. In spite of their good intentions, they deprived Michael of the use of the library, which might have been a major intellectual resource for him. Then they splurged by getting him a children's encyclopedia, but they did not set an example of reading, nor did they read to him or help him learn to read.

It is probable that Michael would score higher than average on an intelligence test if he had been raised in a family that knew better how to give him a good start in reading and in the other skills that are essential to good school work. Nevertheless, Michael is not educationally retarded in relation to his age group and he can finish high school if he wants to do so. He is disadvantaged but not enough so to be considered educationally retarded.

DISADVANTAGED AND EDUCATIONALLY RETARDED

Sam is a ten-year-old boy in the fourth grade of school in a deteriorated section of a large city. He lives with his mother and four other children in a two-bedroom flat. His mother gets a monthly Aid to Dependent Children welfare payment. His father deserted the family five years ago, and the last two children have other fathers who did not marry his mother.

Sam's home life has been chaotic. His father and mother quarreled a great deal when he was very young, and Sam was left to fend for himself. Nobody read to him or paid much attention to him. He played with other children in the back yards of the run-down houses and apartments near where he lived. His mother did not bother to send him to kindergarten. In the first grade he was put in a "slow" group, and he was not reading when he entered the second grade, still in the slow group. Finally he began to read, but not at all well, and he remained in slow sections through the fourth grade, when he repeated a year. He had been mischievous and unruly for two years, and his teacher asked that he be given a psychological examination. It disclosed that he had an IQ of 80. The examiner suggested that Sam probably could do better if he had some systematic tutoring. The examiner did not approve of sending him to a class for the emotionally maladjusted and thought he was within the range of "normal" intelligence. However, he was reading at the second-grade level.

Sam is both retarded and disadvantaged. We can suppose that the disadvantages he suffered at home retarded his mental development.

The Family Experience
of Disadvantaged Children

Disadvantaged pupils should be distinguished from mentally handicapped and physically handicapped pupils. They are those who have been denied certain basic social experiences, in particular certain experiences in the family, that the majority of children have had.

1. They lack a family environment that sets an example of reading and that provides a variety of toys and play materials of colors, sizes, and shapes that challenge their ingenuity with their hands and their minds.
2. They lack a family conversational experience that answers their questions and encourages them to ask questions; extends their vocabulary with new words, in particular adjectives and adverbs; and gives them a right and a need to stand up for and to explain their point of view on the world.

Systematic study of the language behavior of families by Bernstein (1961) and others indicates that when relatively large samples of families are analyzed, there are major differences in the complexity and the content of the language used by the middle class and the working class. Generally, working-class families use a *restricted* form of language, whereas middle-class families use a more *elaborated* form. At the same time, the language of some working-class families is like that of typical middle-class families and vice versa.

A child who has learned a restricted language at home is likely to have difficulty in school, where an elaborated language is used and taught by the teacher; and the child's difficulty is likely to increase as he goes further in school, *unless he learns the elaborated language that is expected in the school.* On the other hand, the child who has had experience with an elaborated language from his earliest years has a relatively easy time in school; he simply goes on developing the kind of language and related thinking that he has already been using.

Deutsch (1963) has studied socially disadvantaged children, using techniques of the experimental psychologist. He finds these children to have inferior auditory discrimination, inferior visual discrimination, and inferior judgment concerning time, number, and other basic concepts. (In this context, *inferior* means inadequate for success in school.) This inferiority, he contends, is due not to physical defects of eyes and ears and brain but to inferior habits of seeing and hearing and thinking. Presumably, the family environment of these children did not teach them to pay attention to what was being said around them or to the visual scene. Then, when they came to school, their school performance suffered because they had not learned to "listen" to the teacher and to their classmates or to "see" the things they are shown in school.

This analysis is based on the proposition that family experience is the dominant factor in the child's cognitive development, and that preschool experience in the family makes the greatest difference between a child who comes to the first grade "ready" to read and a child of equal native endowment who enters the first grade quite "unready" to read.

A more detailed analysis of the nature of this family experience is given by Hess (1964), who describes two examples of mother-child communication. One mother uses a "restricted code" or language, to use Bernstein's term; the other uses an "elaborated code" or language. Hess says,

> Assume that the emotional climate of two homes is approximately the same—the significant difference between them is in style of communication employed. A child is playing noisily in the kitchen with an assortment of pots and pans when the telephone rings. In one home the mother says, "Be quiet," or "Shut up," or gives any one of several short, peremptory commands, and she answers the phone while the child sits still on the floor. In the other home the mother says, "Would you keep quiet while I answer the phone." The question our study poses is this: what inner response is elicited in the child, what is the effect upon his developing cognitive network of concepts and meaning in each of these two situations? In one instance, the child is asked for a simple mental response. He is asked to attend to an uncomplicated message, and to make a conditioned response (to comply; he is not called upon to reflect or to make mental discriminations). In the other example, the child is required to follow two or three ideas. He is asked to relate his behavior to a time dimension; he must think of his behavior in relation to its effect upon another person. He must perform a more complicated task to follow the communication of his mother in that his relationship to her is mediated in part through concepts and shared ideas; his mind is stimulated or exercised (in an elementary fashion) by a more elaborate complex verbal communication initiated by the mother. As objects of these two divergent communication styles, repeated in various ways, in similar situations and circumstances during the pre-school years, these two imaginary children would be expected to develop significantly different verbal facility and cognitive equipment by the time they enter the public school system . . . .
>
> The effects of such early experience are not only upon the communication modes and cognitive structure; they also establish potential patterns of relationship with the external world. It is one of the dynamic features of Bernstein's work that he views language as social behavior. As such, language is used by participants of a social network to elaborate and express social and other interpersonal relationships and used in turn to shape and determine these relationships. The integral association between language and social structure is critical for an understanding of the effects of poverty upon children; within the individual family it emerges in terms of the principles which govern the decision-making activities, which themselves help regulate the nature and amount of social exchange.
>
> The interlacing of social interaction and language is illustrated by the distinction Bernstein makes between two types of families—those oriented

toward control by status appeal or ascribed role norms and those oriented toward *persons*. In status-oriented families, behavior tends to be regulated in terms of role characteristics—children are told to behave in harmony with status and role expectations. There is little opportunity for the unique characteristics of the child to influence the decision-making process of the interaction between parent and child. In these families, the internal or personal status of the children is not influential as a basis for decision. Norms of behavior are stressed with such imperatives as "You must do this because I say so," or "Boys don't act like that," or other statements which rely on the status of the participants or a behavior norm for justification.

In the person-oriented family, the unique characteristics of the child modify status demands and are taken into account in interaction. The decisions of this type of family are individualized and less frequently related to status or role ascriptions. Behavior is justified in terms of feelings, preference, personal and unique reactions and subjective states. This philosophy not only permits, but demands, an elaborated linguistic code and a wide range of linguistic and behavioral alternatives in interpersonal interaction. Status-oriented families may be regulated by less individual commands, messages and responses. Indeed, by its nature, the status-oriented family will rely more heavily on a restricted code. The verbal exchange is inherent in the structure; regulates it and is regulated by it.

In the person-oriented family, children tend to develop a more complex language facility. They learn to express themselves more persuasively because they have more opportunities to state their own points of view. Also, they learn to put themselves in the position of others as they listen to other family members express themselves. They learn to speak about a subject from several different points of view and to entertain contradictory assertions for the sake of studying an argument.

Hess (1964) talked with a variety of mothers of young children, asking them this question:

Imagine your child is old enough to go to public school for the first time. How would you prepare him? What would you tell him?

One mother, who is person-oriented and uses elaborated verbal codes, replied as follows:

"First of all, I would remind Portia that she was going to school to learn, that her teacher would take my place, and that she would be expected to follow instructions. Also, that her time was to be spent mostly in the classroom with other children and that any questions or any problems that she might have she could consult with her teacher for assistance."

Anything else?

"No, anything else would probably be confusing for her at her particular age."

In terms of promoting educability, what has this mother done in this response? First, she has been specific and informative; she has presented the school situation as comparable to one already familiar to the child; second, she has offered reassurance and support to help the child deal with anxiety; third, she has presented the school situation as one which involves a personal relationship between the child and the teacher; and fourth, she has presented the classroom situation as one in which the child is to learn. This orientation toward school fosters confidence and initiative on the part of the child and helps him gear into the school routine by seeing it as an extension of the home situation.

A second mother responds as follows to this question:

"Well, John, it's time to go to school now. You must know how to behave. The first day at school you should be a good boy and should do just what the teacher tells you to do."

In contrast to the first mother, what has this mother done? First, she has defined the role of the child as passive and compliant. Second, the central issues involved in school are in the area of dealing with authority and the institution, rather than having to do with learning. Third, the relationship and roles portrayed are sketched in terms of status and role expectations, rather than in personal terms. Fourth, the entire message is general, restricted, and vague, lacking in information about how to deal with the problems of school except by passive compliance.

Health Status of Disadvantaged Children

In this discussion, the criteria for being considered disadvantaged are mainly social, not physical or mental. However, certain health defects are found more frequently in socially disadvantaged children than in a typical group of American children. The reason for this is that poverty and lack of education on the part of parents lead to inadequate health care for these children.

Some indication of the extent of health defects among disadvantaged children can be seen in the results of medical examinations of Chicago children in the Head Start program in 1966, as reported to the Board of Education of the City of Chicago by the General Superintendent of Schools, November 9, 1966. (Head Start served a considerable proportion of disadvantaged children in certain areas during the summer prior to their entering kindergarten or first grade.)

Number of children examined medically—14,075

Defects—3957 in 2960 children. Major defects included:

286 neurological defects, the majority of which were emotional problems

175 eye defects

138 ear defects

143 nutritional deviations, the majority of which were cases of children being underweight

435 heart defects, of which approximately two-thirds were murmurs; the remainder, congenital conditions and rheumatic heart diseases

775 cases of anemia
  3 cases of tuberculosis: two active cases; one child living in home
  with active case

In addition, 13,513 hearing screening tests indicated 490 (4 percent) "hearing failures," and 13,022 vision screening tests indicated 1077 (8 percent) "vision failures."

We do not have comparable data on a representative sample of American children. On the whole, the Chicago findings do *not* indicate that health and physical defects are a severe problem among disadvantaged children. Still, such data as an 8 percent incidence of "vision failures" indicate a need for medical and optometric screening of children from poor families and for a program of health and corrective services aimed at this particular subgroup.

Economic, Geographic, and Ethnic Breakdown of Disadvantaged Children

Who, then, are the disadvantaged when we attempt to describe them in terms of observable social groups? Most often they are groups with the following characteristics:

1. They are at the bottom of the American society in terms of income.
2. They have a rural background within the last two generations.
3. They suffer from social and economic discrimination at the hands of the majority of the society.
4. They are widely distributed in the United States. While they are most visible in the big cities, they are present in all except the very high income communities. There are many of them in rural areas, especially in the southern and southwestern states.

Another means of describing the disadvantaged would be to locate them geographically. This can be done in a general way by answering the question, Where do the poor people live?

Studies by the federal government provide the basis for the data Tables 1–1 and 1–2 on the numbers and location of children of poor families.[1]

It is important to keep in mind that there is a substantial number (at least half) of each of the groups listed in Table 1–2 who are *not* seriously disadvantaged. But as the proportion of people with a low income and a low educational level increases in these groups, the proportion of disadvantaged children increases.

---

[1] A "poor" family was defined as a nonfarm family of four with an income of less than $3135. For farm families, the dividing line of income was slightly lower.

TABLE 1–1

Geographic Breakdown of Poor Children* in 1965

Location	Percentage of Poor Child Population	Number of Poor Children (in millions)	Percentage Classified Poor
Urban	60	7.5	20
Rural	40	5.0	28

* Aged 5 to 19 inclusive.

SOURCES:
   Adapted from Bird (1965), Orshansky (1965), and United States Bureau of the Census (1960).

TABLE 1–2

Ethnic Breakdown of Poor Children* in 1965

Ethnic Group	Percentage of Poor Child Population	Number of Poor Children (in millions)	Percentage of Each Subgroup Classified Poor
White	69	8.5	18
Black	25	3.1	44
Spanish-American of the Southwest	4	0.5	35
Puerto Rican	1.2	0.15	50
Indian	1.1	0.14	65

* Aged 5 to 19 inclusive.

SOURCES:
   Adapted from Bird (1965), Orshansky (1965), and United States Bureau of the Census (1960).

Summary

The socially disadvantaged child has been described in broad, general terms. Chief among his characteristics is his restricted linguistic code. Although many handicaps and problems are shared by all linguistically different learners, regardless of their ethnic origin, it is important that the unique problems of each ethnic group be considered. Therefore, Chapter 2 focuses on the social backgrounds of specific groups.

2

Social Backgrounds
of Specific Groups

WHITES

Alvin L. Bertrand

VIEWS on who are the disadvantaged in American society are varied.[1] At best, the standards used to determine whether one is disadvantaged are arbitrary and subjective. There is a strong tendency to equate being disadvantaged with low income. Income levels offer a practical basis for programs and policies, but it should not be assumed that the needs of the disadvantaged are wholly economic —they are social, psychological, and educational as well. These other kinds of needs are most prevalent, however, among the economically disadvantaged, and for this reason, income levels constitute a useful criterion for isolating a large segment of the disadvantaged population in order that their other characteristics and needs may be studied.

The Number and Location
of Economically Disadvantaged Whites

In 1968 the United States Bureau of the Census released a monograph dealing with the extent of poverty in the United States. The data in this monograph (for 1966) are based on the definition of poverty developed at the Social Security Administration in an attempt to improve on purely arbitrary income data. The

[1] For a review of the definitions most frequently cited, see Ralph J. Ramsey, *Forms and Scope of Poverty in Kentucky*, Lexington, Ky., Cooperative Extension Service, Resource Development Series 10, 1968.

monograph classifies families and individuals according to an index that takes into account such factors as family size, number of children, and type of residence (farm-nonfarm), as well as amount of income. The poverty levels are based on a minimum nutritionally sound food plan, called the "economy" plan, designed by the United States Department of Agriculture for emergency use when funds are low. The plan assumes that a poor family should spend no more than one-third of its income for food; a household is statistically classified as poor if its total money income is less than three times the cost of the economy food plan. Applied to 1966 incomes, the poverty levels of nonfarm residents ranged from $1560 for a woman sixty-five years or older living alone to $5440 for a family of seven or more persons. A nonfarm family of four was considered in poverty if the income of its members was less than $3335.

According to the monograph, there were 29.7 million persons in the United States in 1966 who were classified as living below the poverty level.[2] Of this number, 20.1 million—two-thirds of the nation's poor—were white.[3] In proportion to their number in the total population, 3.5 times as many nonwhites are living in poverty as whites, but the large number of poor whites—one-third of them children under eighteen—makes this segment of the disadvantaged population worthy of serious concern.

It is surprising to most persons to learn that there is more poverty, relatively speaking, in rural America than in urban America.[4] Some 30 percent of the total United States population live in rural areas, but 40 percent, or 12 million, of the nation's poor live there, about 80 percent of them white.[5] Of the 18 million urban poor, about two-thirds live in inner-city areas and one-third in suburbs. It is estimated that 71 percent of the poor families in inner-city areas are white, and

[2] This total is considerably lower than some earlier estimates because of the effective reduction of poverty within recent years. The number of persons below the poverty level was reduced from 39 million in 1959 to 30 million in 1966. This is a faster rate of reduction than predicted by earlier Census Bureau publications.

Editor's note: The different criteria used to define poverty terms should explain the apparent discrepancies between the number of "poor" children reported by Havighurst in Chapter 1 ("a nonfarm family of four with an income of less than $3135") and the number of economically disadvantaged whites reported by Bertrand (definition based on a minimum nutritionally sound food plan; a household is statistically classified as poor if its total money income is less than three times the cost of the economy food plan).

[3] Persons with Spanish surnames are ordinarily included within the census of the white population. Hence the estimates cited include this subgroup.

[4] The United States Bureau of the Census defines as urban all incorporated communities with 2500 or more inhabitants and the densely settled area around cities with 50,000 or more inhabitants. Rural areas are classified as farm or nonfarm; farms include plots of fewer than ten acres from which sales of farm products amount to $250 or more and plots of ten acres or more from which sales of farm products amount to $50 or more.

[5] For a comprehensive treatise on rural poverty, see *Rural Poverty in the United States*, Washington, D. C., a report by the President's National Advisory Commission on Rural Poverty, 1968.

this percentage could be expected to be even greater in the suburbs. Thus, the white poor are spread across America—in open country, in villages and hamlets, in towns and urban fringes, and in the ghettos of the large cities.

Differences Between White Poor and Other Poor Groups

Specific sociological features distinguish economically disadvantaged whites from other groups of poor. First, there is the factor of *social distance*. By being identified with the racial group generally accorded highest status in our society, poor whites have certain advantages over other poor groups. These advantages include an edge in competition for jobs, welfare, social acceptance, and social participation. In order to preserve these advantages low-income whites are more likely to practice discrimination and to resist integration than middle-income whites. The latter are not in as direct competition for jobs and recognition. The maintenance of social distance affords low-income whites a step up the social ladder.

The second factor that sets poor whites apart from other poverty groups is *socialization*. Again, by virtue of the fact that they have more opportunity to participate in white middle-class society and to be exposed to the ways of speech, dress, and manner that are acceptable in the "outside" world, they have advantages over other groups of poor. Blacks and Indians in particular are likely to be isolated from society at large and to develop patterns that are unique to their subcultures.

The third factor that sets poor whites apart is not generally appreciated. This is the fact that, unlike blacks and Spanish-speakers, poor whites have no special identification that generates a unity of purpose. Thus, they have gone, and probably will continue to go, relatively unnoticed by the mass media and by program- and policy-makers. Were there strong organizations such as the NAACP, CORE, and the Urban League fighting to call their plight to the attention of society, more concern could be expected for this group.

Life Styles of Economically Disadvantaged Whites

Among the white poor there is a greater personal and social diversity than in any other poor group. The significance of cultural differences among the various groups of poor whites can be portrayed most dramatically in terms of their respective life styles. The expression "life style" means the way people in various subcultural groups live in comparison with that of people in other subcultures. The indexes that measure life style are patterns of interaction (who mixes with whom), symbolic possession (what is sought in the way of consumption goods and material belongings), and symbolic activities (recreational patterns, speech habits, and formal social participation). The advantage of using a life-style approach in comparing the various groups of poor whites is that it gives insight into the social intimacy that only occurs among people who look upon and treat each other as equals. Said another way, it spotlights the sociological factors that account for the way people behave toward one another.

Three major groups of poor whites have been selected for special treatment here: (1) those living in the so-called general farming and self-sufficing rural areas of the United States; (2) those living in inner-city ghettos; and (3) those living in typical small towns throughout the nation. These three groups represent the great majority of American poor whites.

RESIDENTS OF GENERAL FARMING AND SELF-SUFFICING RURAL AREAS

Approximately one-fifth of the nation's families live in areas that have been classified as general farming and self-sufficing areas.[6] Most of the inhabitants of these generally mountainous areas, which include substantial parts of Kentucky, Tennessee, West Virginia, Virginia, Pennsylvania, Missouri, Ohio, Vermont, New Hampshire, and small sections in several other states, exist at a subsistence level. The majority are descendents of families who came to America during the colonial period from northwestern Europe, especially England, Scotland, and Northern Ireland. However, a number trace their origins back to Germany, Wales, Holland, and France.

Physical barriers, such as mountains, steep hills, forests, and streams, make modern travel and communication difficult in the general farming and self-sufficing areas. Yet, the people tend to carry on intimate social relationships—they know each other and each other's affairs. Traditionally, social life has consisted of getting together at country stores, post offices, and schoolhouses. There is little formally organized activity except for that in schools and churches. Even there, programs are limited. Family ties are strong, and there is much visiting among relatives.

---

[6] The information for this section comes principally from the following sources: Jack E. Weller, *Yesterday's People* (Lexington, Ky.: University of Kentucky Press, 1965); Thomas R. Ford, ed., *The Southern Appalachian Region* (Lexington, Ky.: University of Kentucky Press, 1962); Hart M. Nelson, "A Review of Literature Pertaining to Appalachia Stressing Attitudes to Social Change and Religious and Educational Orientation," mimeographed, 1967; Carl C. Taylor and others, *Rural Life in the United States* (New York: Alfred A. Knopf, 1949), Chapter 26.

It is not surprising to find that those who live their lives in the general farming and self-sufficing areas have developed a unique subculture in response to their physical environment and their poverty. This subculture can best be described in terms of the behavioral traits of its members.

These mountain dwellers exhibit fierce independence as a result of their long and continuous fight for survival. It has been customary for each family to remain independent, with each household head his own provider, his own doctor, his own teacher, and so on. The independent spirit of the mountain people is a key to their ability to endure poverty. But their individualism and independence often prove to be stumbling blocks when they move to the city, for they are ill prepared to cooperate with others and to understand the necessities for such things as taxes and insurance.

A second trait of mountain people is traditionalism. They are strongly bound to the past and stubbornly resist change. This characteristic goes against the middle-class "improvement" orientation so common in the United States and is one reason programs designed to improve the lot of these individuals have failed. It is difficult to get mountain children to be achievement-oriented, since their families do not stress moving ahead in the world and they have very few contacts with adults who are successful in middle-class terms.

The third trait of the poor whites living in self-sufficing rural areas is fatalism. These people are seldom optimistic and often feel defeated before they have tried new solutions to a problem.

Another characteristic of mountain people is their attitude toward fear. On the one hand they face danger with seldom paralleled personal bravery. It is a matter of intense pride to be able to stand up before man or nature at its worst. By contrast, fear of separation from family and community is openly exhibited.

Mountain people tend to conceive their goals in terms of their relationships to other people in their community. They place more importance on their relationships with people than on material goods and are thus often thought to lack ambition or goals.

Children in the general farming and self-sufficing areas grow up in economic, geographic, and social isolation. They are generally reared impulsively by their parents, with relatively little of the conscious training practiced in middle-class families. Discipline is usually given with no concern for the child's understanding or level of maturity. Punishment is always physical punishment, though it may be accompanied by a verbal scolding. Yet, children in these areas are also indulged in many ways. Rates of school absenteeism are high, for example, primarily because many parents do not value education and therefore do not compel their children to attend school. In essence, the children of the subsistence-level poor in rural areas are monumentally deprived—of a full social life, of many of the basic necessities of life, of a chance to improve themselves, and of an understanding of the behavior necessary for getting along in and contributing to society at large.

THE URBAN VILLAGERS: WHITES IN THE GHETTOS

Gans (1962) has identified as "urban villages" the low-rent districts in urban centers where immigrants first settle. He justifies this term by observing that immigrants usually form a relatively cohesive group in their attempt to adapt their nonurban institutions and culture to the urban milieu. Urban villages populated by whites are found in all major cities. Although the particular ethnic groups that populate them vary, from city to city there is not a great deal of difference in their appearance or in the activities carried on within them. For this reason, it is possible to use Gans's description of the West End of Boston (an area that no longer exists as such) to describe white urban ghettos and white urban-ghetto life.[7]

As one enters a ghetto area, whether it is inhabited by whites or by blacks, he is likely to see what greeted Gans in the West End:

> a series of narrow winding streets flanked on both sides by columns of three- and five-story apartment buildings—many poorly maintained structures, some of them unoccupied or partially vacant, some facing on alleys covered with more than the average amount of garbage; many vacant stores; and enough of the kinds of people who . . . inhabit a slum area.

The latter would be likely to include

> some old people who looked like European immigrants, some very poor people, some who were probably suffering from mental illness, a few sullen looking adolescents and young adults who congregated on street corners, and many middle-aged people who were probably mainly Italian, Russian Jewish, Polish, and Irish in parentage.

The population of the West End typifies the ethnic diversity of white ghettos. It included the following major groups:

1. First- and second-generation Italian households—about 42 percent of the population.
2. First-generation Jewish households—about 10 percent of the population.
3. First- and second-generation Polish households—about 9 percent of the population.
4. A residue of older Irish people—about 5 percent of the population.
5. Other ethnic groups, principally Albanians, Ukranians, and Greeks.
6. Pathological households—that is, a small number of families and individuals who lived in extreme poverty because of physical or psychological disability.
7. Postwar newcomers—gypsies, groups of single men, members of broken families, and people who had fled from other places, for

[7] Gans spent a year in this ghetto as a participant observer.

example, a redevelopment project in the South End. Some were squatters who tried to live in rent-free buildings.
8. Middle-class professionals and students—nurses, interns, doctors, and students from a nearby hospital. (Ghettos usually manage to attract some persons who live according to middle-class standards.)
9. Other hospital staff—service workers who lived here because of the proximity to their work.
10. Artists and bohemians—a small but highly visible group of artists and would-be artists and of people choosing a bohemian way of life.

Life in a white ghetto takes place primarily on the street. Faces become familiar very quickly. Neighbors meet on stairs and in front of buildings. Shopping patterns tend to become routine and provide a set of everyday acquaintances. A common residence and sharing of facilities, as well as the constant struggle against absentee landlords, tend to create "village" solidarity, as do the common problems of illness, job layoffs, school and discipline problems among children, alcoholism, mental illness, desertion, death, serious financial difficulty, and violence. However, emergencies and problems tend to be solved within ethnic or peer groups, and members of the various groups do not mingle freely socially.

Family life in white ghettos is adult centered. Children are not planned but come naturally and regularly. They are not allowed to become the center of family life. As soon as children are weaned and toilet trained, they are expected to behave in ways pleasing to adults. They start assisting their parents by the time they are seven or eight. Although these children are expected to behave like adults at home and to obey their parents, they are completely free when with their peers. Parents are not expected to supervise, guide, or take a part in their activities with their peers. The movement of children into peer groups proceeds gradually, but by the time they are in their teens they are almost completely submerged in these groups. At this time family-taught behavior patterns give way to what have been called the rules of the street. When a boy reaches ten or twelve, his parents may feel that they are no longer responsible for his actions. If he gets into trouble the blame is attributed to the influence of bad companions or to his own moral failings.

The predominant method of child-raising is punishment and reward. White ghetto parents, like parents in rural self-sufficing areas, raise their children impulsively, with relatively little of the conscious purpose in child rearing that is found in the middle-class family. This type of child rearing often develops, in part, because parents have no clear image of the future social and occupational levels they want their children to reach. It is no wonder that the child develops a pragmatic outlook quite early which impresses him with the need to obey only that authority which can implement social power affecting him and to ignore that which cannot.

In brief, the white child growing up in an urban ghetto faces unique disadvantages. First, he must learn to live with economic deprivation. This not only means a meager existence, but one complicated by constant awareness that many others have more than he does. In addition, although he may not be subject to discrimination as are blacks and some others, he may suffer prejudice because of his ethnic origin or his religion. Unlike the child in rural poverty, he lives with problems created by too many rather than too few people. For example, he is able to maintain only a small degree of privacy. Deviant behavior is a way of life where he lives, and this explains the high probability of his having experience with the law and its enforcers. It also explains the early development of a negative attitude toward law and other forms of social control. In short, educational and social opportunities for the white child in an urban ghetto leave much to be desired, although they may not be as deficient as they are for the black or Mexican-American child.

POOR WHITES IN "ANYTOWN, U.S.A."

The third large group of poor whites is dispersed among the literally thousands of small towns, with populations from 2500 to 50,000, that are scattered across the nation. These towns have been studied by many social scientists, and it is possible to determine that the towns share characteristics of social stratification (Hodges, 1964).[8] Each town has what has been termed a "lower-lower" class, comprising 15 to 20 percent of the town's population, within which poor whites are found.

In small towns the neighborhoods where poor whites live can be exemplified by the description Lloyd Warner gave of Jonesville, the setting for his book *Democracy in Jonesville* (1949). The poorest area in town is "south of the Canal and behind the old tannery." In this area "one must drive carefully for the streets are like alleys bordered by broken fences that lean over into them. Old women sit out in the yards in broken-down chairs watching chickens running over the alleys and destroying the yards." He describes the places where people live—abandoned stores, deserted industrial plants, and rudely constructed tar-paper shacks—and notes that there is no planned arrangement of houses.

The residents of lower-lower-class neighborhoods in small towns are a mixed lot. As in the urban ghettos, however, black and white members of the lower-lower class tend to live in different neighborhoods, although in many towns outside the South there are so few blacks that they are more or less a novelty. Most of the white residents of these small towns are relative newcomers. In Jonesville, they were mountain people and Polish immigrants.

Those who have studied the lower-lower-class whites in small towns have found that they are typically unskilled and have marginal and sporadic employ-

[8] Harold M. Hodges, Jr., has summarized the characteristics of social classes in small towns, after a review of the many studies done by social anthropologists, sociologists, and others. The discussion that follows draws from his work. See *Social Stratification: Class in America* (Cambridge, Mass.: Schenkman Publishing Co., 1964), Chapter 4.

ment. The men usually enter the labor market in their middle teens, after dropping out of school (most often before the eighth grade). They marry teen-age brides, who soon bear more children than the family can afford to support. Marriages frequently do not last, and those that do are often strife-ridden. It is not surprising that this class of whites is often hostile to strangers and marked by an overwhelming sense of pessimism and apathy.

It was stated that the white children of the ghettos and of the general farming and self-sufficing rural areas were expected to behave as adults at a very early age. The same is true among economically disadvantaged whites in small towns. Family democracy is a middle- and upper-class trait. A lower-class child is expected to be obedient, quiet, and subservient to parental dictates. The father is frequently an authoritarian patriarch, who rules his family with an iron hand.

It is undoubtedly true that the children of the white poor living in small towns have more opportunities to see and to socialize with middle- and upper-class children than do poor whites elsewhere, since small towns often have only one or two schools. Also, the small size of the community itself enables widespread acquaintance among its inhabitants. Yet, this "high visibility" tends to accentuate certain disadvantages of the poor—namely, social isolation. In school they may be in the same classes with middle- and upper-class children, but they seldom become friends or attend the same functions. Very early a poor child may be made aware that he is not considered proper as a friend and companion to children in the higher social classes. Warner (1949), after careful study, states that "by the time children reach the ages of ten and eleven, they show clear-cut divisions along class lines."

In summary, at least two types of disadvantage mold the characteristics of the children of poor white families in small towns: the physical atmosphere of a substandard housing and living area, and the social atmosphere of strife-ridden authoritarian homes, poorly educated parents and neighbors, a pervasive feeling of hostility and despair, and a pronounced social distance between them and others in their community. A poor white child from a small town has one advantage: he has a greater chance breaking out of his environment than do poor white children in other environments.

BLACKS

Kenneth R. Johnson

MINORITY group membership is not synonymous with being disadvantaged. However, a person's chances of being disadvantaged are increased if he is black instead of white.

Economic and Cultural Deprivation

Discrimination in employment has caused disproportionate numbers of black people to be economically impoverished. The incomes of black families of every level of education are significantly lower than the incomes of white families. For example, a black college graduate earns about the same amount as a white high school graduate, and a black high school graduate earns about the same as a white elementary school graduate. The discrepancy can only be explained by discrimination.

Poverty affects the achievement of many black children in specific ways. Basic needs—for food, clothing, and shelter—often go unsatisfied, and it is difficult for children affected in this way to achieve in school. Poverty also prevents many black children from having the kinds of experiences that support the instructional efforts of the school. Trips to cultural facilities, books in the home, educational toys—in other words, all the objects and services that are commonly part of the experiential background of middle-class children and that satisfy educational needs outside school—cost money, and many black families cannot afford them.

This does not mean, however, that educational experiences—trips to cultural facilities, books in the home, educational toys—are substitutes for money. The basic problem for many black families is a lack of money. They need money to satisfy basic needs first—educational experiences are secondary. Many educators miss this point.

Membership in a minority group increases a person's chances of being culturally disadvantaged. Culture can be defined as a way of life, a design for living, that consists of the attitudes, beliefs, practices, patterns of behavior, and institutions that a group has developed in response to particular conditions in order to survive. In this country the conditions that existed for the majority of the people have produced the response labeled "the dominant culture." Black people, however, have had to respond to a different set of conditions, and they have developed a subculture that is different in many ways from the dominant culture. One of these differences is the matriarchal family structure of many black families. Another is the nonstandard English dialect spoken by many black people.

Membership in the black subculture contributes to cultural deprivation because it prevents black children from acquiring the middle-class cultural patterns on which almost all school curricula and instructional materials are based. Many black children have not acquired from their subculture the language patterns, the value system, the attitudes and beliefs—the entire experiential background— that the school program demands. The readiness of black children for achievement is *different*, not just deficient. This is another point educators have missed; compensatory education programs have aimed to supply disadvantaged black children with a middle-class experience so that they could conform to the expectations of the standard middle-class curriculum. This is impossible, and it may be the main reason for the only moderate success (some would argue the lack of success) of compensatory education. Instead of this approach, educators should discover what kinds of experiences membership in the black subculture affords and what kinds of concepts these experiences yield. The curriculum for disadvantaged black children should be based on these discoveries.

Not all black children are disadvantaged, even though they are members of the black subculture. Many black children have acquired almost the same experiential background that middle-class white children have acquired. These black children, though not assimilated, are acculturated. They are bicultural. Furthermore, not all disadvantaged black children are disadvantaged to the same degree. The disadvantaged population is not as homogeneous as it is often thought to be.

Other Characteristics of Disadvantaged Blacks

In most instances, disadvantaged children live in a negative environment, suffer from family breakdown, lack a tradition of literacy, feel rejected by society, have a poor self-concept, and are linguistically handicapped. Of course, this is not a complete list of characteristics of disadvantaged children; however, it includes those characteristics that affect school achievement most seriously.

NEGATIVE ENVIRONMENT

Many disadvantaged black children live in the negative environment of large-city ghettos. This environment is negative because it restricts the experiences of these children, and the concepts their experiences yield are not those on which the school program is based. Again, it must be pointed out that the experiences and concepts gained from this environment are not deficient, but different. Some educators have erroneously concluded that the ghetto environment is unstimulating. In fact, it is over-stimulating. That is, children living in a noisy ghetto under crowded conditions and surrounded by activity are bombarded with stimuli. They learn to shut out stimuli in order to have peace of mind. This habit becomes a hindrance to them in school because they shut out the instructional stimuli provided by teachers. For example, ghetto children frequently do not have the same ability as the majority of children to distinguish meaningful sounds.

Ghetto life generates a value system that is often in opposition to the value system of the school. For example, ghetto children tend to be very aggressive, and they value aggressiveness over intellectualism. Aggressive behavior is a survival pattern in the ghetto; thus, it is a necessary pattern. One of the reasons that these children often cannot work well in groups is that they are accustomed to using threats or physical force as a means of persuasion instead of cooperation and discourse.

The pattern of aggression derived from ghetto living also explains why disadvantaged black children do not like to be touched by teachers in a stress situation. In a stress situation, teachers should not touch disadvantaged black children because the children are apt to interpret any physical contact, even the middle-class "pat on the back" to communicate concern, as an aggressive act.

Ghetto living also generates anti-intellectualism because ghetto children see few benefits of intellectualism in their environment. Therefore, behavior appropriate in school is considered nonfunctional. On the other hand, black people recognize that education is a means for advancement.

In an environment scarred by age, neglect, abuse, and overuse, it is difficult to develop respect for property. Moreover, economic deprivation prevents private ownership of property, a common source of pride for more affluent families.

No disadvantaged black child living in the ghetto can escape being marked by it. Blacks in the ghettos are trapped behind invisible social barriers that prevent their escape to a more promising environment—sometimes prevent even their coming into direct contact with the outside world, the dominant culture. The world presented in textbooks is populated by strangers who inhabit a strange environment unlike anything in their experience. Because these barriers keep disadvantaged black children out of touch with the dominant culture, the ghetto subculture is perpetuated with all the handicaps of restricted experiential development.

FAMILY BREAKDOWN

The "Moynihan report," issued by the United States Department of Labor in March, 1965, revealed that male absenteeism is common among poor black families. Too often, women have had to become both breadwinners and caretakers for their families.

To understand the development of the matriarchal family structure of disadvantaged black families and the absenteeism or weak position of the black male, it is necessary to examine the institution of slavery in America. Marriage between slaves was not recognized as a sacrament. Slave families were frequently separated by the sale of the father to one buyer and of the mother and children to another. The father was permitted to visit his family only at the whim of his master. The disruption of families through selling and separate plantation living helped to establish the pattern of male absenteeism. In addition, white plantation-owners fathered many children who remained with their black mothers. This frequent miscegenation also contributed to the establishment of the matriarchal structure of the black family as something common. Thus, the institution of slavery very early placed the black woman in a position of prominence and power in the family.

The second factor behind the establishment of the matriarchal structure of black families is the precarious economic position of black males in the American employment market. Black women have always been able to obtain employment more easily than black men, and they have often been able to obtain steadier employment. As a result, they often hold the purse strings in the family, and whoever controls the purse strings usually holds the power.

It is ironic that our welfare systems have supported and perpetuated the matriarchy of disadvantaged black families. Many welfare systems deny families financial help as long as an employable male lives at home. Some black women, realizing that the family income from welfare is greater than the income of the black male working at menial and intermittent jobs, simply force their husbands to leave home. Frequently too, black men realize that their families would be better off financially without them and simply leave voluntarily. It may be that many leave "on paper" to qualify their families for welfare, and that the absenteeism rate may not be as high as it appears.

The father's absence does not necessarily mean that a disadvantaged black child is not able to achieve in school. Many disadvantaged black children come from wholesome families without fathers—families that supply basic needs, love, and security. When these children fail, it is due to other factors. Teachers must realize that a black mother and her children (often, the grandmother and the mother and her children) are a functioning family. When a disadvantaged black child from a fatherless home fails, the direct cause of his failure may be economic: no man is present earning an income to satisfy his basic needs. (Of course, there are other reasons that these children fail; this is just one of the reasons.)

Teachers must understand that since the mother usually holds the power in a disadvantaged black family, even when the father is present, she is the one to deal with when contacting the family.

The absence of the father often has a particularly debilitating effect on boys. Too many black boys grow up in families without a male model and attend schools dominated by females. They learn their male roles the best way they can, often in the streets of the ghetto. The most attractive, and apparently the most successful, male adults in ghetto communities are those who are making money, including the men who have been led perhaps by discrimination in employment to apply their talents to illegal activities. These undesirable models do not make school seem attractive or even necessary to the boys who wish to emulate them. (In fact, education does not make a significant difference in the income of blacks: black high school graduates earn only slightly more than black high school dropouts.)

The precarious economic position and high rate of absenteeism of black fathers and the dominance of black mothers rob black boys of appropriate models. Therefore, ghetto schools—particularly ghetto elementary schools—should hire more male teachers, preferably black males.

Finally, the position of the mother in a black family explains something that teachers—white teachers in particular—are often puzzled about: many black children react violently to any derogatory statement or implication about their mothers. (Talking in a derogatory way about another's mother is "playing the dozens" in the idiom of the black subculture.) Teachers should understand that much more often for a black child than for a white child the mother is the only source of love and security, the one person in life on whom the child can depend. Teachers should avoid making overt negative judgments about the mothers of black children.

TRADITION OF ILLITERACY

The black subculture lacks a tradition of literacy. Before the Civil War it was illegal in many southern states to teach slaves to read, and even after slavery was abolished, black people in the South were not encouraged to become literate. The schooling that was provided for them produced semiliterates. In addition, the sharecropping economy in which most blacks in the South were ensnared prevented them from completing many years of schooling. Illiteracy prevailed among blacks in the South until very recently.

Furthermore, the reality of discrimination, until recent years, has preempted the necessity for many blacks to acquire an education. Even if blacks became educated in academic areas other than teaching, the ministry, medicine, and social work (the professions traditionally open to blacks), they could not easily obtain employment. This situation discouraged academic aspiration and consequently academic achievement. The situation, however, is changing. Black college graduates in every field of study are in great demand now. This demand must be communicated to disadvantaged black children to inspire them to set their academic goals high.

Even though black people lack a long tradition of literacy, they generally have a positive attitude toward education. This appears to be a contradiction. However, black parents realize that education is one way their children can improve their standard of living. Consequently, they encourage their children to go to school. Education probably follows employment and housing on the list of priorities of most black people. However, their own ignorance, lack of education, or economic poverty often prevents them from knowing just how to support the efforts of the school.

FEELING OF REJECTION AND POOR SELF-CONCEPT

Many black children rightfully feel that society has rejected them. Furthermore, they have concluded that they have been rejected by society simply because they are black. This feeling of rejection has produced a poor self-concept in many black children. These children learn at an early age that they are black, and that they are somehow inferior because they are black.

Black children develop this self-concept in a social context. In making qualitative judgments about themselves they take cues from those who are unlike them as well as from those who are like them. For example, they observe the way black people in our society are treated by many whites. They respond to our language—specifically, to the negative connotations of the word *black* in many contexts.

For many blacks, the unalterable color of their skin has been an outward sign of their inferiority. This traditional attitude is changing, however. The "Black Revolution" is giving black people—particularly the younger ones—a new dignity and a new pride in themselves. Because of their increased dignity and pride, many black people have adopted a new label for themselves: *black*. They have also adopted a new hair style: the natural or Afro style. They no longer wish to conform to white America's beauty standard of straight hair. These two cultural changes are expressions of a healthy self-concept.

LINGUISTIC DISADVANTAGE

Many black children are linguistically disadvantaged: they speak a nonstandard dialect of English that a number of educators and linguists believe interferes with their attempts to learn to read and to speak standard English.

Teachers often react to the use of nonstandard dialect by telling the children that their language is "bad" or "sloppy." Since language is an identifying label, teachers who reject the language of disadvantaged children reject the children themselves and those who speak the same dialect (their friends and families)— indeed, the whole culture from which the children come.

It is unlikely that these children will accept the language of the school and teacher if the school and teacher do not accept their nonstandard dialect. Disadvantaged children whose native language is not English—Mexican-Americans, Puerto Ricans, and Indians, for example—often receive sympathy from their teachers, whereas black children who have a similar but not so obvious interference problem generally do not. Teachers of disadvantaged black children frequently follow a "don't say it like that, say it like this" approach. Before they are likely to learn standard English, these children need specialized help, not unlike that given pupils learning English as a second language. In other words, the points of interference between their dialect and standard English must be dealt with systematically. This is not often done in language programs.

A similar program should be followed for reading instruction. Children should have a reading program that takes account of the phonological and structural differences between their nonstandard dialect and standard English, in particular those that produce interference. This means that the reading program must be custom-made for disadvantaged black children, and it must be coordinated and conducted concurrently with the language program. Instead, the approach usually followed in teaching reading to disadvantaged black children is to give them a remedial reading program—which too often means the regular reading program administered in smaller doses and in diluted form, with no attention given to the interference caused by their nonstandard dialect.

In order to provide effective language arts and reading programs, teachers should be educated in the phonology and structure of the nonstandard dialect of disadvantaged black children as well as in second-language teaching techniques, and instructional materials must be prepared that take into account the special linguistic and cultural features of this group.

Another common fault of the language program for disadvantaged black children is that standard English is taught as a replacement dialect rather than as an alternate dialect. This approach is faulty because as long as these children live in a cultural environment in which the nonstandard dialect is functional, they will not discard it. The goal of language instruction, then, should be to give pupils language flexibility.

The Black Revolution

Black people cannot be discussed without taking note of the "Black Revolution" that is occurring. This revolution touches the lives of everyone—white and black. For many Americans the phrase "Black Revolution" calls to mind sit-ins, demonstrations, arrests, riots, and destruction. These are some features of the revolution, but their dramatic quality tends to blot out the most significant feature, the search for identity. The essence of the revolution is that black people are now defining themselves. They are looking inward and discovering what kind of people they are, and what they are discovering is their identity—their black identity, their membership in a unique subculture. Furthermore, they are discovering valuable and positive aspects in themselves and their subculture.

The term "black," which they have adopted as their total identifying label, is a racial label and a psychological, sociological, and cultural label. It refers to an individual who shares a common experience with twenty-two million others, characterized in part by a common will to survive in a hostile racist society. This self-discovery, or self-definition, is the most significant feature of the revolution. Black people are asserting that they will no longer allow white people to define them and that they will no longer look upon anything identifiably black as automatically inferior.

As black people look inward, many have grown revengeful as they contemplated the accumulated injustices perpetrated on them by a white racist society for over three hundred and fifty years. Young black people are particularly revengeful, and their attitude toward white society is often violent, as the Kerner

Commission revealed in its report on violence in American society, published in March, 1968.

This revengeful attitude causes young blacks to reject, often justifiably, the three authority figures of the white society that they come into contact with most frequently: the white businessman, the white policeman, and the white teacher, who symbolize exploitation, brutality, and neglect. In the near future white teachers will probably find it increasingly difficult to work with black pupils because of their revengeful attitude.

The revolution—the process of self-definition—should become as much a part of the curriculum as math or science or history. It is particularly important as part of the secondary-school English program. Language arts activities—reading, writing, speaking, drama, debating—can be structured around the wealth of materials and topics presented by the revolution, which is the most significant event in the lives of many black pupils.

Instead of making the Black Revolution a part of the curriculum, many whites have tried to shut it out. They may feel threatened because the revolution presents a new image of the black man, not what many whites want him to be. This tendency is reflected in the kinds of black people included in textbooks. Although blacks appear in textbooks in increasing numbers, those included are usually "safe Negroes," such as Booker T. Washington, Dr. George Washington Carver, Dr. Percy Julian, Dr. Charles Drew, Marion Anderson, Ralph Bunche, and Jackie Robinson—"safe" because their achievements are not concerned with current crises. Instead, their success carries the message "Be good, be outstanding in one attribute, and white people will accept you." The fallacy is that only a few black children can become as outstanding as these "safe Negroes." The majority will continue to be unacceptable by these standards. A few revolutionary blacks, too far removed in history to be relevant to today's revolution, Nat Turner and Denmark Vassey, for example, may be included in an ineffective attempt at a balance.

But black people esteem other kinds of blacks than those included in textbooks. For example, Adam Clayton Powell, Rap Brown, Stokely Carmichael, Malcolm X, Muhammad Ali, and the Reverend Jesse Jackson are black men who have fought oppression, speaking in a way white people do not want to accept. They present a much more aggressive model to black children. These men have not waited for or asked politely for civil rights. Instead, they have spoken defiantly in response to racism, demanding civil rights for black people. This kind of action has earned them the esteem of fellow blacks.

In addition, the reading curriculum must include black writers who are relevant to today. In addition to works by Paul Lawrence Dunbar, Countee Cullen, Phillis Wheatley, and James Weldon Johnson, the reading curriculum should include the writings of W. E. B. DuBois, Richard Wright, James Baldwin, Malcolm X, Eldridge Cleaver, Le Roi Jones, and other relevant black writers. These writers are excluded on the grounds that they are "controversial" or "too mature."

The first excuse is intellectually dishonest, and the second is nonsense. Many young blacks have already discovered these writers. In fact, their works are nearly all they are reading with fervent interest. Little else in American literature speaks directly to them.

A study of these writers will not increase black pupils' anger and revengefulness, as some white educators may fear. Instead, it will help black pupils to go beyond these feelings to self-definition. Anger and desire for revenge are temporary emotions, and they will cease when black people realize that they consume both the subject and the object. A study of these writers will speed this realization, by focusing attention on the main issue of defining black people. When this definition is completed, white teachers will be able to work effectively with black children—but it will be a new relationship of equals.

SPANISH–SPEAKERS

William Madsen

WHENEVER we teach a "subject" to a child we are doing more than merely adding one more skill to his total abilities. We are affecting the total configuration of his personality and thereby his patterns of interaction with others. This is especially true when we are teaching something as symbolically and socially significant as a language. Therefore, we have not only the problem of how the individual will try to use his new skill but also that of how society will react to his attempts to use that skill. This interaction will produce changes in the total social arrangement.

Language and Social Goals

It is important that we attempt to conceive our total goals when considering specific problems such as teaching English to Spanish-speaking groups. In almost every sphere of our society we are at a crossroads in regard to our goals. To a large extent this has always been true in our society: the United States has always been characterized by rapid social change and adjustment. However, never before have the changes been so rapid nor the goals so difficult to define. Moreover, today the possibilities have been greatly increased, so that a decision made at one crossroad will negate or modify a decision made at another. For example, many people today sense a conflict between the value of freedom of choice in association and the principle behind legislated and enforced integration.

Regardless of the stresses involved, we are now pledged to integrate minority groups into the normative patterns of the larger society. As the older values of both dominant and subordinate groups are modified, sensitivities of members of both groups are intensified. Both those seeking to preserve the old ways and those seeking the new are prone to feel threatened by any direct or indirect reference to societal values. Individuals in this setting tend to seek and reinforce association with others sharing their own values, and the times are fertile for the formation of hate and action groups. When a language difference, such as that between Spanish and English, is primarily associated with the differences between a dominant and a subordinate group, enormous emotional sensitivity is associated with these languages.

In this changing and stress-filled situation we are relying on education as one of our major tools to achieve the goal of successful integration. In part, we are assuming that when Spanish-speakers have mastered English much of the threat felt by some other whites, or Anglos, will be removed. However, the knowledge of English will also, as intended, open new job opportunities for the Spanish-speakers. Anglos already in these job categories may develop an increased hostility toward their new competitors for employment. Thus, reaction against integration in many work situations may be increased. Spanish-speaking pupils should not be led to believe that a firm knowledge of English by itself will open the gates to a friendly and rich world.

The Role and Responsibility of Teachers

Teachers are in the sensitive and delicate position of bridging the gap for their pupils between real and ideal situations as well as moderating between conflicting parental values that may find their way into the classroom. Their best aid in this situation is familiarity with the formalized goals of the society as a whole and with the subsocietal values facilitating or hindering the achievement of these goals. They should also try to recognize clearly their own values within this configuration so that they can, as far as possible, avoid unconscious reinforcement of barriers to the achievement of the formal goals. At the same time, to avoid introducing added strain to the pupil's home life, teachers must be careful in trying to modify values acquired from parents.

An awareness of the value conflicts involved in formal goal achievement may not be enough. The fact that teachers must now concentrate on correcting "handicaps" of the Spanish-speaking pupils, such as inadequate English, may easily change for the worse their real or apparent attitude toward these pupils. Through such language teaching, teachers may violate the very concepts of individual and group worth that they should be trying to strengthen. In our historical past, when an ethnic or racial group was thought to be socially subordinate, it was still seen as having a meaningful and permanent, even if inferior, place in our total social structure. Its members were accepted in well-defined and socially approved roles.

Today, however, with the goal of total integration, the tendency is to see such a minority as "deviant" rather than "subordinate." The individuals in that group are no longer accepted as a valuable lower level of society. Rather, they are viewed as joining the ranks of those who do not conform to the norms of the larger society. Inadvertently, then, the Spanish-speaking citizens may be lumped into a larger "social pathology" with other deviants. The desire to change someone implies a disapproval of what they are even if their "deviancy" is attributed to societal rather than moral failings. To allow a pupil to sense such disapproval can prove disastrous.

It would be wise for teachers to consider seriously how much of the Spanish-speaking "deviancy" should really be changed. Since the purpose of improving a pupil's English is to involve him more fully in the Anglo manner of life, it may be mistakenly assumed that when he improves his English he will simultaneously abandon much of his culture associated with the speaking of Spanish. Is our ultimate goal an equality so complete that individual and group differences are to be traded for a technically more efficient society of interchangeable human robots? If we should choose to retain our traditional value of allowing the individual to seek excellence according to his own unique abilities, should this right not also be offered to minority groups that wish to avoid complete absorption into normative Anglo culture? Many Spanish-speaking citizens do wish to preserve much of their cultural heritage. However, the very concept of total integration almost prohibits the possibility of ethnic group identity.

On the other hand, when teachers recognize a pupil's ethnic identity, they can easily fall into the psychological and semantic error of stereotyping. Whenever we classify any group of objects or people with a common word or phrase, we tend to minimize the differences between the members of that group. The fewer the traits used for the classification, the fewer will be the other shared attributes. Unfortunately, the classificatory lumping of humans on the basis of language use frequently carries an erroneous assumption of the sharing of extensive cultural and psychological traits.

Such inaccurate stereotyping in this country is all too often observable in our use of the rubric "Spanish-speaking." In practice, this classification is usually restricted to those who trace their ancestry to Cuba, Puerto Rico, and Mexico, since these countries are the sources of the major migrations from Spanish-speaking nations. Still, these individuals come from vastly different cultural backgrounds, even though each of these countries of origin shares an important Spanish heritage. Different Indian cultural admixtures and distinctive histories have produced national cultures that differ significantly. Many Spanish-speakers have great pride in their national origins and resent being lumped with others on the basis of language alone. Others are proud of identification with regions within the United States where historical events have produced distinctive sub-cultures. The Spanish-American of New Mexico, for example, has significant linguistic and cultural differences from the Mexican-American of Texas. Both groups see themselves as different and apart from the Puerto Ricans of Spanish Harlem. Other group differences between our Spanish-speaking citizens are produced by class, religion, and political ideology. These differences frequently reflect varying degrees of acculturation to the dominant culture. The attitudes, beliefs, and self-image of a recently arrived Mexican peasant will differ drastically from those of a fourth-generation Spanish-speaking citizen in Chicago. Such differences can color the classroom environment. In order to relate successfully to Spanish-speaking pupils, teachers should be aware of such group differences as well as of the fact that every individual is above all unique.

At the same time that teachers are guarding against stereotyping their Spanish-speaking pupils, they should remember that they are probably being seen as stereotypes by many of these pupils. If the teacher is an Anglo, he may be regarded as merely an interchangeable unit of the dominant society. If he is from a Spanish-speaking background, he may be viewed as typical of those who have "sold out" their cultural heritage for power or money. It may be that from a sociological standpoint, a teacher from another ethnic faction, black or Oriental, would be in the best position to teach American culture to Spanish-speaking pupils.

AMERICAN INDIANS

Miles V. Zintz

AMERICAN Indians were living throughout the United States when the conquistadors moved into the Southwest in 1540 and when the English colonists began settling the Atlantic seaboard in 1607. It has been estimated that there may have been about one million Indians in the United States at that time.

Because the Indians were living on land and using resources that the "white man" desired, it is not surprising that the white man soon began pushing the Indians farther and farther westward from the Atlantic shores. The conquistadors did not exercise the same militant stand, continually making war, as the English settlers did, but they did have the same general notions about their value system as contrasted with that of the Indians.

Settlers from northern Europe tended to label the Indians in terms of their relationships with them at a specific time. Washburn (1957) points out that when the Indians taught the New England colonists how to plant and fertilize their gardens and even loaned them food from their storehouses, the colonists called them "noble savages." Later, when the colonists tried to push the Indians off their lands and make treaties to take control, the Indians sometimes burned their homesteads and generally fought back; then the settlers labeled the Indians "treacherous savages." When the Indians were later confined to reservations with their life style completely destroyed because they did not accept the ways of the white man, the white man chose to describe the Indians generally as "filthy savages."

Many Indian groups are still struggling with the problems of transition from their traditional way of life to the dominant culture. Washburn suggests that the members of the dominant society are apt to label them, and accept them, as "incompetent savages" and continue to deny them the social and economic status that they should enjoy.

Changes in the Indian Way of Life

CULTURAL PATTERNS AND VALUES

Reifel (1957), himself an Indian, analyzes cultural factors affecting social adjustment of Indians and emphasizes four principal differences between the American way of life and the traditional pattern of Indian life.

1. While the thinking of the dominant culture is future-oriented, Indians may be prone to live in the present—to take care of their needs today and to let tomorrow take care of itself. While the thinking of the dominant culture has at its roots the idea of a "mastery over nature," the Indians believe in a "harmony with nature." Reifel emphasizes this difference in behavior: the dominant society lives in a state of anticipation, whereas Indians find the essence of living in the present.
2. Viewing time, in terms of hours and minutes, with subservience to clocks and calendars, is not important to the Indian way of life.
3. Saving as a means of achieving economic development has not been a part of Indian economic life. While competition is an integral part of the white man's behavior, cooperation is more characteristic of the Indian's.
4. Habituation to hard work, particularly for the men of the tribe, is not a part of the Indian system.

The psychological principles that most Anglo teachers have internalized in the process of learning to be teachers may not apply when they attempt to teach the prescribed course of study to Indian children, who have been taught values in their homes and in their communities that are different from those of their teachers. In every culture, value is placed on whatever works best to achieve the goals that society has determined are important. And the goals with which Indian children come to school may not at all be the goals the elementary school teacher thinks are the best for American society.

Further, because through history Indians have been made to feel that they must surrender their way of life in order to accept the white man's, there has been a general resistance to learning the English language well, a fundamental requirement for success in our schools. The fact is that because of differences in language, culture, and experience, Indians are culturally *different* rather than culturally deprived.

Assimilation and change has taken place among American Indians during the past four hundred years. From earliest times, when one group obtained steel knives or efficient tools from another group, they were quick to see their advantage. In 1868 a band of Navajos made their way back to their former homes in northeastern Arizona after being detained for five years in eastern New Mexico in a futile government effort to train them to be farmers. During the long trek the Navajo women learned of the long skirts and velvet blouses of the pioneer women and adopted this manner of dress—and continue it to this day. Pick-up trucks have proved to be invaluable both for providing automobile transportation and for replacing the horse and wagon in hauling produce. The radio and to some extent television have brought Indians many new desires, so that they are trading their agrarian subsistence living more and more for participation in the money economy. They need dollars to make weekly installment payments on television sets, automobiles, washing machines, sewing machines, and many other items of middle-class life.

THE BASIC INSTITUTIONS OF LIVING

There are certain basic institutions in all societies. These may generally be classified as some type of religion, education of the young, family life, health practices, economy, government, and recreation. The way of life in a given society depends on the interaction of these basic institutions. If one institution is lost or undergoes a rapid radical change, it has a disorganizing effect on the other institutions.

In the Navajo culture, for example, one of the primary focuses of daily living is on maintaining or regaining one's health. Religious ceremonies used to be the means of regaining harmony with nature, pleasing all the gods, and restoring the balance in nature. With the advent of medical services provided by the United States Public Health Service, however, many Indians find that they can keep healthy without any of their traditional religious rituals. In other words, the rapid change to the use of white man's medicine has also made serious inroads into traditional religious practices.

Indians quickly see the desirability of modern goods that the mass media advertise so effectively. The new need for a weekly pay check and money to meet installment payments regularly is destroying the old subsistence, agrarian economy.

Formal education replaces the traditional way of learning from the old people. The Navajo Tribal Council, using royalties from oil, gas, and uranium mines on the reservation, established a ten-million-dollar investment fund; the revenue is used for scholarships for Indians in institutions of higher education. This plan had its inception, perhaps, with Manuelito, an old chief of the Navajos. Underhill (1953) reports him to have said, "Education is the ladder. Tell our people to take it."

Since the advent of the Economic Opportunity Act in 1965, Indian groups have been most alert in organizing at the grass-roots level and requesting teachers with communications skills in English for their preschool children.

So, with radical changes in the basic institutions, the processes of cultural change work rapidly, and the values of the Indian young people become more like the values of young people growing up in the dominant culture.

Effect of Cultural Differences on Learning in the Classroom

The danger of stereotyping is ever-present in attempting to make generalizations about behavior. It appears best, then, to limit this description of cultural differences to Pueblo Indians of the Southwest. Even attempting to group all the Pueblos of the Rio Grande River Valley together is not completely safe because, of course, there are certain differences among them. However, the general behavior of a traditional Pueblo Indian child may be contrasted with that of his Anglo teacher in the following ways (Zintz, 1962, 1963).

The Pueblo Indian child is likely to be taught at home to value:	*The Anglo teacher is almost sure to place the highest value on:*
1. Harmony with nature.	Mastery over nature.
2. Mythology. (The supernatural is feared, and sorcerers and witches are thought to cause unexplained behavior.)	Scientific explanations for everything (Nothing happens contrary to natural law.)
3. Present-time orientation.	Future-time orientation.
4. Working to satisfy present need.	Working to get ahead.

5. Time as infinite.	Efficient use of time. (Time can never be regained.)
6. Following the ways of the old people.	Climbing the ladder of success.
7. Cooperation.	Competition.
8. Anonymity.	Individuality.
9. Submissiveness.	Aggression (socially acceptable).
10. Humility.	Striving to win.
11. Sharing.	Saving for the future.

With such a value system the Pueblo child is unlikely to be sensitive to some of these admonitions from his teacher: "Try to get through with the problem *first*"; "What you did yesterday wasn't quite good enough. Do a little better next time"; "Everyone must read well."

All children do have the same basic psychological needs. Problems arise from the fact that a teacher's successful response to any child requires some understanding of his cultural background: the teacher must know *how to respond* so that the child will derive the satisfactions he needs. For example, where the definition of sex roles of boys and girls is different from that in the dominant society, the way a teacher communicates reward and punishment, praise and blame, or even affection, even to six- or seven-year-old pupils, should be gauged by the way the children think, act, and feel. Further, if a child believes that witches, not germs, cause disease, the teacher must know how to explain the germ theory without alienating either the child or the child's parents.

The three illustrations that follow emphasize for the teacher that an Indian child's "readiness" for classroom learning is not the same as the child's whose cultural heritage has already given him many of the values taught in the school. Wauneka (1962) reports the medicine man's explanation of the cause of tuberculosis in the following way:

> I asked the medicine men what they thought caused the lungs to be destroyed; what caused the coughing and the spitting up of blood. According to the stories learned from their ancestors, tuberculosis is caused by lightning. If lightning struck a tree and a person used that tree for firewood or anything, it would make him sick, cause blisters to develop in his throat and abscesses in his lungs.

Anthropological literature contains many illustrations of the differences in behavior between Indians and non-Indians. Wax and Thomas (1961) report:

> From childhood, white people and Indians are brought up to react to strange and dangerous situations in quite different ways. The white man who finds himself in an unstructured, anxiety-producing situation is trained to react

with a great deal of activity. He will begin action after action until he either structures the situation, or escapes from it, or simply collapses. But the Indian, put in the same place, is brought up to remain motionless and watch. Outwardly, he appears to freeze. Inwardly, he is using all of his senses to discover what is expected of him—what activities are proper, seemly and safe. One might put it this way: in an unfamiliar situation a white man is taught to react by aggressive experimentation—he keeps moving until he finds a satisfactory pattern. His motto is "Try and try again." But the Indian puts his faith in observation. He waits and watches until the other actors show him the correct pattern.

Spang (1965) points out that Indians are likely to have a low level of aspiration: they generally lack information about a wide range of occupations; they may have no available role models to identify with; they may have no great desire to leave the reservation; they may see no reason to achieve if "father is on relief and has enough money to live on." A young Indian might not even want a permanent job because his relatives might move in with him, and he would be supporting not only himself and his family but also a host of others.

Conflicts in "Perceiving, Behaving, Becoming" a Fully Functioning Self

It is possible for teachers and professors oriented to the middle-class life style to forget that there are large segments of the population that have a very different outlook.

In *Perceiving, Behaving, Becoming* (1962) Kelley makes several statements about the dominant society and about the needs of students in general that Anglo teachers working with Pueblo Indian children should interpret in terms of traditional Pueblo cultural values. For example, Kelley says, "We live in a moving, changing, becoming-but-never-arriving world." But a Pueblo Indian child has likely already learned that nature provides and that man's objective is to remain in harmony with nature. The dances, rituals, and seasonal prayers are learned perfectly and passed from one generation to another in an effort to maintain and restore harmony.

He continues, "[The pupil] needs to see process, the building-and-becoming nature of himself. Today has no meaning in the absence of yesterdays and tomorrows." But, a Pueblo child may believe that there is an essence of timelessness in the way night follows day and seasons pass slowly in succession. His life has been concerned with the here and now. Accepting nature in its seasons, man will live through the years one at a time.

According to Kelley, "The growing self must feel that it is involved, that it is really part of what is going on, that in some degree it is helping to shape its own destiny." So, too, a Pueblo child early in life is made to feel that he is involved and personally responsible for doing his part so that all of life—village life, the natural order, all the cosmic forces—is kept running smoothly and harmoniously. Thus, a Pueblo child may be *more* actively involved, and have more specific tasks to perform, than a middle-class child.

However, the goal of a Pueblo child's involvement will not likely be to change his destiny, which is determined by the older and wiser members of the community. Each individual best fulfills his destiny by remaining an anonymous member of his social group, accepting group sanctions, and placing primary emphasis on conformity.

Kelley says, "The acceptance of change as a universal phenomenon brings about modifications of personality . . . one who accepts change and expects it, behaves differently." But, a Pueblo child has probably already learned that one may follow in the ways of the old people with confidence. Young people should keep quiet because they lack maturity and experience. This behavior deemphasizes experiment, innovation, and change.

Finally, "One sees the evil of the static personality because it seeks to stop the process of creation. . . . Life . . . means discovery and adventure, flourishing because it is in tune with the universe." But, a Pueblo child believes that if the things he is doing are good now, to be doing these same things all his life will be good. Leadership evolves; one does not seek to dominate others. (In sports, for example, if one wins once, he should then let someone else win.)

Accepting these cultural factors in the traditional ways of life of a people and recognizing the general axiom that cultures change very slowly, we know that much of the behavior of Indian children today either is largely controlled by the traditional values of their ancestors or is moving on a long continuum toward acculturation in the American middle-class society. We may, then, ask, What is the role of the school in meeting the needs of these children who come to school with this different set of cultural values?

Accommodations Within Different Cultures

Under certain conditions two cultures may exist side by side and maintain their cultural integrity, each continuing to practice its habits and customs. Indians and the Spanish settlers in the Southwest maintained such an existence for more than 150 years. However, when the Anglo-Americans came their culture became dominant and influenced the cultures of the other ethnic groups. Whether cultures can continue to exist side by side, then, is determined by the continued independent operation of their basic institutions, for example, economy, health practices, education, religion, and family life.

Can the traditional economy of simple agriculture, based on gardens of beans, squash, corn, and chili, continue to provide for the needs of Indian families when the products of the dominant culture—televisions, radios, pick-up trucks, refrigerators, and freezers—must be paid for on an installment plan that calls for a weekly pay check? *Economy* is probably the pivot on which the stability of a way of life depends.

What of health practices? Reducing infant mortality and using miracle drugs are efforts that, once demonstrated with modern medical practices, everyone wants continued and expanded. Modern medicine competes effectively with the curing rites of the medicine man, and since curing rites are parts of religious ceremonies, the close interdependence between health and religion determines that both of these basic institutions will be changed.

Of course, new specific practices do get incorporated into the behavioral patterns of a group. For example, the shalakos, or priests, of the Zuñi tribe now come up from the river to bless new houses most often on Friday or Saturday night. More and more Navajo girls are not going through the traditional puberty rites before their third menstruation. The more acculturated the parents are, the less they consider the ceremony necessary.

Education is changing very rapidly as Indians struggle to obtain formal education. To fail to give them an opportunity for education will be to bequeath them only the most limited economic opportunities when they attempt to move into the mainstream of American life.

In an informal talk with school administrators in Albuquerque, New Mexico, in 1963, Harvard sociology professor Florence Kluckhohn suggested that Indians' increasing acceptance of the life practices of middle-class America is inevitable and that the responsibility of educators is to make the transition as easy and as painless as possible. This means that we must try to offer the kinds of educational experiences that make it possible for Indians to provide for their families as quickly as possible in the general competitive world. If, through education, they can meet the economic challenge, then they must in their own good time work out the solutions to problems of changing family life and religion. These are areas in which the white man may offer much support, but they are also extremely personal and must be met by each individual in his own way.

3

Economic Backgrounds:
Their Impact on Schoolchildren

Robert W. MacMillan

POVERTY is not racist. Whether a person is economically disadvantaged or deprived does not depend on race or other ethnic consideration. Membership among the economically disadvantaged group includes people of every race—black, red, white, yellow, and any intermediate hue.

There is a tendency, however, to identify poverty with one group. When problems of the economically disadvantaged are discussed and policies and programs set forth, the group most closely linked with being disadvantaged is the black. Blacks comprise approximately 11 percent (22 million) of the total population in the United States. In order to meet its needs, this significantly large group has formed organizations dedicated to furthering the black cause and black demands. The NAACP (National Association for the Advancement of Colored People) and CORE (Congress on Racial Equality) have been instrumental in pushing programs and legal reforms designed to assist the black population. Other organizations, either more or less militant, also are directly concerned with upgrading the economic and social status of the black man.

It almost has become a truism that when we speak of the disadvantaged, we are speaking of blacks. Yet, in absolute numbers based on the government's criterion for classifying disadvantaged (an income of $3135 or less annually for a family of four), more persons of other races, and specifically whites (Witmer, 1964), can be classified disadvantaged than blacks. In its 1968 television series "Hunger in America," the Columbia Broadcasting System emphatically pictured the plight of Indians, Mexican-Americans, and Appalachian whites, as well as that of blacks. Probably the most startling and depressing aspect of this exposé was the effect extreme deprivation has on children caught in the poverty cycle.

One ethnic group caught in the throes of extreme poverty and largely ignored is the Mexican-American. The socioeconomic plight of Mexican-Americans has been described as "America's best kept secret" (Sitomer, 1965). In view of the amount of publicity given to such places as Appalachia and to particular ethnic groups such as the black population, the description may be appropriate. There is no national Mexican-American voice similar to the NAACP for the black man. And yet, in certain geographic areas of the United States, Mexican-Americans are living in a state of deprivation greater than that of blacks or Appalachian whites. One might say, in light of federal and state emphasis, that the tragedy of Mexican-Americans is that by act of Congress they have been classified as white.

American Indians constitute a third and extremely disadvantaged group. In actual numbers, the Indian population is smaller than either the black or the Mexican-American, yet it is the only group of the three with its own federal bureau—the Bureau of Indian Affairs. Nevertheless, American Indians are as disadvantaged as either blacks or Mexican-Americans, if not more so in some areas.

The history of American Indians has been well documented (although at times one-sidedly) by writers, historians, and others through various media—books, magazines, movies, radio, and television. In considering the present socioeconomic status of American Indians, we have to depend on sources such as Census Bureau reports, congressional records, and studies by the Bureau of Indian Affairs that at times are not at all consistent with each other. For example, educational data differ depending on what source is used. To some extent the same is true for income and population data. Projects such as Havighurst's comprehensive study of American Indians, funded by the United States government, may aid in the establishment of more definitive data.

The general purpose of this chapter is to describe socioeconomic conditions prevalent in the culture of the poverty-stricken that influence children of school age, using examples from both nonwhite and white populations. Specific attention is paid to three groups—blacks, Mexican-Americans, and Indians—and comparisons are drawn between these groups and the Anglos, the white population minus Mexican-Americans.

Populations: Size and Location

The United States Bureau of the Census estimated that in 1967 approximately 21,983,000 blacks were living in the fifty states (United States Department of Commerce, 1968). The ratio of black population to total population has changed little in this century. From 1900 to 1960 the black race increased 113 percent;

the white race, 137 percent; and other races, 227 percent. The most startling change in the black population was not in increase in numbers but rather in mobility. Blacks have consistently moved from the farm to the city, from rural areas to urban—that is, according to the Census Bureau definition, to cities, boroughs, towns, or villages with twenty-five hundred or more inhabitants. In the South, where we would expect most blacks to be living in rural areas, three out of five are urban dwellers. Blacks in other sections of the country are predominantly city dwellers (United States Department of Labor, 1966).

However, in 1968 only one major city, Washington, D. C., had more blacks than whites. "In all other cities of 250,000 population or more, the ratio of Negroes to the total population was 40 percent or below in 1960; and in most instances, it was less than 30 percent" (United States Department of Labor, 1966).

Spanish-speakers comprise one of the next largest groups in the country. According to the 1960 Census Bureau report, *Persons of Spanish Surname*, there were approximately 3.5 million Spanish-speakers in the United States. This figure is believed to be inaccurate,for it takes into account only the five southwestern states.[1] *Newsweek* magazine (March 23, 1966) reports the actual figure may be closer to 10 million; Chicago alone has over 200,000 Spanish-speaking residents. In New England there has been a great influx of Spanish-speakers, with resulting confusion in educational circles. One small community opened school to find, unexpectedly, thirty-five Spanish-speaking children enrolled. The superintendent immediately formed a special-education class for them in order to receive more state aid and, probably, if the usual practice is followed for children placed in special-education classes, as a "final solution."

The bulk of Mexican-Americans are assumed to be concentrated in the five southwestern states: Arizona, California, Colorado, New Mexico, and Texas. They are the largest minority group in these states (see Table 3–1). Some 33.5 percent of the total Mexican-American population live in fourteen cities. Manuel (1965) reports that in two Texas cities, Brownsville and Laredo, Mexican-Americans are actually in the majority—73.8 and 82.1 percent, respectively—and that in three others, Corpus Christi, El Paso, and San Antonio, over 30 percent of the population is Mexican-American. This is a greater concentration than that of blacks in metropolitan areas.

The American Indian population is presently far smaller than the black and Mexican-American populations. When Spanish explorers came in the sixteenth century to what is now the United States, there were an estimated one million Indians. By 1910, however, the Indian population had declined to about 220,000. It seems that a great many Indians died in wars and from disease and other

[1] In this chapter, government data on Spanish-surname persons are taken to refer to Mexican-Americans, since the data are based on figures for the five southwestern states only—Arizona, California, Colorado, New Mexico, and Texas—whose Spanish-surname residents are predominantly Mexican-American.

52   *Backgrounds*

TABLE 3–1

Ethnic Composition of the Population
of the Southwest in 1960 (in percent)

| | White Population | | Nonwhite Population | |
	Anglos	Mexican-Americans	Black	Other Races*
Arizona	73.4	16.4	3.3	6.9
California	82.0	10.0	5.6	2.4
Colorado	87.0	9.9	2.3	0.8
New Mexico	61.0	31.1	1.8	6.1
Texas	71.1	16.3	12.4	0.2

* Other races, as defined by the Census Bureau, include American Indian, Japanese, Chinese, Filipino, Korean, Hawaiian, Asian Indian, Malayan, Eskimo, and Aleut.

SOURCES:
Adapted from United States Bureau of the Census (1960c, 1960e, 1960f).

causes that were probably closely associated with the white man's subjugation of the Indian race.

The Indian birth rate since 1960 has been approximately double the rate of the general population. In 1961, the latest year for which a figure is available, the estimated Indian population exceeded 600,000, with almost 400,000 living on or near reservations.

The following states have the largest Indian populations (given in round figures), according to the United States Commission on Civil Rights (1968):

Arizona	85,000
Oklahoma	65,000
New Mexico	57,000
Alaska	50,000
California	40,000
North Carolina	40,000
South Dakota	30,000
Montana	22,000
Washington	22,000

Indians are predominantly rural dwellers: over 69 percent of the population, according to the 1960 census, lived in rural areas, although the majority were classified nonfarm. Table 3–2 shows the breakdown by geographic area.

The assumed correlation between a highly rural population and socioeconomic deprivation is substantiated by the following data. According to figures presented to the United States Senate Committee on Labor and Public Welfare on August 29, 1967, by Senator Paul J. Fannin of Arizona, over 50 percent of employable Indian males are unemployed. Ninety percent of Indian housing is substandard.

TABLE 3-2

Breakdown of Indian Population by Geographic Area

Area	Total	Urban	Rural Nonfarm	Rural Farm	Percentage Rural
Northeast	34,906	23,028	11,162	716	34
Northcentral	105,048	39,160	57,440	8,448	63
South	132,576	39,668	60,262	32,646	70
West	273,698	64,066	173,353	36,279	77

SOURCE:
United States Bureau of the Census (1960e).

The average life span of the Indians is 42 years, which is over 20 years below the national average of 62.3 years. Infant mortality is double the national average, and the tuberculosis rate is seven times the national average.

The combined 1969 black and Spanish-speaking populations are estimated to be over thirty million persons, or over one-seventh of the total United States population. This is a significant number and the necessity of identifying characteristics that may influence school performance is apparent.

Income Levels

The number of blacks who fall into the poverty category is out of proportion to their number in the general population. In 1964, for example, 37 percent of the country's blacks had annual incomes below $3000,[2] whereas only 15 percent of the white population could be classified poor on this basis.

Many blacks have succeeded in pulling themselves out of the poverty category. In 1967 alone, over one million nonwhites were able to rise above the poverty level (United States Department of Labor, 1968). A similar rise occurred in 1966. The change in the status of whites has not been as dramatic. In 1967 there remained, however, 8.3 million poor blacks who were below the poverty level. This figure represents approximately 35 percent of the total black population.

A comparison of Mexican-American income with that of the general population gives an indication of the degree of economic deprivation found within this minority group (see Table 3-3). Of the total Mexican-American population, more than one-third of the families existed on annual incomes of less than $3000 in 1960.

[2] There are many indexes used to determine poverty. The $3000 figure is one of the most commonly accepted, and when absolute figures are used, it generally develops data equal to the other criteria, such as education levels, housing, and so on.

TABLE 3–3

A Comparison of Family Income
of Anglo, Mexican-American, and Nonwhite Populations
in 1960 (in percent)

	Ari-zona	Cali-fornia	Colo-rado	New Mexico	Texas	South-west	United States
Under $1000							
A	3.7	2.9	3.2	3.6	5.2	3.7	4.4
M-A	7.3	4.6	6.5	11.3	13.6	8.8	—*
NW	26.9	6.3	6.3	28.2	18.0	14.1	15.4
$1000–2999							
A	12.7	9.9	13.5	12.0	16.1	12.2	13.7
M-A	23.7	14.8	28.6	30.2	38.1	25.9	—
NW	30.4	18.5	21.2	28.0	29.6	27.6	32.5
$3000–4999							
A	19.7	14.8	20.6	18.6	21.3	17.5	19.7
M-A	32.4	23.9	29.7	28.4	26.8	26.1	—
NW	23.0	25.5	29.8	21.9	26.5	25.9	24.9
$5000–6999							
A	24.4	22.6	24.8	24.1	23.1	22.9	23.8
M-A	21.4	26.3	19.7	16.7	12.8	19.8	—
NW	11.1	22.9	21.8	11.2	10.0	16.7	14.4
$7000–9999							
A	22.1	26.0	22.3	22.6	19.7	23.6	21.2
M-A	10.6	19.9	10.8	8.8	6.1	12.8	—
NW	5.6	16.8	14.2	7.0	4.2	10.4	8.7
$10,000–14,999							
A	12.1	16.5	11.1	14.1	9.9	13.8	11.2
M-A	3.8	8.3	3.9	3.4	2.0	5.2	—
NW	2.2	7.6	5.3	2.7	1.2	4.3	3.4
$15,000 and over							
A	5.3	7.3	4.5	5.2	4.7	6.3	4.9
M-A	0.8	2.4	0.8	1.0	0.6	1.4	—
NW	0.5	2.1	1.1	0.5	0.2	1.1	0.8

* No figures are available for the whole country.

SOURCES:
Adapted from United States Bureau of the Census (1960c, 1960f, 1960i).

One caution should be observed in interpreting income data for black, Mexican-American, and Anglo populations. If only the figures for males are used for computation purposes, the difference between median incomes of blacks and Mexican-Americans is reduced. The probable reason for this is the large number of black women in the labor force. Black women work "intermittently and for low wages" (Browning and McLemore, 1964). They tend to gravitate toward two occupational categories, private household and service work (United States Bureau of the Census, 1960b). Of the total of black women in the labor force, 55 percent are included within these categories (United States Bureau of the Census, 1960a). In Texas, the percentage is 71.8 (United States Bureau of the Census, 1960a).

In Appalachia, a much publicized and subsidized poverty area, almost one in three families lives on an annual income of $3000 or less (Page and Huyck, 1964). The actual percentage of families living on incomes of $3000 or less in Appalachia in 1960 was 30.7, only slightly less than the 34.7 percent of Mexican-American families with annual incomes of less than $3000 (United States Bureau of the Census, 1960f).

On the surface it may seem that Appalachian whites are as economically deprived as Mexican-Americans. There are, however, two considerations that influence interpretation of these data: (1) rural families generally have lower incomes than urban families; and (2) the cost of living is lower in rural areas than in urban areas. Of the total population in Appalachia, 52.5 percent is rural (Page and Huyck, 1964). The rural Mexican-American population in the Southwest is 20.8 percent of the total Mexican-American population there. The higher percentage of rural residents of Appalachia tends to account for the lower level of income. The greater urbanization of the Mexican-American population increases the difficulty of living on an annual income of under $3000 (United States Bureau of the Census, 1960f). Thus, although Mexican-Americans have about the same level of income as Appalachian whites, their standard of living is somewhat lower.

In New Mexico, over 40 percent of Mexican-American families have incomes of less than $3000; in Texas the figure is over 50 percent. Tuck wrote in 1946, "Leaders among the Mexican-Americans recognize that [the] economic disadvantage. . . . one could say degradation . . . of their group, constitutes its greatest problem." Twenty years later, the same type of situation is still in evidence (Browning and McLemore, 1964; Manuel, 1965; Sitomer, 1965).

Despite occasional financial windfalls, such as oil discoveries, Indians comprise one of the most economically deprived groups in the United States. An indication of Indian deprivation, in addition to the 50 percent unemployment rate among Indian males, is income level. According to the 1960 census, the median income of all Indians was $1348 (United States Bureau of the Census, 1960g). By contrast, the median income of blacks was reported to be $1519. By 1967 the average annual Indian family cash income was $1500 (according to the Bureau of Indian Affairs)—a gain that did not, however, keep pace with normal inflationary increases over this seven-year period (United States Commission on Civil Rights, 1968).

The degree of economic deprivation of Indians is further indicated by the number of families "existing" on annual incomes of less than $3000, as reported in the 1960 census. Of a total of 90,560 Indian families in the United States, 54 percent were living on annual incomes of less than $3000. Twenty-two percent of the families had incomes of less than $1000 per year (see Table 3–4). Although Indians living on reservations receive free medical care and educational assistance, the actual amount of fringe benefits equated in terms of dollars and cents would be quite small.

TABLE 3–4

Income of Indian Families in the United States in 1960

	Number of Families	*Percentage of Total*
Under $1000	20,367	22
$1000–2999	28,837	32
$3000–4999	19,373	21
$5000–6999	11,750	13
$7000–9999	6,986	8
$10,000–14,999	2,649	3
$15,000 and over	598	1
	90,560	

SOURCE:
United States Bureau of the Census (1960d).

In comparing Indian income with black income, the usual extreme variations are found (see Table 3–5). Of the six states surveyed—Arizona, California, New Mexico, North Carolina, Oklahoma, and Texas—only in Texas was there a greater percentage of black males than of Indian males earning less than $1000 annually. More Indian males than black males earned under $3000 annually (based on percentages) in all states except Texas and Oklahoma. Almost 87 percent of Indian males in North Carolina earned less than $3000.

RELATIONSHIP BETWEEN FAMILY INCOME
AND CHILD'S SCHOOL PROGRESS

The relationship between income and school progress can be readily described. In the age group ten to thirteen, approximately 30 percent of Indian children and 20 percent of black children were enrolled in grades below that expected of them based on their age—a high retardation figure. In the age bracket fourteen to fifteen, the figures increase to 42 and 31 percent respectively. By contrast, other minority racial groups have succeeded. Japanese and Chinese children in the lower age category had a 5 percent retardation rate and in the upper age category a 4 percent rate (Folger and Ram, 1969).

TABLE 3–5

A Comparison of Income of Indian and Black Males
in Six States* in 1960 (in percent)

	Arizona	California	New Mexico	North Carolina	Oklahoma	Texas
Under $1000						
I	44.0	20.7	36.9	53.0	39.3	25.9
B	24.3	14.1	15.1	42.7	35.2	31.6
$1000–2999						
I	29.3	33.4	32.4	34.6	33.6	44.4
B	37.8	27.0	47.9	43.2	38.3	41.5
$3000–4999						
I	18.8	25.9	20.7	9.8	17.1	17.5
B	28.7	33.8	27.6	11.9	21.2	21.5
$5000–6999						
I	6.5	14.3	8.2	2.2	7.4	6.9
B	7.8	19.8	6.7	1.6	4.2	4.5
$7000–9999						
I	1.2	4.3	1.4	0.1	1.9	4.0
B	1.0	4.3	1.9	0.4	0.7	0.7
$10,000 and over						
I	0.2	1.4	0.4	0.3	0.7	1.3
B	0.4	1.0	0.8	0.2	0.4	0.2

* Comparative figures were available for only these six states.

SOURCE:
Adapted from United States Bureau of the Census (1960e).

Of schoolgirls ten to thirteen years old of all races whose parents earned less than $3000 annually and had not completed eighth grade, 26 percent were found to be behind expected grade level; whereas only 10 percent were behind grade level whose parents had not completed eighth grade but had an annual income over $7000. The level of family income affected children's school progress even in families in which the parents were high school graduates: in families with incomes of $3000 or less, the retardation rate was over 5 percent compared with a retardation rate of 2 percent in families with incomes of $7000 or higher (see Table 3–9).

The relationship between family income and the child's school performance is obvious when one considers the statistics. However, the relationship becomes more apparent upon visits to homes and schools in poverty-stricken areas. For a child to compete within the school environment, a home situation conducive to study is needed. In most low-income families this is an impossibility, for proper facilities are not available, due in a large degree to lack of money.

Mexican-Americans of San Antonio comprise one of the most economically disadvantaged groups in the United States. As long ago as 1954 San Antonio was described as having one of the worst slum areas in the United States (Burmer, 1954). In the 1968 television program "Hunger in America," CBS concentrated on this area. Low incomes force the Mexican-Americans to live in some of the most dilapidated housing imaginable; housing that is, at the least, a handicap for positive school incentive.

In a study of a particular area of San Antonio (MacMillan, 1966), the following home conditions facing the school child were described. A group of eleven crib-type tenements (*vicinidad*) was found to contain approximately fifty-seven children of elementary-school age. Each unit contained approximately 260 square feet and there were on the average seven or eight persons per unit. For light, there was one ceiling fixture. Heat, if any, was usually from a potbellied stove. Indoor plumbing facilities were nonexistent. One outhouse in the courtyard served over ninety people. Water for washing, cooking, and all other needs was drawn from one outdoor tap, which was attached to the rear of the outhouse. There was usually only one bed, probably reserved for the adults. Other members of the family slept on the floor, or, at most, on a mattress. If there was no mattress, a blanket sufficed for comfort, warmth, and health. To compound matters, many of these "subhuman" dwellings were subrented in order to share rental expense. The area rented might be simply a curtained-off section of the one room. This form of home environment can only be classified as hostile or foreign to that which children need in order to compete in our present school situation.

Disadvantaged Mexican-American children are struggling against a tremendous handicap beyond their control: the subjection of their culture, which is older and in some respects more deeply rooted than the dominant culture of the Anglos. The result is a further strengthening of the cycle of poverty.

Occupations

In any study of a group's economic status, occupation should be considered. Income, occupation, and education are closely related. The type of occupation an individual enters is usually influenced by the amount of schooling completed; income in general depends on the level of occupation; and the lower the occupation, the less income a person enjoys.

A comparison of occupational status using 1960 census data of Mexican-Americans, blacks, and Anglos in the southwestern states (MacMillan, 1966) indicates that most Mexican-Americans have traditionally been employed in unskilled or semiskilled occupations. Being employed in the unskilled or semiskilled ranks from one generation to another is an important example of the perpetuation of economic deprivation. Of the Mexican-American group, Browning and McLemore (1964) state that "natives of native parentage" have not materially improved their occupational position in comparison to that of "natives of foreign or mixed parentage." We would expect those who have been in the United States longer to have improved their occupational status. However, this is not true of Mexican-Americans. The continuous poverty pattern from one generation to another seems to have caused regression in the occupational status of Mexican-Americans (Browning and McLemore, 1964).

According to the 1960 census, over 60 percent of blacks and Mexican-Americans and 63 percent of employable Indians were employed in the five lowest occupational categories. In contrast, only about 27 percent of the Anglo group were employed in the same categories. At the other end of the occupational scale, a little over 18 percent of Mexican-American males are employed in the top five categories. Close to 20 percent of black males and 23 percent of Indian males are similarly employed. Anglo male workers comprise by far the dominant group within these five top categories: almost 50 percent of the total Anglo male working force are employed in a professional or technical capacity, or as managers, clerks, and sales workers.

A study by the United States Department of Labor (1968), indicates that for the first time over 50 percent of all nonwhite workers are employed as white-collar workers or skilled craftsmen. Blacks have been improving their occupational positions rapidly, particularly in recent years. In some areas, such as government service, their gain has been very large, even disproportionate to their percentage of the total population, reports the *Austin American* (February 15, 1966). Mexican-Americans do not seem to be keeping pace with blacks. Indeed, they are probably being penalized because of the concentration of interest on blacks by many national groups (Sitomer, 1965).

RELATIONSHIP BETWEEN PARENT'S OCCUPATION AND CHILD'S SCHOOL ACHIEVEMENT AND IQ

The occupation of the parent is a factor in the attitude of the child toward society, family life style, social adequacy, and finance. Moore and Holtzman (1965) contend, "Children of unskilled workers, rural or urban, are much more negatively oriented to society than young persons from other occupational groups." They also state that children whose parents are employed in "skilled, white collar, ownership" positions give "evidence of more adequate achievement in school." Parents who are unskilled workers earning low incomes often convince their children "that it is hopeless to consider jobs other than those currently held by the majority of their group" (Morris, 1964). Laswell (1965) states that a parent's occupation is interrelated with attitude, income, and values and has an important effect upon his child's school achievement.

Another indication of the importance of the parent's occupation for the child's scholastic achievement can be found by analyzing the winners of National Merit Scholarships. Although the scholarship program was designed to help children from low economic families attain higher educational levels, the results have been just the opposite. Laswell (1965) describes the results of a study by Horace Mann Bond that demographically illustrated that a disproportionate number of National Merit Scholars came from families in the higher occupational categories. Out of 510 scholarships awarded in 1956, 349, or 68.4 percent, of the winners came from families within the two highest ranking categories (professional and technical workers; and managers, officials, and proprietors). These two highest occupational categories comprised 15.7 percent of the male working population in 1960 (United States Bureau of the Census, 1960a). Fifty-one winners, or 10 percent of the total, came from families in the five lower occupational categories (operators, private household workers, service workers, farm workers, and laborers except farm and mine). Over 30 percent of all male workers are included in these groups (United States Bureau of the Census, 1960a).

In a more recent study Nicholas and Davis (1964) found the imbalance still prevailed. They reported that there were approximately twice as many Merit Scholars who came from families with over $15,000 in annual income, had parents with college educations, and had fathers in the professional category as there were Merit Scholars from lower status groups.

The following data are further indicative of the influence of parents' occupation on the school achievement of the child. In a study (MacMillan, 1966) of Mexican-American first-grade children, the occupations of the parents were correlated with the school achievement of the children, as measured by the Metropolitan Readiness Test, Form A, and a significant relationship was found ($r = .30, p < .01; N = 305$). An analysis of variance also was computed among the occupational groups using first the Metropolitan Readiness Test as the criterion and second the IQ of the child as measured by the Goodenough-Harris Draw-a-Man Test. In the first test (using the Metropolitan Test as the criterion) a significant difference was found among the five occupational categories (F-ratio = 8.794; $p < .01$). These groups with their respective N's, numerical designations, and criterion means were as follows:

	Occupational Category*	*Occupational Numerical Designation*	*Means***	*N*
1	High	12	60.70	10
2	High medium	16	59.79	47
3	Medium	20	60.42	40
4	Low medium	24	54.66	98
5	Low	28	48.39	110
				305

* Categories are relevant only to the group studied.
** F-ratio = 8.794; $p < .01$.

Relative to the test of significant difference among the five parental occupational categories using mean IQ of the children as the criterion, the following was determined:

Occupational Category	Mean IQ
High	91.80
High medium	96.28
Medium	93.60
Low medium	89.01
Low	87.30

There is a significant difference among the IQ levels of the children for the five parent-occupation groups. A difference of 8.98 points exists between the high group's mean and the low group's mean. One should keep in mind that the designation "high group" is not the same as upper class as defined by most sociologists. These were the occupations determined to be high as they related to this particular extremely deprived Mexican-American group. The difference of 8.98 points between the high and low groups would probably have been greater if there had been a greater spread of occupations. For example, in one study (Eells and others, 1951), a 15- to 25-point difference was reported in mean IQ's of children of parents in the higher occupational categories as compared with children of parents in the unskilled occupations.

Levels of Educational Attainment

Growth in income and occupation, and the concurrent rise in social status, is largely influenced by the level of education attained. During the last few years, blacks have shown their awareness of this by concentrating a large amount of pressure in the area of education. In 1960 the education gap between whites and nonwhites was one and one-half years; by 1967 the gap had been reduced to approximately one-half year (United States Department of Labor, 1966).

In all five southwestern states blacks have achieved a higher level of education than Mexican-Americans. In California, where one cause of the black riots in 1965 was said to be the low level of education, blacks have better than one and one-half years more education than Mexican-Americans. In Texas, Mexican-Americans have approximately three years less formal education than blacks, with the resulting loss of job training and other skills.

It is in the area of educational attainment that Mexican-Americans are most deprived. In the five southwestern states, Mexican-Americans have the lowest median number of school years completed when compared with blacks and Anglos. Mexican-Americans in Texas have a lower median number of school years completed, 4.8, than in any other southwestern state—some 3.7 years less of education than Mexican-Americans in California. For a comparison of black, Mexican-American, and Anglo educational levels, see Tables 3-6 and 3-7.

TABLE 3-6

A Comparison of School Years Completed by All Anglos, Mexican-Americans, and Blacks Twenty-five Years Old and Over in the Southwest in 1960 (in percent)

MALES

School Years Completed	Arizona			California			Colorado			New Mexico			Texas			Southwest		
	A	M-A	B	A	M-A	B	A	M-A	B	A	M-A	B	A	M-A	B	A	M-A	B
None	0.8	14.7	6.4	1.0	10.3	2.3	0.8	7.3	2.5	0.7	9.2	4.1	1.2	22.2	5.4	1.0	14.8	4.7
Elementary:																		
1-4 years	3.4	22.9	18.9	2.9	15.5	9.8	3.0	17.3	6.7	3.5	21.2	12.8	6.2	29.2	18.2	3.9	21.5	16.4
5-6 years	4.6	14.4	13.6	4.0	11.5	10.4	4.1	14.2	7.5	4.5	14.2	12.8	8.2	15.2	15.0	5.4	13.4	13.2
7 years	4.7	6.8	9.1	4.3	5.9	7.6	4.4	8.6	5.9	4.3	8.4	7.4	7.5	5.5	10.1	5.2	6.1	8.9
8 years	15.8	15.1	15.0	14.2	13.7	13.3	18.3	17.3	13.0	13.7	13.8	10.9	11.6	6.7	11.4	13.7	11.3	11.9
High school:																		
1-3 years	19.3	11.9	18.9	19.7	18.9	23.8	17.4	17.4	20.9	18.9	14.2	17.8	20.2	8.7	19.0	19.6	14.2	19.8
4 years	25.2	8.9	11.2	25.7	14.5	19.1	26.0	11.0	24.5	26.7	10.9	23.4	21.6	7.2	12.5	24.5	11.1	14.6
College:																		
1-3 years	13.3	2.9	4.2	14.6	6.1	9.7	12.1	3.9	10.6	13.3	4.5	6.2	11.6	3.1	4.4	13.4	4.6	6.8
4 years or more	12.9	2.4	2.7	13.6	3.6	4.0	13.9	3.0	8.4	14.4	3.6	4.6	11.9	2.2	4.0	13.3	3.0	3.7
Median number of school years completed	12.1	6.7	8.1	12.1	8.5	9.8	12.1	8.1	11.1	12.4	7.7	9.3	11.3	4.8	7.6	12.0	7.1	8.6

FEMALES

None	0.7	11.9	3.3	0.9	8.5	1.6	0.7	6.6	2.3	0.7	9.3	2.8	1.0	23.6	4.3	0.9	14.7	3.1
Elementary:																		
1–4 years	2.3	20.2	11.7	2.3	13.3	7.1	2.0	16.5	5.3	2.4	19.4	7.9	4.1	28.3	14.9	2.8	20.3	11.4
5–6 years	3.7	16.3	12.3	3.6	12.1	9.4	3.2	14.5	7.3	3.7	14.4	11.6	7.2	16.7	14.3	4.6	14.4	12.2
7 years	3.7	7.5	10.2	3.5	5.9	7.3	3.3	9.2	4.4	3.5	8.5	9.4	6.7	5.4	10.3	4.5	6.1	9.0
8 years	13.7	15.7	15.2	13.4	14.7	13.2	15.4	17.0	13.7	10.8	14.5	11.2	10.9	6.5	12.1	12.7	11.6	12.6
High school:																		
1–3 years	20.9	13.3	22.9	20.5	20.5	25.2	18.2	17.1	21.3	20.2	15.1	23.3	22.5	8.2	21.0	20.9	14.7	22.7
4 years	32.6	12.1	14.4	33.6	18.4	22.3	34.1	13.8	28.7	33.7	14.0	21.4	28.7	8.2	14.1	32.2	13.4	17.8
College:																		
1–3 years	13.6	1.8	6.2	14.2	4.6	9.9	14.0	3.6	10.6	14.7	2.7	7.7	11.5	1.9	4.4	13.4	3.2	6.8
4 years or more	8.8	1.2	3.8	8.0	2.0	4.0	9.1	1.7	6.4	10.3	2.1	4.7	7.4	1.2	4.6	8.0	1.6	4.4
Median number of school years completed	12.2	7.2	8.8	12.2	8.7	10.4	12.2	8.2	11.4	12.3	8.8	9.9	11.7	4.7	8.5	12.1	7.1	9.2

Anglo and Mexican-American percentages and medians are based on absolute figures derived by subtracting Mexican-American from Anglo.

Black percentages and medians are based on absolute figures for Arizona, California, and New Mexico. Colorado and Texas percentages and medians were based on nonwhite figures because the Census Bureau did not differentiate between nonwhite and black in these states. Nonwhite as defined by the Census Bureau includes black (92 percent of all nonwhite), Japanese, Chinese, American and Asian Indian, Filipino, Korean, Hawaiian, Malayan, Eskimo, and Aleut.

Medians were computed using the method described by George A. Ferguson, *Statistical Analysis in Psychology and Education* (New York: McGraw-Hill, 1957), p. 47.

SOURCES:
Adapted from United States Bureau of the Census (1960c, 1960e, 1960f).

TABLE 3–7

A Comparison of School Years Completed by Anglos,
Mexican-Americans, and Blacks, Twenty-five Years Old and
Over in the United States in 1960 (in percent)

School Years Completed	Anglos	Mexican-Americans	Blacks
	MALES		
None	1.7	14.8	6.3
Elementary:			
1–4 years	5.2	21.5	21.9
5–6 years	7.1	13.4	15.3
7 years	6.6	6.1	8.7
8 years	18.5	11.3	12.3
High school:			
1–3 years	19.0	14.2	17.3
4 years	22.4	11.1	11.3
College:			
1–3 years	9.1	4.6	4.1
4 years or more	10.4	3.0	2.8
Median number of school years completed	10.7	7.1	7.7
	FEMALES		
None	1.6	14.7	4.2
Elementary:			
1–4 years	3.9	20.3	15.6
5–6 years	6.2	14.4	15.0
7 years	5.6	6.1	9.6
8 years	17.9	11.6	13.3
High school:			
1–3 years	19.7	14.7	20.6
4 years	29.4	13.4	14.3
College:			
1–3 years	9.6	3.2	4.1
4 years or more	6.1	1.6	3.3
Median number of school years completed	11.3	7.1	8.4

All percentages are based on absolute figures. The Anglo figure was computed by subtracting the Mexican-American from the general white population. Figures for Mexican-Americans are for the five southwestern states only.

SOURCES:
Adapted from United States Bureau of the Census (1960e, 1960f).

If a comparison is made between blacks and Mexican-Americans, using national figures for the blacks, Mexican-Americans still have a lower level of education (see Table 3–7). The national figures for blacks include figures for the deep South, which has the effect of depressing their median number of school years completed, but not enough to lower the median to the level of the Mexican-Americans.

Over 35.6 percent of Mexican-Americans have less than a fifth-grade education; the national figure for those with less than five years of formal education is 8 percent.

Over 14.7 percent of Mexican-Americans have no education at all. Mexican-Americans comprise only 1.6 percent of the total general white population. However, of that segment of the general white population listed as having no education (1,720,154 in 1960), Mexican-Americans comprise 12.5 percent, or almost eight times the expected proportion (United States Bureau of the Census, 1960j).

In the area of education, American Indians, like Mexican-Americans, are extremely disadvantaged. In 1967 the median number of school years completed for the Indian was reported to be five (United States Senate, 1967). The indication is that on the basis of the number of school years completed, most American Indians should be illiterate.

According to the 1960 census, in the three states of Arizona, New Mexico, and North Carolina, approximately 50 percent of male American Indians over twenty-five years of age have an educational level of less than fifth grade. In Arizona and New Mexico, over 30 percent of male Indians over twenty-five years of age have had no formal schooling (see Table 3–8).

In the area of educational attainment, American Indians are generally more disadvantaged than blacks. In the six states where a comparison was possible—Arizona, California, New Mexico, North Carolina, Oklahoma, and South Dakota (see Table 3–8)—only blacks in South Dakota are more disadvantaged if educational levels below the fifth grade are considered. There are approximately 800 blacks in South Dakota, which may negate some of the significance of the percentages. The widest differences between the educational levels of Indians and blacks were recorded in Arizona and New Mexico, where the median level of schooling of Indian males is over four years below that of black males.

The "vanishing American" may no longer be vanishing. American Indians are increasing at approximately double the rate of the general population. However, in the important categories of income and education, they are acutely disadvantaged. One major difficulty in assisting Indians in their battle against poverty is their resistance to acculturation into the white man's society. Attempts have been made to bring about such assimilation but most have ended in failure.

TABLE 3-8

A Comparison of School Years Completed by All Indians and Blacks
Twenty-five Years Old and Over in Six States in 1960 (in percent)

MALES

School Years Completed	Arizona		California		New Mexico		North Carolina		Oklahoma		South Dakota	
	I	B	I	B	I	B	I	B	I	B	I	B
None	32.1	6.4	5.4	2.3	34.0	4.1	10.9	8.1	6.2	5.2	1.9	1.8
Elementary:												
1–4 years	17.5	18.9	10.2	9.8	14.7	12.8	32.5	31.6	17.7	18.1	7.1	22.6
5–6 years	12.7	13.6	9.7	10.4	9.5	12.8	15.9	18.3	11.3	13.5	19.3	5.8
7 years	5.2	9.1	6.6	7.6	5.1	7.4	12.0	10.0	7.9	7.7	11.9	1.3
8 years	9.1	15.0	16.9	13.3	9.1	10.9	7.3	7.8	16.4	14.4	21.8	15.2
High school:												
1–3 years	13.9	18.9	23.3	23.8	14.4	17.8	10.9	12.1	18.5	18.2	23.7	10.3
4 years	7.2	11.2	19.5	19.1	9.8	23.4	5.9	6.9	12.9	12.8	9.7	23.0
College:												
1–3 years	1.9	4.2	5.9	9.7	1.9	6.2	2.2	2.5	6.8	5.8	3.0	8.8
4 years or more	0.4	2.7	2.5	4.0	1.5	4.6	2.4	2.7	2.3	4.3	1.6	11.2
Median number of school years completed	4.0	8.1	9.1	9.8	5.1	9.3	4.4	5.6	7.4	7.4	7.4	8.5

FEMALES

None	40.1	3.3	6.3	1.7	39.8	2.8	7.0	4.9	5.8	4.5	2.7	—
Elementary:												
1–4 years	12.4	11.7	9.2	7.1	11.2	7.9	23.6	20.1	14.7	12.2	8.9	6.7
5–6 years	12.4	12.3	9.4	9.4	9.1	11.6	18.4	18.2	13.2	12.4	17.5	4.6
7 years	6.4	10.2	5.4	7.3	5.0	9.4	12.1	12.9	8.4	8.4	10.0	3.5
8 years	8.8	15.2	18.4	13.1	8.4	11.2	10.1	10.1	16.1	15.3	20.0	8.6
High school:												
1–3 years	10.8	22.9	22.1	25.2	14.0	23.3	16.9	16.7	19.7	22.2	23.4	20.7
4 years	7.4	14.4	21.0	22.3	9.3	21.4	7.3	10.4	15.3	15.2	14.3	34.9
College:												
1–3 years	1.3	6.2	5.6	9.9	2.0	7.7	2.1	2.5	4.8	5.0	3.2	11.3
4 years or more	0.4	3.8	2.6	4.0	1.2	4.7	2.5	4.2	2.0	4.8	—	9.7
Median number of school years completed	3.5	8.8	8.1	10.4	3.9	9.9	6.1	6.5	7.5	7.8	7.6	9.1

SOURCES:
Adapted from United States Bureau of the Census (1960c, 1960e).

RELATIONSHIP BETWEEN PARENT'S EDUCATION
AND CHILD'S SCHOOL PROGRESS

As Table 3–9 demonstrates, there is a significant correlation between the parent's education and the child's school progress. There is a steady decline in the retardation rate of all three groups of children from ten to seventeen years old, both male and female, as the parent's level of educational attainment increases (except for a slight upward turn where the father is a high-school graduate but earns less than $3000). It is interesting to note, then, that although family income correlates significantly with a child's school progress, the parent's education seems even more important.

TABLE 3–9

The Percentage of Scholastically Retarded Children in the Child Population Aged Ten to Seventeen Years, Living with One or Both Parents, in 1960

Education of Parent* and 1959 Family Income	Male			Female		
	10–13 years	14–15 years	16–17 years	10–13 years	14–15 years	16–17 years
Less than 8 years	28.9	35.6	34.9	18.3	24.1	23.0
Under $3000	36.9	47.7	47.4	26.4	33.3	33.6
$3000–4999	24.5	33.6	35.7	16.2	22.7	22.3
$5000–6999	18.3	28.4	28.3	11.4	18.0	16.6
$7000 and over	15.0	21.6	21.8	9.5	13.0	13.1
8–11 years	11.0	15.6	17.3	7.1	9.1	10.0
Under $3000	17.4	23.9	25.0	10.6	14.4	16.0
$3000–4999	12.9	18.3	20.9	7.6	11.0	12.2
$5000–6999	9.7	14.2	16.9	5.2	8.4	9.9
$7000 and over	7.6	11.3	13.0	3.9	6.1	6.8
12 years or some college	4.8	7.1	8.5	2.7	4.1	4.9
Under $3000	8.3	12.4	13.4	5.2	7.1	8.7
$3000–4999	7.0	10.6	12.4	3.9	6.0	7.2
$5000–6999	5.2	7.8	9.7	3.0	4.7	5.7
$7000 and over	3.6	5.6	6.9	2.0	3.2	3.8

* Education of parent refers to father's education when child was living with both parents or father, and to mother's education when child's father was not living with the household.

SOURCE:
United States Bureau of the Census (1960h).

INFLUENCE OF PARENTAL
ATTITUDE TOWARD EDUCATION

The attitude of parents is an important factor in school achievement. Madsen (1964) has concluded that the attitude of Mexican-American parents toward education is negative: "The father regards his children as unworking members of the family and envisions their future as a duplication of his own life. For this kind of life, formal schooling is unimportant."

Madsen's conception of parental attitude toward education agrees with Saunders' (1954): "Eight years of schooling have been thought by many mothers and fathers to be enough; if a child failed to complete that small amount of formal education they have shown no great concern."

Murray (1954) and Manuel (1965) disagree with the above argument. In her study of 118 families in San Antonio, Murray indicated that only 10 percent of her sample voiced a negative attitude toward education. Manuel claims Mexican-American parents do have a positive attitude toward education; however, they feel stymied because of their poverty.

In an attempt to determine attitudes of parents (and of children) toward school, a study was made (MacMillan, 1966) using attendance figures of first-grade black, Mexican-American, and Anglo children. The rationale for using school attendance as the criterion is best described by Moore and Holtzman (1965): "It is common knowledge among school administrators that regular school attendance is largely dependent upon motivation of children and youth by parents. Support in keeping children in school has to do with parents' academic achievement and overall attitudes toward education."

It was determined that with zero rainfall and a temperature of 60°, Mexican-American and black children of low status would attend school at approximately the same rate as middle-class Anglo children. There are certainly many factors contributing to attendance patterns of school children. Yet attendance itself is a prime indicator of attitude.

To obtain a deeper insight into the possible effects of temperature and precipitation on the three ethnic groups, expected attendance values were computed using a temperature range of 30° to 60° F and a precipitation range of 0 to 2.5 inches. Of the days used in this study (September 21 to April 27), 119 had 8:00 A.M. temperatures within the 30° to 60° temperature range selected. There were no days during this period that had more than 2.5 inches of rain.

Table 3–10 shows expected attendance percentages for each of the ethnic groups at 30° and 60° using arbitrarily set precipitation figures of 0, 0.5, 1.0, 1.5, 2.0, and 2.5 inches.

Although Anglos are adversely affected by weather conditions, they are not as affected as blacks or Mexican-Americans. As precipitation is increased and temperature is held to the 30° to 60° range, the difference between the expected percent of attendance for the three groups widens. With 2.5 inches of precipita-

TABLE 3–10

Effects of Temperature and Precipitation
on School Attendance (in percent)

	0	.5	1.0	1.5	2.0	2.5
MEXICAN-AMERICAN						
30°	85.01	75.50	66.02	56.52	47.03	37.54
60°	91.01	88.11	85.22	82.32	79.43	76.53
BLACK						
30°	85.30	70.52	55.74	40.96	26.18	11.40
60°	88.00	84.02	80.04	76.06	72.08	68.10
ANGLO						
30°	86.33	82.38	78.43	74.48	70.53	66.58
60°	91.73	90.73	89.85	88.83	87.93	86.93

tion and 30° temperature, there is an expected difference of approximately 55 percentage units between blacks and Anglos, and almost 18 percentage units when the temperature is 60°.

The startling effect of weather conditions on these groups is quite conceivably due not only to attitude but to their state of poverty. Anglo children can, if necessary, be given some form of transportation to school in order to protect them. Black and Mexican-American children who have no access to this luxury and whose parents have a "why bother" attitude are at a disadvantage. Lack of clothing can become terribly important when the weather turns bad. A lack of proper diet can bring on sicknesses more easily warded off by the more affluent. In addition, inoculations for the prevention of diseases are more readily available to the affluent than to the poor.

Attendance is not only an indicator of attitude, it is a significant predictor of achievement (MacMillan, 1966). When a child is continually absent, particularly in the lower grades where basic patterns and structures are developed, his present and future achievement are bound to suffer.

OTHER EDUCATIONAL HANDICAPS

Black and Mexican-American children are faced with other similar handicaps in regard to school achievement. Besides easily identifiable handicaps such as income and housing, there are handicaps not as easily measured or tested statistically but certainly educationally significant. These include segregation, language difference, and teacher attitudes.

Segregation has been a part of the school culture of Mexican-Americans and blacks alike. Whereas blacks have been segregated on a racial basis, Mexican-Americans have been segregated on a linguistic basis. The argument used is that a child will feel more comfortable and be better able to achieve by associating with those using a similar language (Tuck, 1946).

Tuck also mentions the fact that although some teachers know a few words of Spanish, they may be forbidden to use them. Techniques of teaching reading were, and continue to be, predicated on the student having a sizable English vocabulary. Yet, to most beginning Mexican-American first-graders, such "interesting and stimulating" dialogue as "Look, Jack," "Run, Jack, run," and "See Spot run" is a collection of nonsense words.

A parental attitude can be highly influential in the child's school achievement; a teacher's attitude can also be a significant factor. Teacher acceptance of the child, whether by verbal or nonverbal means, can be a highly potent weapon in influencing the child's image, his aspirations (realistic or unrealistic), his actual achievement, and his IQ (Rosenthal and Jacobson, 1968).

In conversation with teachers and administrators, MacMillan (1966) was confronted with arguments that Mexican-Americans were natural slow-learners and were not studious. These arguments coincide with studies made by Woods (1956) and Saunders (1954) and are not limited to any particular ethnic group. Similar assumptions have been made concerning blacks, Italian-Americans, Irish-Americans, and other groups.

Many Mexican-American children are faced with the additional handicap of being members of migrant families. Manuel (1965) reported an estimated total interstate migration for labor purposes of 90,000 people nationwide. Of these, approximately one-third were children under sixteen years of age. Migration in 1961, according to Manuel, "interfered with the schooling of some 15,000 children of Texas migrant workers . . . enough children for five hundred classrooms."

Among the difficulties with schooling faced by migrant children are low attendance due to frequent moves, lack of a positive school attitude on the part of the parents, lack of proper records of previous school experience, and inability of schools to accommodate large increases of nonresident children and adapt school curriculum to their needs. Another difficulty is the negative attitude of the community toward migrant families.

Summary

The general socioeconomic status of blacks is fairly well documented. The status of American Indians, although not as well-documented as that of blacks, has also been the subject of studies and congressional action. The status of Mexican-Americans has not been as well publicized. The latest data gathered, tabulated, and analyzed by the federal government take into account blacks, Indians (and other nonwhite races), and the general nonwhite population. Yet, as far as can be determined, little statistical data on Mexican-Americans have been gathered recently. In some respects being declared "white" by an act of Congress has proved to be a detriment for Mexican-Americans. Yet, the deprivation of the three groups is almost equal, with Mexican-Americans and Indians considerably lower in the all-important area of educational attainment. Like the blacks, Mexican-Americans experience the handicap of segregation. There is, however, the added handicap for Mexican-Americans of having a first language other than English. The language difference and extreme poverty place Mexican-American children at a disadvantage in trying to cope with the middle-class, English-language-oriented school curriculum. Generally, blacks are primarily handicapped by poverty and segregation. However, segregation prevents Mexican-Americans not only from being able to be socially and economically assimilated into the dominant Anglo culture but also from gaining needed fluency in English.

American Indians are, and have been, segregated on reservations. It is not the same form of segregation experienced by blacks and Mexican-Americans, for they are faced with segregation while attempting to live within society. American Indians live within their own societies on the reservations. There have been a number of attempts through federal action to bring about assimilation of Indians into the "white man's" culture. The Indian Reorganization Act of 1934 and two federal measures passed in 1953 that have as their intent the elimination of federal control over Indians are examples of the government's attempt to hasten assimilation. However, many Indians have voiced their opposition to assimilation, wishing to maintain their own separate culture.

Poverty has become a part of the Mexican-American, Indian, and black heritage. Although large percentage gains have been made in the education and income of Mexican-Americans, absolute gains have been relatively small compared with those of blacks and Anglos. Indians have made even smaller gains in these areas. Mexican-Americans and Indians are actually falling behind Anglo and black rates of growth. This is a cycle—a cycle of poverty—that has become hereditary in an environmental sense.

Due to extreme poverty, existence is a day-to-day chore. Education and its related philosophy of deferred gratification has to take a backseat to a more immediate and pressing item—living.

Scholastic achievement suffers because of poverty. Children do not have a proper diet, adequate clothing, and other material items necessary for complete involvement in school activities. Visiting classrooms in economically deprived areas, one has no problem in finding examples of how economic deprivation can restrict learning. Children fall asleep from lack of proper sleep and food; skin discoloration and other physical defects caused by malnutrition are common sights. One of the more startling revelations is to walk into a classroom of thirty to thirty-five first-graders on a hot spring or fall day and be confronted with a strong stench of urine. This has been enough to turn many a student-teacher or first-year teacher away from teaching in deprived areas. In some communities schools serving this type of child are called "retirement schools." Teachers who are close to retirement are sent there—the "Siberia" of the education world. Yet these children are neither basically filthy nor inherently dull. Their problem is a need for the basic supports of life—food, shelter, clothing, sanitation—and for the fundamentals necessary to compete successfully in the classroom.

4

Correlates with
the School Success and Failure
of Economically Disadvantaged Children

Newton S. Metfessel
Mark W. Seng

FROM 1964 to 1969, more than three thousand children from the western part of the United States were the focus of a study called Project Potential,[1] an investigation into the general achievement patterns of children from the culture of poverty. This investigation identified individual correlates with academic success and disability, and in particular with success and disability in reading. These correlates are used in this chapter in five ways: (1) to draw a profile of the low achiever and identify the characteristics that correlated with poverty and school disability; (2) to draw a profile of the successful pupil and to identify the characteristics that correlated with poverty and school success, particularly in reading; (3) to describe possible treatments for low achievers based on the low achiever's profile; (4) to draw a profile of the poor reader and identify the characteristics that correlated with current reading difficulty as a means of suggesting possible causes and treatments; and (5) to draw a profile of preschool readiness skills that correlated with subsequent school success and to show how they may form the basis for a formalized preschool readiness program. One note of caution: To avoid the over-use and repetition of qualifying statements, for example, "in most cases," "tends," and so on, the writers have used phrases such as "The low achiever will . . ." These statements are not to be regarded as "facts" or "fictions" per se but as *probability* declarations for which unique exceptions are recognized.

[1] This investigation was supported in part by a grant from the U.S. Office of Education, Basic Research Project No. 2615, Contract OE 4–10–219, 1964–69. It was conducted by the senior author, Newton S. Metfessel, who served as Project Director; Newton S. Metfessel and Mark W. Seng collaborated on the interpretations in this chapter and on the writing of the manuscript.

The correlates are based on several assumptions. First, correlation is not causation (the *post hoc* fallacy). Second, a pupil can have many of the positive characteristics cited and yet be a poor reader. Third, conversely, a pupil can have many of the disabilities cited and demonstrate adequate reading skills. Fourth, not all possible correlates of either reading success or disability were explored in the study.

The more than three thousand individuals studied included: (1) black children and youth from the Watts ghetto in Los Angeles and surrounding environs; (2) Mexican-American children from the East Los Angeles ghetto and surrounding suburbia; (3) Indian children whose families had lived over six generations in the rural poverty area of San Jacinto, which includes the Soboba Indian reservation; (4) Mexican-American children from the rural poverty areas in Blythe, Coachella Valley, and Indio; (5) migrant poor children from rural areas in Merced, San Joaquin, and Stanislaus counties, including populations of Mexican nationals as well as Mexican-Americans from Texas, New Mexico, and Arizona; (6) black rural poverty youth, both resident and migrant, from Tulare County; and, finally, (7) Oriental and white poor children and youth not included in but representative of these geographical areas.

This chapter focuses on economically poor children who are having difficulty succeeding in the school culture. The problem of definition is critical, however. Poverty and being "disadvantaged" are not synonymous. For example, semi-literate maids from Mexico raise many upper-middle-class children who have reading problems. And many children from sixty-thousand-dollar homes in which there are more bottles than books have serious reading problems that are remarkably similar to those of children from the culture of poverty.

Profile of the Low Achiever

Some twenty-seven characteristics that correlated with poverty and school disability constitute a profile of the low achiever. There are several ways in which one might group these characteristics. Five categories have been selected that contain them in a useful way: (1) learning style, (2) value framework with emphasis on the child's perception of his own worth, or his self-concept, (3) existing cognitive structure, (4) models of behavior, and (5) home environment. The categories are not mutually exclusive; some characteristics might have been placed in other categories. The purpose of the categorization is to sketch a profile that is accurate yet not rigid.

LEARNING STYLE

Low achievers characteristically demonstrate a cognitive learning style that responds more to visual and kinesthetic signals than to oral or written stimuli.

They have a poor attention span when presented with too many stimuli at one time. Thus, they tend to persevere longer in a task involving one activity. They learn more readily by inductive than by deductive approaches. They also learn less from what they hear than their middle-class counterparts. They are typically at a marked disadvantage when placed in timed-learning and test situations perhaps because of their lack of self-confidence and negative self-concept.

VALUE FRAMEWORK AND SELF-CONCEPT

These children expect to fail and therefore seldom develop the habit of achievement; they frequently have had little experience in receiving approval for success in a learning task. They are "today" oriented and have difficulty responding to long-range goals. They are not encouraged to engage in fantasy and imagination. In general, they are characterized by weak ego-development, a lack of self-confidence, and a negative self-concept. They expect to fail and when they do, the failure reinforces their feelings of inadequacy. At home they are typically disciplined by physical force. This is in contrast to the school culture, where discipline is usually through reason (insight building) or loss of privilege.

COGNITIVE STRUCTURE

These children often have important gaps in fundamental knowledge, concepts that some teachers might assume they have. Their intellect is unevenly developed, in part because they have not been encouraged by their family to ask questions. For example, they are typically crippled in language development because they have varying degrees of awareness of the fundamental concept that objects have names, that it is desirable to "label" or name all things. They may use a great many words with fair precision but unfortunately not those words useful in or representative of the school culture. Even more important than the child's existing intellectual development, perhaps, are the models of human behavior to which he is exposed and which he values.

MODELS OF BEHAVIOR

Low-achieving children typically have parents who simply do not model language skills appropriate for school and whose values do not encourage intellectual development. On the contrary, the children observe parental models using oral language that may be considered inappropriate for the culture of the school. The parents work at jobs that do not require much education. Children may assume that the skills learned at school are unimportant, since they are not necessary to achieve the "success" of the parental models. To further complicate the situation, the parents' attitude toward the school may be negative because of the high percentage of unfavorable communications from the school. The parents typically feel, for example, that the needs of the family are more important than school-attendance laws. They lack a basic understanding of what education consists of; school is a place where magic occurs—the child learns to read, write, and spell, but without parental involvement in or commitment to the learning process. Perhaps following parental models, or else simply because of frustration, these children typically have great difficulty in handling feelings of hostility through words rather than force, in part probably because they see physical force used frequently in their home environment.

HOME ENVIRONMENT

The physical environment, often overcrowded and noisy, works against the development of listening skills. Low achievers frequently come from homes empty of stimulating objects that would enhance their conceptual development. There are few luxuries such as toys and games and play materials of different colors, sizes, and shapes. With little in the house itself, the children typically have few or limited out-of-school experiences relevant to the school culture. However, not all pupils from the culture of poverty are unsuccessful in school. Some children do quite well, in particular those whose mothers value education.

Profile of the High Achiever

Project Potential research focused on ten attitudinal and behavioral factors significantly correlated with poor pupils who succeeded in school in general and in reading in particular. In the discussion of low achievers, correlates were categorized into five divisions: learning style, values and self-concept, cognitive structure, behavior models, and home environment. To heighten the contrast between low and high achievers, the same categories are employed here. Characteristics of the high achiever tend, as one might expect, to be opposite from those of the low achiever. It is particularly interesting to observe the differences in two areas: values and self-concept, and behavior models. These appear to be the key areas that correlate with success, with the mother's value for education being of singular importance.

LEARNING STYLE

As a general rule, high achievers, and reading achievers in particular, tend to have study plans and to be tenacious in complying with assignments. They tend to succeed by conforming to assignments. Their ability to plan includes planning for college and for careers. Achievers also tend to anticipate a high socioeconomic status in adult life. In marked contrast to low achievers, successful pupils seem able to persist toward long-range goals. They also demonstrate the ability to defer gratification, showing a fundamental difference in their value framework.

VALUE FRAMEWORK AND SELF-CONCEPT

No other area so clearly differentiates high achievers from low achievers as value framework and self-concept. Essentially this category encompasses what a person deems important, worthwhile, or valuable. How a person *feels* about himself in terms of how others react to him is what is meant by self-concept. Therefore, the classification includes all those items that contain the concept of value or worth, positive and negative. In the sense that self-concept reflects how one values his own worth, it is used here to encompass one's willingness and ability to relate to others.

Successful pupils from the culture of poverty relate well to adults. They tend to accept and be accepted by their peers, including those from other ethnic groups, and to have close and valued peer relationships. In contrast to low achievers, they receive approval for their efforts from teachers *and* parents. Their parents approve of the children's choice of friends, especially those doing well in school. With this amount of approval, it is not altogether surprising that success-ful pupils tend to demonstrate a pattern of deferred gratification as opposed to the "today" value orientation of low achievers. High achievers are pupils who have experienced success in the past, tend to set realistic goals, and have positive expectations for future success. In short, they have a very strong sense of per-sonal worth and little feeling of fatalism. Self-sufficient and independent, they tend to experience few conflicts, and generally feel secure, confident, and content with themselves. They recognize that their parents "accept" them; they consider the expectations of their parents realistic and reasonable, and they try to fulfill them. Thus, they tend to accept the similar values of their parents, teachers, and other "successful" adults. Consequently, their values are "socially acceptable" in middle-class terms. Typically, reading achievers tend to feel stimulated by and involved in school work, which they perceive as relevant to their future. They find school personally rewarding. In marked contrast to low achievers, they are motivated by challenging experiences and tend to enjoy proving themselves against competition.

In summary, one might say reading achievers perceive themselves as possessing competent skills and abilities, as accepted by others, and as experiencing few fears and anxieties.

COGNITIVE STRUCTURE

High achievers often have a variety of hobbies and outside interests that motivate and spark their school endeavors. They are often motivated by spontaneous in-terests, evidence of a growing intellectual curiosity. This expanding mental and emotional growth is undoubtedly influenced by their perception of peer and adult models.

MODELS OF BEHAVIOR

School achievers emulate successful teachers. Their parents want them to be educationally and vocationally successful. They identify with adults other than teachers or parents, adults who have specialized abilities. In general, they have successful, positive relationships with a variety of adult models. They tend to feel close to adult authority figures and to feel confident of their ability to communicate with them. They tend to associate with older pupils and to feel socially at ease with adults and peers. In choosing friends, they tend to select other achievers. Their friends also exhibit positive attitudes toward school, studying, and home. Achievers surround themselves with models of success, models whom they admire and emulate. These models are successful and, therefore, the achievers tend to gravitate toward upper socioeconomic levels.

HOME ENVIRONMENT

One would suspect that parents who typically value education would make reasonable efforts to provide circumstances conducive to academic success. The parents who do not have the financial resources for such things as manufactured games and toys might make an effort to provide stimulating homemade playthings as well as to encourage use of free public facilities that enhance educational progress. Some effort is made to provide out-of-school experiences that bear upon school achievement in general and reading achievement in particular, especially as the mother provides *early* readiness experiences. Even more important is the value for education that she communicates—the most important correlate with school success of over two hundred studied by Project Potential.

Some Possible Treatments for Low Achievers

Profiles have been sketched of the low achiever and of the high achiever, both from the culture of poverty. There appear to be some clusters of correlates that characterize the successful pupil. From the correlates that Project Potential identified as being characteristic of low achievers and high achievers, what reasonable treatments (though not empirically demonstrated) can be inferred? Teachers might profitably put forth effort in six areas: (1) providing opportunities for academic success, (2) structuring learning tasks carefully, (3) presenting stimuli appropriate to low achievers' needs, (4) developing fundamental concepts, (5) providing appropriate models, and (6) involving parents in the educational process.

ENSURING ACADEMIC SUCCESS

Low-achieving children typically demonstrate not only failure but the expectation to fail as well. So deeply is this attitude ingrained that they are not able to persist in activities in order to achieve success. Therefore, it is incumbent upon teachers to provide activities in which the children will be successful. This may demand activities seemingly so "fail-safe" and easy as to seem unsuitable for the academic environment. Successes must be continual and sequential until such a point is reached that activities may be suggested that challenge the child. First, however, the child must develop the confidence that he can succeed. With a background of success, he will be able to move forward to areas where success is not so guaranteed. This step is necessary because the child must perceive the learning situation as one in which real success can occur. And success cannot occur without the possibility of failure. That possibility, however, must remain remote until, in the teacher's professional judgment, the child is able to cope with it. For some children, this process may take many months or even years.

STRUCTURING LEARNING TASKS

Low achievers, as was pointed out, tend to persevere longer when engrossed in a task involving a single activity. They are distractible. They learn more readily by inductive than by deductive processes. Because of their poor attention span, they need instruction in small steps. These factors may often be combined in long-range thematic units of instruction that stress gradual integration of small parts into larger and larger concepts in innovative settings. A central interweaving theme contributes to the cohesiveness of what otherwise might be disconnected bits. This strategy combines the best aspects of learning in small steps in which the children may achieve success, with the advantage of increasing their attention span.

Low-achieving children, it was pointed out, do not function well in timed situations. Indeed, it is valid to call timed situations "time bomb" learning situations: the teacher lights the fuse; the children begin work and strive to complete the task before time runs out. It is crucial that teachers not equate slowness with mental incapacity. It really does not matter ultimately if a child needs more time to learn skills; the important point is that he learn them eventually. If time pressure decreases his learning, it appears sensible to remove the factor whenever possible.

PRESENTING APPROPRIATE STIMULI

Low achievers may seem to lack skills in dealing with symbolization. This does not mean that they are totally lacking in capability to deal with symbolization, but that their skills in such areas as abstraction have not developed. Teachers can facilitate learning by providing direct experiences rather than symbolic representations. For example, such activities as field trips will complete basic gaps in their cognitive structure in a way that will be both pleasant and effective. Successful trips demand careful preparation and postevaluation to help children relate what they have seen to what they already know.

This emphasis on learning through visual and motor experiences involving the presentation of concrete rather than abstract or symbolic stimuli will facilitate learning and increase the probability of success, while enhancing intellectual development. Low achievers do not respond to oral and written stimuli as well as to visual and kinesthetic presentations. A task for teachers, then, is to identify and teach those basic concepts the child lacks in a way that will prove fruitful and pleasant for him.

DEVELOPING FUNDAMENTAL CONCEPTS

Underachieving children typically lack concepts basic to further intellectual growth. Consequently, teachers may wish to bring to bear rationales exemplified by various taxonomies (e.g., Bloom, 1956) in which intellectual skills are isolated in a hierarchical manner. Attention may be focused on development of listening skills concomitantly with other learning objectives such as improved receptive and expressive language skills. Teachers may also include, if appropriate, training in color concepts, directionality, position, and relative size. Attention and emphasis should be placed on the habit of "labeling," and the utility of labels should be made clear to the child. By its nature, such labeling increases the vocabulary and conceptual development of the child, which in turn facilitate future learning of a more symbolic nature. Practice is usually needed in identifying similarities and differences among related stimuli to reach a personal generalization about a new stimulus containing the relevant attribute. Of course, such a process is one type of concept learning called abstraction.

PROVIDING APPROPRIATE MODELS

Children are surrounded by people who may serve as models for them of desirable or undesirable behavior. Achievers value such models as their teachers, parents, other successful adults, and peers who share their values. Teachers have the opportunity to serve as most important models for their children if they are able to establish rapport with them. If they can create an atmosphere that is sincere, warm and friendly, in which the children experience success, it is possible that the children will emulate them and perhaps assume some of their values. Teachers can also introduce desirable models from the children's own ethnic group. One would suggest models who are likely to be admired and who have achieved their success as a consequence of their education.

INVOLVING PARENTS IN THE EDUCATIONAL PROCESS

Parents, however, present at once both the most important models and the most difficult for classroom teachers to reach. It might be sensible to restrict communications from the school that are negative in tone while making an effort to send positive messages that the parents will value. In this way, a beginning can be made to involve parents in the educational process, to engage their support of the school's objectives and perhaps affect their behavior to the point that their child perceives them as models who support the value of education.

Profile of the Poor Reader

Profiles have been drawn of the low achiever and the high achiever, and suggestions for treatment have been made based on the failure of the former and the successes of the latter. At this point it is appropriate to focus more specifically on poor readers from the culture of poverty and what can be done to help them develop reading skills. These individual correlates of reading disability are placed within the conceptual context of the Herr model (1955) of symptoms, causes, and treatment. It must be stated that many poor readers from the culture of poverty lacked up to 30 percent of the specific symptoms cited. Yet, each of the following categories did correlate with reading disability as measured by standardized tests at the 5 percent level of confidence: (1) physical, (2) mental, (3) emotional, (4) social, and (5) instructional. The correlative symptoms are discussed, followed by hypothesized causes and recommended treatments.

PHYSICAL

Vision difficulties may be indicated if a child squints, holds his book close to his eyes, or shows a lack of persistence in study. Typical complaints include headaches, muscular awkwardness, swollen eyes, and dizziness. These symptoms might be caused by defective vision or reduced visual perception that results from eye strain, poor lighting in the room, glare, or a bad seating arrangement. Small type could also cause such symptoms. Other physical causes might include poor coordination, disease, affective disorders, or malnutrition.

Suggested treatments would include glasses, large type, better lighting, and improved seating arrangements. Relaxation intervals with shorter work periods would reduce physical strain, as might the use of opaque, dull-finished paper.

Hearing difficulties will be shown by inattention or indifference. The child will not be able to understand or follow directions given in a low voice. He will confuse letters and sounds, have defective speech, or a poor auditory memory.

Causes might include defective hearing or too much noise in the room or on the playground. The teacher might talk too low. The child might have difficulty in associating meaning and verbal symbol, perhaps because of an inadequate vocabulary.

The child should be examined to determine hearing response. A quieter room and grounds might help as might changing the child's seat. Rhyming songs facilitate comprehension. The instructor can teach differences in words and provide a good speech model.

Poor general health will cause a child to be nervous or tired or to seem lazy. He will have poor posture, be pallid, complain, and be irritable. He will have a poor attention span and be absent from school frequently. Undernourishment, improper diet, or irritation because of disease or defect might impair the child's health and result in retarded growth or inhibited function.

Treatment would involve examination of the child's diet and general health habits. Special treatment would be warranted in case of defects, diseases, or functional disturbances.

MENTAL

Mental immaturity will cause inability to learn at the appropriate grade level. The child will experience difficulty in following directions or be slow in understanding assignments. He will often misbehave. Mental immaturity will also result in a limited vocabulary, poor word recognition, inattention, and speech problems. Inherited differences will cause individual differences. Grade placement might be improper. Instructional emphasis on content might disregard individual differences. The child might be striving for attention. His immaturity might be caused by a bilingual home in which the child is not facile in either language. Reading before prerequisite skills have been developed might also cause these problems as might discipline for failure.

Treatments include proper grading and classifying, adjusting assignments to the pupil's ability and developmental needs. Appropriate classroom activities would include a variety of experiences including dictated stories.

EMOTIONAL

A child who is temperamental, extremely fearful, easily angered, embarrassed, timid, or stubborn may have emotional difficulties. Such a child will often have tantrums, brag, and show feelings of superiority. He will cry often or be pugnacious. He will lack ordinary poise and find it difficult to get along with his peers. Poor independent work habits will prevent him from completing tasks. He will have short recall and overall difficulty in adjusting to school. Causes might include word-blindness or word-deafness, feelings of inferiority, or a lack of readiness for school. He might be prone to failure and find the work too difficult.

Initial treatment would include parental conferences, a change in environment, and perhaps a change in disciplinary methods. The teacher should make an effort to establish rapport with the child by promoting friendly relations and in so doing secure the child's cooperation. His attitude should be supportive and encouraging rather than discouraging. He should seek to identify and remove the cause of the disturbance. Extensive individualized activities would be appropriate as would an extensive readiness program.

Speech defects will be exhibited by faulty speech, monotone, or stammering. (Emotional causes are frequently involved, but see also the discussion of poor oral reading below.) Causes might include a bilingual home, emotional instability, self-consciousness, poor teeth, and poor muscular coordination.

Treatments suggested for speech defects would include instruction in standard American English. The teacher can help by providing careful instruction in proper breathing and correct tongue placement and by providing a speech pattern. An important point is to put the child at ease.

SOCIAL

A meager or limited vocabulary will produce accent, hesitation in reading, and slow vocalization. The child will learn in a parrotlike manner. He will have difficulty in interpretation and not find stories interesting. He will have difficulty in following directions and show a general lack of understanding. A meager literary background in the home will be manifested by poor vocabulary or poor school attendance, indicating a parental lack of value for education. The child will be inattentive, unable to adjust, or nervous. Possible causes would include foreign parents or broken homes. His mother might not be literate. A foreign language as well as English might be poorly used in the home. His classwork might not seem meaningful because he does not see its relevance to his future.

Treatments would include building up a rich background of experiences with special help in vocabulary. Oral language should be stressed. The meaning of the lesson should be carefully developed so that the child perceives the point and direction of the activity. The child should be induced to do a great deal of simple reading. There should be more concrete illustrations with a continuing pattern of relating what the child is learning to something he already knows. He should be helped to develop a healthy self-concept. Development can be enhanced by establishing communication between his home and the school and emphasizing the positive aspects of such communication. The child and his family should be able to perceive themselves as accepted and welcome at school. The classroom environment should be happy and relaxed.

INSTRUCTIONAL

Poor oral reading will result in a retarded rate of vocalization with frequent halts, confusion, word reading, and omissions. Other symptoms of poor oral reading include guessing, mispronunciation, the omission of word endings, repetitions, carelessness with little words, and lack of comprehension, as well as poor expression and phrasing. The child will ask for help on common words and exhibit no interest in reading but will like to be read to. He will encounter difficulty in attacking new or unfamiliar words and will tend to transpose words. His voice will reveal poor tonal quality, be monotonous; he will read too rapidly and insert words that do not appear on the page. He will have too many eye fixations per line, and the fixations will be too short.

Causes of poor oral reading might be a meager vocabulary and lack of phonetic power and perhaps a short span of perception. The child might read too much from context and exhibit short attention and short eye-voice span. His apperceptive power might not be developed. He might show a general lack of comprehension and fail to appreciate language relations. He might select inappropriate reading materials. His breath control and phonetic facility might be inadequate. He might fail to pay attention to context or be inattentive in general. The return sweep of his eye might not be true nor his eye movements rhythmic. Too great an emphasis on sounding out words might interfere with smooth oral reading. He might have formed other bad habits in early grades. In general, he might reveal a poor attitude toward the subject and might enunciate ineffectively.

Treatments for poor oral reading could well start with an effort to increase vocabulary through content areas and an attempt to improve reaction time. There should be enough word analysis to give the pupil independence, and he should be supplied with a quantity of material suited to his abilities. His attention should be drawn to the tactic of recognizing the word by its context. Training would increase his span of perception. Short exposure exercises would be indicated to remedy oral-reading problems. His speed might be increased by timed exercise; oral language instruction such as enunciation drills would probably help him. Exercises would help him make his voice more pleasing and help him control breathing, but they should be planned with care in order to avoid fatiguing the child. A high level of attention should be established when the child reads. Reading should fit the experiences of the child as closely as possible. The teacher should aid in an analysis of types of imagery, group the children according to the types of errors they make, and encourage each child to keep graphic charts of his progress to focus his attention on his success. Providing an audience is another way to motivate children toward improved oral reading.

Poor silent reading will result in the inability to follow directions. The child will tend to look only at the pictures in the book. His reports in social studies will be inadequate because he finds it difficult to use indexes or look up references. He will be slow in finishing assignments or fail to finish them. He will tend to have no interest in reading for pleasure. When he is reading silently, he will move his lips, with too many line fixations, reading word by word rather than in groups of words. He will vocalize inwardly and reveal poor comprehension of what he has read. He will lack word-analysis skills.

One cause of poor silent reading might be inadequate vocabulary. The child might have experienced an overemphasis on vocabulary study, phonetics, and other analytic drills. Language forms might not be automatic, and he might read word by word. Another cause might have been overemphasis on reading too large units in the beginning, causing him to fake comprehension of difficult material. The child might find it difficult to interpret meaning or be unfamiliar with the subject. The problem might stem from an inability to organize, to abstract meaning from sentences or phrases. There might have been an overemphasis on oral reading with too great vocalization. The child might not have been encouraged to use context as an aid in recognizing unfamiliar words. He might have failed to receive training at certain critical periods. He might have too narrow a span of perception, show a general slowness in all responses, or find the material uninteresting.

Treatment of poor silent reading would include diagnosis and removal of vocabulary difficulties by specific teaching. The teacher could use standard word lists and tests to check practice. The child should be trained to recognize words by context. Special exercises might increase his speed. The teacher could decrease vocalization by direct appeal and by the use of timed devices. The child should be encouraged and helped to develop motivations for reading. The teacher should give special treatment to each content subject. Workbooks might prove helpful, and the child might be taught how to study most effectively. The teacher should make assignments clearly and explicitly. The child should be taught to summarize, to pick out the central idea, to organize and retain important ideas.

The child should learn to read with a specific purpose in mind. Practice material should be similar to the test that revealed the child's weakness. He should be made aware of his reading habits so that he can actively seek to improve them. The teacher can show the value of silent reading and can use enough easy material to increase the child's confidence and to assure that he will indeed practice. The child should learn how to interpret paragraph units. However, the material must be of suitable difficulty and contain real thought units that require comprehension constantly. Different types of reading—narration, description, and poetry—can be taught as well as the appreciation of literature.

Inadequate reading will result in a meager knowledge of facts, information, and basic concepts. The child will lack interest in literary masterpieces that typically appeal to his group. Materials that are interesting, varied, and appropriate should be supplied. Besides lack of suitable materials, other causes might be low intelligence or content that is too difficult. The child will reveal unsatisfactory appreciations, preferring comic books, popular fiction, thrillers, and questionable publications. He will show an inordinate interest in obscene writings and drawings. He will show poor reading skills, be inattentive, and reject completely or simply dislike reading. These symptoms might result from too much analysis of the mechanics of writing with a lack of choice or variety. The child might have insufficient knowledge of life, health habits, and wholesome living, evidenced by an undue interest in obscene writings. Lack of vocabulary, inability to read, and meager out-of-school experiences as well as a lack of value for education in his home will produce symptoms of inadequate reading or unsatisfactory reading appreciations.

Treatment of inadequate or inappropriate reading appreciations would first of all include providing a variety of reading materials suited to individual needs, interests, and mental maturity. Literature should be assigned for enjoyment rather than for study until the child learns to value his reading skill. A wide choice in the field of literature should be allowed, with emphasis on reading for pleasure rather than analysis. The child should have more literature with simple vocabulary. Assignments should be short at first, and then gradually increased. The teacher should assign reading materials that correlate with concrete experiences. The teacher should read to children, and the children should keep charts of their own progress. The child should be encouraged to develop wholesome ideals and attitudes toward the broad goals of education.

Profile of Prerequisite or Readiness Skills

On the basis of correlates identified by Project Potential research, treatments for low achievers and for poor readers in particular have been suggested. Remediation, however, is less satisfactory than prevention. Therefore, the findings of Project Potential were set to use in an attempt to describe an early childhood education program to ensure subsequent school success. There appears to be a need for such a program.

In regard to early childhood education Sears and Dowley (1963) claim "there has been little or no attempt to integrate a set of theoretical concepts." A preliminary approach to this task has been set forth in terms of the model depicted in Table 4–1. Following research, these Project Potential findings later became the formalized objectives for the preschool programs in the Los Angeles city schools and the State of California Migrant Education Projects and have also been the basis for a reading series developed by Black and others (1968). The model is divided into four columns.

First, the objectives of the preschool and kindergarten reading-readiness programs are set forth. Classification has been made in terms of the three major categories of human learning: (1) perceptual-motor, (2) social-emotional, and (3) intellectual-academic. Within each of these areas, specific developmental tasks appropriate to the age level of the participants were selected with emphasis upon those considerations that would also permit a smooth transition to formalized reading. Second, the importance for attaining these objectives is described with emphasis given to those facets of the developmental task that at the preschool age level are basic to concurrent and continuous growth patterns. Third, the theoretical orientation of the objectives deals with the relationship of the objectives to research findings. Fourth, implications are drawn with attention to experiences to assist in the attainment of the developmental task involved.

The basic premise or assumption underlying the model in Table 4–1 is that a conducive environment can stimulate reading readiness in a child with normal faculties who fails because of environmental factors to demonstrate readiness appropriate to his age level.

Correlates related to later reading success appear in the first column of Table 4–1 formally classified as objectives; these objectives appear in the table as follows:

1. *Perceptual-motor:* These objectives stress the physical readiness of the child in terms of neurological input-output functions.
   - a. Body image and differentiation of body parts
   - b. Laterality and eye-hand coordination
   - c. Directionality and eye-hand coordination
   - d. Space-world perception; reality-centered observation skills
   - e. Form perception; part-whole, figure-ground
   - f. Sensory discrimination; tactile, auditory, visual, kinesthetic
   - g. Muscle coordination; large, small
   - h. Flexibility in motor control and ability to stop

2. *Social-emotional:* These objectives stress the readiness of the child in terms of independence and interaction functions.
   - a. Group participation and sharing skills
   - b. Socially acceptable means of channeling expressions of feeling
   - c. Social interaction skills with adults and peers
   - d. Utilization of social-practical tools
   - e. Sensitivity to and expression of humor
   - f. Problem-solving attitudes in terms of perseverance
   - g. Skills in self-help and independence functions

3. *Intellectual-academic:* These objectives focus on the child's ability to approach the more formalized instructional processes of the regular school program.
   - a. Receptive-language skills; understanding vocabulary
   - b. Expressive-language skills; working vocabulary
   - c. Problem-solving skills
   - d. Ability to follow directions

TABLE 4-1

Correlates with Later Reading Success

Objectives for the Readiness Programs	*Importance of Attaining Objectives*
1. *Perceptual-motor*	
a. Body image and differentiation of body parts	Body is the point of origin for all movements and all interpretations of outside relationships (Kephart, 1960).
b. Laterality and eye-hand coordination	Before a child can follow directions or draw a square, he must be able to distinguish between his left and right side and to control the two sides of his body separately and simultaneously (Douglass, 1965; Muehl, 1963).
c. Directionality and eye-hand coordination	Without laterality and directionality there is no difference between letters like p and q; thus reading becomes a difficult if not impossible skill to achieve (Kephart, 1960; Hendrickson and Muehl, 1962).
d. Space-world perceptions; reality-centered observation skills	An adequate space-world is necessary for the observation of similarities and differences basic to conceptualization.
e. Form perception; part-whole, figure-ground	It would appear that there is a significant relationship between form perception and reading achievement (Vernon, 1960; Corah, Jones, and Miller, 1966).
f. Sensory discrimination; tactile, auditory, visual, kinesthetic	A child who has many opportunities to touch, taste, smell, hear, and see, and to manipulate and enjoy all the forms of sensory exploration has a better chance to develop in every way than one less fortunate (Clark, 1963).

Theoretical Orientation	*Implications for Facilitative Processes*
An individual's conception of his body appears to be closely related to his self-concept; if he is self-rejecting, he rejects his body image (Fisher, 1965; Simon, 1959).	Observing the movement of different body parts in relation to each other and to external objects helps in the formation of body image.
There is no well-established theory about laterality. The cerebral-dominance theory, once widely accepted, is now considered at best speculative and at worst wrong.	By experimenting with the movement patterns of objects in space, the child learns left-right discrimination within himself.
Directionality is a learned concept and follows laterality, i.e., development is from egocentric localization (subjective space) to objective localization (objective space).	Through experience based on right-left discrimination of objects in relation to himself, the child translates right-left discrimination to objects outside himself.
Spatial perception is the most complicated and the last of the readiness skills to develop (Strauss and Lehtinen, 1947).	Activities that require a child to keep a moving object constantly in view help to develop the ocular control necessary for spatial perception.
Form perception is developed sequentially from *global* to *analytic* to *synthetic* (Hanley and Zerbollo, 1965).	Opportunities to learn part-whole, figure-ground relationships are provided by puzzles (stressing picture form rather than individual shapes) and pegboard activities.
Sensory discrimination is achieved through reduction of every phase of one's surroundings to an "alphabet" of aspects (James, 1966).	Sensory discrimination is developed through opportunities to experience similarities and differences in many sensory modalities.

Correlates with Later Reading Success—*(continued)*

Objectives for the Readiness Programs	*Importance of Attaining Objectives*
g. Muscle coordination; large, small	Differentiation of hand and finger movements from movement of the organism is essential to the tasks of drawing and writing (Kephart, 1960).
h. Flexibility in motor control and ability to stop	If change in direction of ongoing movement is to take place, the child must be able to stop and initiate movement in another direction (Ryan and Moffitt, 1966).

2. *Social-emotional*

a. Group participation and sharing skills	Learning to cooperate with others, and to follow as well as lead, is basic to other stages of social development (Erikson, 1956; Zunich, 1963).
b. Socially acceptable means of channeling expressions of feeling	"Successful achievement leads to happiness . . . while failure leads to unhappiness in the individual [and] disapproval by the society . . ." (Havighurst, 1953).
c. Social interaction skills with adults and peers	How a child reacts to adults and peers while transforming organic patterns to uniquely human patterns may become an established mode for perceiving the world (Frank, 1958; Estvan, 1966).
d. Utilization of social-practical tools	Children who have acquired mastery of certain social-practical skills in their environment have acquired the means of developing manners and social graces (Emmerich, 1966).

Theoretical Orientation	*Implications for Facilitative Processes*
Direction of growth and motor development is cephalocaudal (line of development from the head downward), proximodistal (line of development from the center to the periphery) (Conner, 1966).	The child is helped to develop the ability to maintain a flexible postural adjustment under varied conditions through experiences requiring balancing.
The stimulus for stopping is very weak and is a combination of perceptual data and imagery (Maccoby and Bee, 1965).	The child is helped in anticipating a stopping point by the number of clues available to him.
Learning the process of belonging to and becoming a member of the family and the social group is a developmental task of early childhood (Gellert, 1962).	Intentionally planned play situations can provide opportunities for children to live in a social order.
Achieving emotional release through sensory experiences is a developmental task of early childhood.	In words, gestures, dramatic play, and manipulation of plastic and graphic materials, the child is able to find more mature expressions of his emotional reactions without having to repress them.
By the time most children are four years old they are actively interested in social cooperative behavior with adults and peers (Martin, 1960–61; Stevenson and Stevenson, 1960).	In various play situations the child may discover new ways of relating himself to others through cooperative play.
Exercises of practical life, i.e., useful things adults do in the home, assume major importance in the initial phases of an educational process.	Developing skills for using social-practical tools is helped in part by an environment that provides motivation for such development.

Correlates with Later Reading Success—*(continued)*

Objectives for the Readiness Programs	Importance of Attaining Objectives
e. Sensitivity to and expression of humor	"Humor is a most valuable human trait . . . it is too precious to be left to chance; the child with it will meet life better than the child without it" (Antonitis, Frey, and Baron, 1964).
f. Problem-solving attitudes in terms of perseverance	The whole process of arriving at some conclusion may be influenced by personality and values.
g. Skills in self-help and independence functions	"Successful achievement leads to . . . success with later tasks, while failure leads to . . . difficulty with later tasks" (Havighurst, 1953).
3. *Intellectual-academic*	
a. Receptive-language skills; understanding vocabulary	Children understand speech before they can make themselves understood (Bernstein, 1961).
b. Expressive-language skills; working vocabulary	The reaction of others to a child's language patterns has a dramatic influence on his self-concept and school adjustment (Deutsch, 1964).
c. Problem-solving skills	The ability to solve problems when confronted by obstacles is essential to goal attainment (Russell, 1956; Montague, 1964; Amster, 1966).
d. Ability to follow directions	The ability to respond to verbal directions is basic to expressive language.

Theoretical Orientation	*Implications for Facilitative Processes*
Emphasis has been placed on developmental factors in concepts of humor; however, a sense of humor is possible for children without real self-objectification (Russell, 1956; Larder, 1962).	Social settings may be considered to provide opportunities for development of concepts of humor.
During the preconceptual stage the child attempts to solve each new problem with the expectations of past assimilations (Braine, 1962).	An active curiosity and motivation to overcome difficulties give children a good start as problem solvers.
Achieving independence in caring for oneself as an individual is a developmental task of early childhood (Havighurst, 1953).	A child achieves this task as he learns to dress and undress himself, get out and put away his toys, and use the toilet independently.
At every age children's passive comprehension is always greater than their active vocabulary.	Abstractions, symbolic meanings, and concepts are dependent on word usage. Words grow and change in meaning for the child as the experiences he brings to those words change and develop.
Learning communication and symbolization progresses from jargon to words, from words to phrases, from phrases to sentences (Bereiter, 1961).	The child's opportunities to practice using words and sentences has an effect on the development of language skills.
The problem solving of young (preschool) children should be considered as taking place in concrete, immediate situations rather than as occurring in abstract.	Children achieve the ability to solve and work out perplexing problems as they manipulate words, sounds, and playthings.
The child concomitantly alters his perception of the world and his conduct responsive to that perception of social order (Frank, 1958).	The distinction should be made on the part of adults whether the four-year-old child is defying adult commands in keeping with his age or is unable to follow directions, which is characteristic of younger children.

Summary

This five-year research was concerned with the identification of correlates dealing with the school failure and success of children from the culture of poverty. First, some twenty-seven characteristics of low achievers were grouped into five categories: learning style, value framework and self-concept, cognitive structure, models of behavior, and home environment. Second, the ten attitudinal areas studied in Project Potential that relate to school achievement in general and reading in particular were grouped into the same five categories. Third, based on a contrastive analysis of the failures of low achievers with the successes of high achievers, treatments were suggested for helping low achievers. Fourth, characteristics of poor readers identified by Project Potential correlates were used to draw a profile of the poor reader that was accompanied by a discussion of possible causes and treatments. Fifth, an attempt was made to integrate a set of theoretical concepts in regard to early childhood education. Based on the correlates that identified preschool skills needed for subsequent reading success, a series of objectives was outlined. The justification for and theoretical orientation of each objective were given, and processes to facilitate attainment of each objective were suggested. Through integration, theoretical concepts (objectives, justifications, theoretical orientation, and processes) became formalized objectives. They have been formally adopted for several preschool and migrant education projects and have been published as a comprehensive reading program. These findings, however, were presented as *probabilities* rather than as "facts" or "fictions" per se. As Project Potential research continues, a new task awaits completion: ranking the hundreds of correlates identified according to the priority each deserves from program developers and teachers.

II
Language

5

The Linguistically Different: Learning Theories and Intellectual Development

Mark W. Seng

MAN IS characterized by thought and feeling, which he communicates through language. Language, then, is symbolic thought, symbolic feeling. The formulation, expression, and exchange of ideas depends on language. Thus success in using language determines success in school and almost without exception in later life.

The purpose of this chapter is (1) to explain the function of language including its relation to intellectual development; (2) to identify and describe four learning theories that underlie a bilingual or bidialectal education program; (3) to illustrate how these theories can be incorporated within instructional materials; and (4) to suggest ways in which teachers with a grasp of the underlying learning theories can teach linguistically different children more effectively and creatively.

The Function of Language

Man benefits from language in two ways. It gives him an instrument to communicate his ideas, and it influences his intellectual capability. Psychologists seem to agree that it is language that distinguishes man from animal. For example, Pavlov maintained that man has two signaling systems. The higher system (i.e., language) enables man to achieve a "new type of neural activity-abstraction" (Rivers, 1964). Apparently, it is the lower system of automatic response that is common to both man and animal. Other psychologists have modified Skinner's applied psychology, which attempted to explain language in terms of the same principles as nonverbal behavior, by including the concept of *mediation*, that is, the interaction between observable stimuli and observable responses. These "neobehaviorists" have developed theories (or more appropriately sub-theories, since they tend to describe only certain types of human behavior [Klausmeier and Goodwin, 1966]) that facilitate language teaching by describing how learning occurs (e.g., Staats and Staats, 1964).

Human learning may usually be assigned to one of three categories of skills: intellectual, motor, or attitudinal. Language learning, however, requires simultaneous consideration of all three categories. For example, as pupils learn to produce physically the sounds of a new language, they also must develop intellectual linguistic concepts. Thus they are required to develop motor and intellectual skills simultaneously. Teaching must be carried on in a way that develops positive attitudes and maintains pupil interest and morale. It is important to underscore this third category because a person's language repertoire reflects his innermost self, because language reflects cultural attitudes, and because it is desirable that the learning process be perceived as pleasant by the pupil.

If bilingual or bidialectal language programs are to achieve success in terms of pupil and teacher acceptance, they must consider intellectual skills, attitude formation, and oral skill development. Children, consequently, must have adequate opportunity as well as stimulation for oral skill development. Pupils should practice oral language skills as much as possible while developing concepts, *and* the process should be enjoyable. A child in such a program will grow intellectually more competent, more proficient in expressing his own expanding universe of ideas, and confident of his own intrinsic worth. The program demands that every possible insight gained by learning theories and supported by experimentation involving human beings be put into play. In addition, it must be put into practice by teachers in a sensitive, sensible way.

Learning, Laws of Learning, and Three Learning Theories

What is meant by *learning?* If, after some experience, a child is able to do something he previously was unable to do, the child is said to have learned (Klausmeier and Goodwin, 1966). Learning can be distinguished from performance, which provides us with observable evidence that learning has occurred. In other words, one may learn but not be called upon to demonstrate that he has learned. Learning, as will be shown later, can also occur without a person's being aware that he has learned. One type of such learning is called *conditioning*.

A law of learning is a generalization about some aspect of learning that has proved valid over a period of time. For example, it has been proved that spaced practice (e.g., shorter, more frequent practice sessions) is more effective than massed practice. A learning theory attempts to assemble these laws in a compatible manner. It may describe a theoretical "model," which can then be used to guide program developers in the creation of instructional programs and by teachers in the actual use of the programs in learning situations. A learning theory is not a teaching theory; it must be interpreted and applied. Such intellectual leaps require imagination, intuition, and insight—first by program developers and then by teachers. Learning theories at present are still only intellectual candles. Nonetheless, teachers who understand the learning theories used to guide the development of a program can implement the program in a way appropriate for their pupils and their individual teaching styles and still maintain the learning-theory rationale behind the program.

One occasionally hears instructional materials described as teacher-proof; these materials will prove successful despite the teacher. Success in teaching linguistically different learners, however, demands a high level of professional competence and judgment. Because there remain so many unknowns, success is contingent on the teacher's sensitivity to and perception of pupils' problems and on his sensitive use of materials and strategies. In short, the program is highly teacher-dependent. Boring, ineffectual classes can result if a teacher blindly follows superficial rules. However, teachers who understand the learning-theory rationale can teach creatively; they derive security from understanding the reasons why certain procedures have been suggested and realize that the procedures call for their professional interpretation in specific instances. From the many learning theories extant, four theoretical models, or paradigms, seem particularly relevant to bilingual or bidialectal programs: classical conditioning, operant conditioning, modeling, and cognitive field.

CLASSICAL CONDITIONING

Brooks (1964) describes only two types of learning theories, one of which is classical conditioning. Pavlov demonstrated that pairing two stimuli several times ultimately caused the first stimulus to elicit responses previously evoked only by the second stimulus. Essentially, association of two stimuli is *classical conditioning*. For example, assume you have read the popular comic strip "Peanuts" many times. The name *Linus* (Stimulus 1) soon calls to mind the thought of a blanket (Stimulus 2). Classical conditioning has been shown by Staats and others to be a process by which words acquire meaning (e.g., Staats and Staats, 1964). Through classical conditioning children learn that such phrases as "Fine," "Very good," and "Well done" have favorable connotations. It has been found that attitudes are also established through classical conditioning. Children learn quickly that a smile indicates approval and acceptance. Teachers who enjoy their work and express this feeling openly usually foster favorable attitudes in their pupils.

OPERANT CONDITIONING

We initially learn our first language through a second type of learning. According to Brooks (1964), at four weeks an infant is "heedful of sounds; at sixteen weeks, he babbles, coos." Brooks cites Osgood and Sebeok, who state in *Psycholinguistics* that "profiles of sounds produced by newborn infants show no differences over racial, cultural, or language groups." Brooks states that many people falsely believe that a child makes the first breakthrough into language (voluntarily matching an object in the environment with the appropriate vocal sound) by imitating those around him. He cites many scholars to disprove this commonly held assumption. For example, he quotes McCarthy, who writes of the "tremendous psychological gap which has to be bridged between the mere utterance of the phonetic form of a word and the symbolic or representational use of that word."

What actually occurs is this: by trial and error, a baby approximates a sound, perhaps of *Mama*, and the nearby mother interprets this as actual speech. She reinforces that sound immediately by picking the baby up or by feeding it, until that tremendous gap is bridged when the baby does indeed *intentionally* pronounce that word. According to Brooks (1964), Helen Keller's autobiography provides the only account we have of a mature mind recalling the initial insight of language as symbolization. That vivid moment on a summer's day when she felt the stream of water splash on her hand as her teacher spelled out the word *water* was the instant she learned that words stand for things.

Trial and error learning, often called *operant conditioning*, was initially described as part of a learning theory by Skinner. Essentially, it refers to the phenomenon of rewarding a desired behavior *if* and *when* it occurs. At first, experimentation was limited to animals. Now, however, there is a vast amount of research concerning this type of learning with humans, and an extensive amount of literature describes its operation in human verbal learning. Krasner (1961) published a review of operant-conditioning experiments, listing numerous studies based on verbal conditioning using such reinforcers as "Good" and "Right." A variety of different human behaviors were effectively developed using this procedure. Successful application of operant conditioning requires an understanding of the theory. The key concept is the reward or, more accurately, the reinforcer. A reinforcer may be defined as anything that when presented immediately after a response causes the same response to occur more frequently in the future (e.g., Staats and Staats, 1964). It is interesting to note that the definition does not prejudge what is and is not a reinforcer.

Teachers assume that words of praise, recognition, or encouragement are rewarding or reinforcing to children, and that children want this type of verbal reward. Most of the time, the assumption is valid. However, especially when working with children whose backgrounds are quite different from those of their teachers—as is usually the case with linguistically different children—teachers should be aware that what they assume to be reinforcing to the children may not be in reality. For example, if children come from homes where attention is given only when punishment is meted out, one would not expect them to want attention in school until they realized that attention in school might mean favorable recognition and thus be desirable. Like attention, money is not always a reinforcer. It has no importance for young children; its importance is learned. Whatever the children perceive as important, then, becomes rewarding or reinforcing. What is important to them forms the essence of their motivation and the basis for their value framework. The effectiveness of operant conditioning depends on the teacher's awareness and use of those things perceived as important by the children. A brief example of operant-learning theory in use will clarify the role of reinforcers and illustrate the fact that their use can accomplish more than one objective at the same time.

In the classroom, one can usually safely assume that recognition from the teacher in the form of "That was well done" constitutes a verbal reward or reinforcer. (Incidentally, that expression acquired its value through classical conditioning.) Verbal rewards must be given only if and when a child responds appropriately. The factor of contingency is essential. If overused, words of praise lose their value, and children sense that the recognition is insincere if it is neither earned nor deserved. The expression "OK" has lost much of its reinforcing power, since it has often been used transitionally or as filler to the point of saturation. It still functions as a reinforcer in one way, however; it provides information, or feedback, that the answer was correct.

Besides indicating to a child that his response was correct and increasing the likelihood that he will respond correctly in the future, reinforcement has a third effect. It increases the child's desire for additional reinforcement; that is, it increases his motivation. Verbal rewards play a fourth role by providing an opportunity for children to hear correct language modeled by the teacher at a time when they are paying special attention. Again, then, the important factor is the teacher's rapport with his pupils. It is the pupils' perception of teachers that ultimately determines the effect of teachers' comments on pupil learning. It does little good to suggest to teachers that they use verbal rewards if they have not established rapport with their pupils. It is equally ineffective if teachers are told to use verbal rewards but find their use artificial and inappropriate for their teaching style.

Teachers can strengthen verbal rewards by pairing them with nonverbal rewards, such as a smile and a pat on the back (provided physical contact is regarded positively). Including the child's name as he likes to hear it ("James" rather than "Jim") will almost always increase the effectiveness of the reinforcer.

One can summarize the chief concepts of operant conditioning by stating that the initial task of teachers is to build rapport with their pupils so that what they say, especially in praise or in recognition, is perceived as valuable by the pupils. Then they should use praise or recognition in a way appropriate to their teaching style *if* and *when* pupils exhibit appropriate or improved responses. Reading, for example, does not have to be perfect to earn praise, only better, in the teacher's judgment, than before. Motivation is the perennial problem for all teachers, especially for those teaching the disadvantaged. Understanding the principles of reinforcement can enlighten teachers to those things that are important to children. Staats and Staats (1964) have expressed the point well: "Thus, perhaps a primary concern of an account of human motivation should be with the sources of reinforcement." Do teachers recognize desired behavior in a way that is perceived as genuine, sincere, and natural by pupils? If so, pupils will learn faster and show increasingly higher levels of motivation. The teacher who understands the wealth of research supporting operant conditioning will recognize its power, but, more important, will be able to apply the theory to a variety of situations in a creative manner. Besides, as Rivers (1964) says, "From the teacher's point of view, the more frequently the correct response occurs the more economical is the teaching procedure."

MODELING

A related learning theory incorporates some aspects of operant conditioning but describes social learning that takes place through a technique known as *modeling* (Bandura and Walters, 1963). Bandura and Walters have shown a young child can learn complex skills very quickly simply by observing another person demonstrate those skills. The procedure is enhanced, their research has shown, if either the person who acts as the model or those imitating the model are reinforced for exhibiting the desired behavior.

In this technique, for example, the teacher illustrates the correct way to pronounce a word, a phrase, or a sentence. This model gives the children a head start in developing the motor skills necessary to produce the sounds. However, developing those skills requires that the children practice oral language in a way that will minimize errors. Making errors does not help a child. In addition, these errors provide a deviant model for the other children. To minimize mistakes and to make the activity interesting, the class may be divided into different groups. Such structured lessons should be kept short and lively with choral recitation before individuals are called on to recite (Rivers, 1964).

Rivers (1964) cites Politzer, who says that "the real skill of the teacher lies not in correcting and punishing wrong responses but in creating situations in which the student is induced to respond correctly." Rivers goes on to say:

> This has been the basis of many effective teaching procedures in foreign-language classes: choral recitation of responses by the class after the teacher before individuals are called on to recite; drills and exercises in which a minimal change has to be made; question-and-answer procedures in which the student's response involves, for the most part, repetition of materials contained in the question; and the use of memorized dialogue material in re-creations of everyday situations.

THE FACTORS OF AGE, SETTING, AND GOALS
IN LANGUAGE LEARNING

The fact that a child can learn to pronounce a second language without accent is generally accepted. It is no longer generally accepted that children learn second languages more efficiently than adults. Politzer and Weiss (1969) described why and how children *seem* to demonstrate superior ability in language learning:

> We believe that our findings furnish at least a partial clue to the puzzle that the child's superior ability to learn is, as Carroll pointed out, almost invariably demonstrated in a natural setting rather than a school situation. The natural setting does not tend to set a limit to the number of repetitions necessary to achieve criterion, while the school situation, with a limited number of class periods (and in FLES [Foreign Languages in Elementary Schools] instruction usually very short periods), tends to do the exact opposite. No wonder, then, that the experts find that ideally the best language learning takes place out of school and that the school setting seems to become more suitable to successful language learning to the degree in which it approaches the natural setting.

One of the important advantages of a bilingual program is that it provides a basic amount of structured material that the child and teacher can use as a point of departure for expansion during the day. Thus, the teacher can build language skills based on a minimal amount of structured activity. It is the child's unique advantage of minimal interference from his native language that allows him to learn a second language more thoroughly when such learning is combined with practice in as natural a setting as possible throughout the day. When the child speaks appropriately, he is reinforced instantly. When he is searching for a word, that word is supplied and the resulting use also reinforced. With operant conditioning, pupils may not even be aware of the relationship between the teacher's reinforcement and their own learning.

In speaking of operant and classical conditioning, Lambert (1963a, 1963b) also discusses the potential value for teachers of these learning theories and the extensive documentation that supports them. Again, it is implied that teachers must gain their pupils' esteem and must understand the teaching techniques that may be inferred from modern learning theory. Lambert (1963a) says, "These developments can be of immediate importance for language teachers who can be either effective or ineffective as social reinforcers of their students' attempts to develop appropriate verbal habits."

Psychologist-linguist Lambert (1963b) speaks from an impressive background of research in bilingual education. He discusses the notion of how bilingual persons can learn two symbols that refer to the same concept and "yet manage to use each language system with a minimum of inter-lingual interferences." The pupil learning the second language in the same context will, according to Lambert (1963b), become a *compound* bilingual, for whom "the symbols of both languages function as interchangeable alternatives with essentially the same meanings. A 'coordinate' system would be developed when the language-acquisition contexts were culturally, temporally or functionally segregated." If the goal is to develop pupils who are bicultural, then it would seem advisable to point out differences between words referring to essentially the same concepts. When one discusses the word as a symbol, one is then discussing meaning, or experience referents. Language, as was pointed out previously, serves as a vehicle for communication, but it also comprises at least one aspect of intellectual competency. The more that one knows, the easier it is to learn new concepts.

Concepts and a Fourth Learning Theory

What is a concept and what is its relation to intellectual development, to language, and to learning theory? The word *concept* is widely used. Yet, if asked to define the word, many people would find themselves hard put to express the "concept of a concept."

Davis (1966) calls *concept learning* "probably the most important of all instances of learned human behavior." However, he points out the difficulty in clarifying what a concept is and how it is learned.

One type of concept learning may be called *categorization*. In this sense, the word *concept* refers to a category into which a number of items may be classified. The category has certain limitations or attributes that are common to all instances of a given concept. For example, the concept might be "round." Into this category would fit all objects that exhibit the quality of roundness—a button, a coin, a dish, a paper circle, and so on. Davis (1966) points out that researchers refer to this type of concept learning as a process of abstraction, or *abstraction learning*. For this type of learning the concept is the category itself, which does not exist as a separate entity. What do a bus, a bicycle, and a plane have in common? Obviously, they are vehicles that are used by human beings. In speaking of classroom learning, Davis says that "whether one speaks of forming concepts in childhood, learning concepts in the classroom, or identifying 'concepts' " in psychological experiments, all the child's responses in which he places an item in the right category are reinforced. Davis then explains that the learning principles involved are those of operant conditioning. The reinforcement serves primarily as feedback to the pupil.

Therefore, the teacher may present examples of the conceptual category with nonexamples to enable the children to abstract the concept. For example, a child may be asked to select the form that has the shape of a circle from a group of assorted forms including squares and triangles. The psychological rationale underlying one aspect of the science program relies upon operant conditioning to help the child abstract those concepts selected as having the greatest ultimate value. Geometric shapes provide only one example of a concept of lasting value.

However, while the child is abstracting the concept, the opportunity also presents itself for oral language development. The critical point here is that the teacher may use operant-conditioning learning theory simultaneously for two completely different types of learning that occur concomitantly: science-concept formation and correct oral language development. It is exceedingly important that the teacher *not* operantly reinforce a response correct for one type of learning but not for the other. For example, if a child responds, "This is a circle," when indeed it is a circle, but mispronounces *is* (*ees*), the teacher should not reinforce the response. Reinforcement will make it far more difficult for the child to learn the correct pronunciation of *is* for the following reasons. First, he was reinforced after he said *is* incorrectly. Second, in addition to reinforcement he was given feedback that his response was correct. Third, the wrong response was reinforced on an intermittent schedule.

Ferster, Skinner, and many others have conducted extensive research on schedules of reinforcement, that is, reinforcing all or some correct responses or varying the time intervals (e.g., Ferster and Skinner, 1957). Definitive research findings conclude that responses reinforced intermittently are extremely difficult to extinguish. Thus, telling a child "That's right," referring to the correct science concept expressed in unacceptable language, is far worse than no reinforcement because the wrong language response will persist that much longer. Learning theory suggests that the appropriate technique would be to repeat the child's response immediately in correct language, then add a verbal reward.

One type of concept learning is abstraction. A second type Davis (1966) refers to as *acquisition of meaning*. For example, you probably have the concept of the words *Charlie Brown*. The words elicit a series of meaning responses. You might think of a small boy, a dog, baseball, Linus and Linus' blanket, happiness, and perhaps many other things. You have learned these responses because you have seen pictures of Charlie Brown in conjunction with the other responses. You have enjoyed reading the comic strip, which would explain the nonverbal, generalized response of humor. "Thus," Davis says, "principles of *classical conditioning* would seem to describe concept learning as the acquisition of meaning responses to a concept name."

It may appear that the two types of concepts—concept instances and meaning responses—are almost reciprocal, mirror images. Each has that element essential to a concept, the notion of commonality. A group of concept instances, for example, a group of round plates, have common features that allow them to be placed in a category. By contrast, the meaning concept "Charlie Brown" evokes a string of responses that all have *one* thing in common. They all relate to Charlie Brown. The first type of concept learning requires that the child learn that there are several criteria (or things in common) that objects must meet to be placed into a particular concept. For meaning responses, there is only one criterion, the concept itself.

FIGURE 5-1

Two Types of Concept Learning

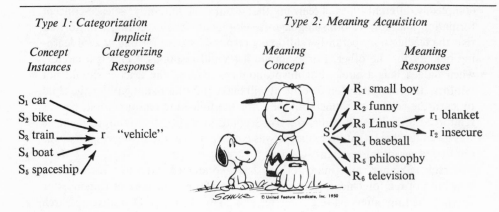

Type 1: Categorization		*Type 2: Meaning Acquisition*	
	Implicit		
Concept	*Categorizing*	*Meaning*	*Meaning*
Instances	*Response*	*Concept*	*Responses*

SOURCE:
Adapted from Davis (1966).

In Figure 5-1 the series of vehicles in Type 1 concept formation have arrows directed toward the inclusive conceptual category. The vehicles are stimuli producing a common response. In Type 2 the category is the stimulus that elicits a string of meaning responses. Therefore, a category may be either response or stimulus depending on whether it is a Type 1 or Type 2 concept. Besides this reversal, there are other differences. The number of items that will fit the category "vehicle" is finite. Type 1 instances must somehow meet the criteria implicit in the category. There is no such limit to the theoretical number of meaning associations that may be attached to Charlie Brown. The associations, classically conditioned, may be arbitrarily selected. For example, Charles Schulz, the creator of Charlie Brown, may associate him with anything from baseball to Broadway. A fascinating aspect is that this interpretation of what a concept is may be used to explain intellectual development.

RELATIONSHIP OF CONCEPTS
AND INTELLECTUAL DEVELOPMENT

A concept has two functions or characteristics. First, it has the notion of commonality, something in common. Second, it has the notion of association. Each conceptual example (exemplar) shares one or more features or attributes. The car and the bus have in common the fact that they are both vehicles. Linus, a small boy, and baseball have in common the fact that they are meaning responses from the stimulus words *Charlie Brown*. Besides the idea of something in common, concepts have the characteristic of association or relationship with a large number of different ideas. We learn something new much faster and retain it much longer if we can relate it to something we already know. The learning that occurs when we cannot relate the new fact with an old one has been defined by psychologists as rote learning. For example, suppose you wish to remember the letters and numbers of the license plate on your car. If the initial letters are XPA, the task will be more difficult than if the initial letters are SIT, which you may associate with the idea that you sit in your car.

The task of program developers and teachers is to help children develop those concepts that will prove of most value to them, to deal with things that are important to them, and to include in the programs a number of related concepts. How can program developers and teachers guide concept learning? The following examples of conceptual buildup for oral language development in a first-grade science program and in a first-grade social studies program are drawn from the bilingual education program produced by the Southwest Educational Development Laboratory (1968).

CONCEPTUAL DEVELOPMENT IN A SCIENCE PROGRAM

The science lessons are carefully structured to facilitate concept learning by presenting the child with concepts that may be rather quickly differentiated. It is for this reason that, for example, a circle, a square, and a triangle are presented in the first lesson, with similar careful structuring following in the other lessons. Davis (1966) points out that the recommended way to teach this type of concept is contiguous presentation of examples with immediate feedback; teachers should bear in mind that what the child must learn are those abstract cues that define the concept.

CONCEPTUAL DEVELOPMENT IN A SOCIAL STUDIES PROGRAM

Important concepts are those that can be divided into smaller, more precise concepts, such as this excellent example of a social studies concept, "How Do We Live?" How does the idea of how we live relate to the notion of *association?* Why was this concept selected to establish a conceptual base? Considered as a category, "How do we live?" can include a number of very important subconcepts. The illustrative topic "school" is selected for its immediacy and relevance to children and serves to illustrate how society's needs are served by basic social institutions. It can be seen immediately that the concept "How do we live?" includes many ideas important to children as well as to adults. To enable children to learn this concept and to attach meaning to it, specific content areas that are encompassed by this concept may be presented. Teachers should always begin with concrete objects and experiences that the children can readily perceive and that they consider important. Different aspects of the school would be those initially suggested in the social studies program. ("School" is a category or concept itself that is encompassed by the larger concept of "How do we live?") The concept of school grows in meaning as children are presented with concrete examples that they can perceive directly through various senses. Within the children's minds, the conceptual category of school gradually develops clarity and stability. Expressed in another way, the word *school* acquires meaning for children in the same way that the much less sophisticated concept of Charlie Brown acquired meaning for us. In addition, children learn those items that fall within the category "school" and those that do not.

CONCEPTS AND WORDS

Words may serve as concepts or categories into which new ideas may be placed. The larger the number of words children have learned, the higher the probability that they will be able to establish a relation between something new and some concept or concepts previously learned. In this sense, language increases intellectual capability. Note that the term "intellectual capability" has been used with deliberate avoidance of the term "intelligence." It does seem obvious that children with a large number of concepts at varying levels of inclusiveness will learn more easily because they can relate new material to the concepts they know. In addition, children learning new material will be able to learn a new idea more precisely if they have a concept in which it is tightly enclosed. Assume, for example, that children have begun to develop the large concept of the school, enclosed in the much larger concept of "How do we live?" Within the concept of school, they have developed the smaller, more precise concept that some items within the school building belong to the teachers, some to themselves, and some to other children. They will be able to use this concept of ownership to create the concept of nonownership in terms of public property. The contrast between the concept of nonownership and the concept of ownership gives children the opportunity to create a new conceptual category and to associate quite precisely the new idea with what they already know.

It is essential, therefore, to aid children in developing first those concepts that they can use to encompass new material of greatest importance to them and for them. If they have no concept that will include new material, they must learn the new material by rote, which psychologists have proved to be the least effective means. Rote learning is the most boring and frustrating learning activity for children (e.g., Ausubel, 1963), and material learned by rote is forgotten most quickly.

The intellectual development of children (and adults) is directly dependent on the number of concepts or categories comprising their knowledge, the importance or relevance of those concepts to new learning, and the clarity with which those concepts are formed (that is, the degree to which concepts contained within larger concepts may be separated from those larger concepts). Children who develop concepts in order of importance and who learn them clearly will be able to draw on those concepts to facilitate new learning. This facilitation is referred to by psychologists as *transfer*. Thus, it is essential that teachers relate new material to what children already know. They may, for example, call attention to the fact that the earth is shaped like a pear or point out that black is the opposite of white. When this process occurs in an organized manner, children will learn quickly while retaining what they have already learned. This expanding and sophisticated organization of concepts, sometimes called cognitive structure, will at the same time enable children to express themselves more easily and to communicate with others more effectively (Ausubel, 1963).

In relation to language, a word children learn may become a concept that permits them to use it to relate to new materials while allowing them to operate at a higher intellectual level. One aspect of thinking involves the use of words other than for communication. Sometimes studied as subvocal speech, it is the process by which we think to ourselves in terms of words. As we think, we instantaneously call on words. Each word brings with it all the meaning associations it has acquired for us, and it also functions as a category into which we can place new ideas. The sheer number of words we know is a major factor in terms of both our "intelligence" and our ability to express our thoughts to other people.

This description of intellectual development in terms of concept formation corresponds to the learning theory of Ausubel (1963). He speaks of a "cognitive structure" that may be interpreted as the sum total of concepts and their interrelationships. He emphasizes the importance of having concepts or "subsumers" that will either perfectly enclose or directly contrast with new material. Existing concepts can be expanded to contain new ideas. In effect, what he says is that it is crucial for teachers to develop new concepts in pupils and then to use these new concepts as starting points to enable the pupils to relate and categorize still other new material.

Language learning incorporates all three types of human learning: pure concept formation, development of attitudes toward ourselves and others, and development of physiological motor skills to form new sound patterns of pronunciation. Unless teachers understand that practice by modeling and imitation in a drilling procedure is helpful, that more is being learned than to form sounds, then the activity will seem almost purposeless to both teachers and pupils and will result in negative attitudes. It has been shown that it is possible to develop syntactical concepts in children (a central purpose of pattern drills) without their being aware that concepts are being developed. Children may also learn appropriate science and social studies concepts at the same time. However, it is important that teachers be aware that learning is occurring, for if they view an activity as meaningless, their attitude will quickly be communicated to sensitive children and result in an artificial, unpleasant learning situation. Familiarity with their pupils' cognitive structures is a prerequisite for the teachers who seek to point out the relationships of new ideas.

COGNITIVE STRUCTURE
OF THE LINGUISTICALLY DIFFERENT

An obvious and important but difficult fact for teachers to bear in mind is that disadvantaged children frequently have had many experiences totally different from their own. If these children have never had the experiences that the majority of children have had as a matter of routine, their classroom behavior may be such that they are labeled at best, naive; at worst, stupid. It is quite possible that many of these children are very intelligent when viewed from the standpoint of their cognitive structure. *The traditional micrometer of IQ is an invalid instrument.*

Let us briefly consider intelligence and its composite factors from the point of view of a learning theory based on a cognitive structure paradigm. How would you measure intelligence, and what would constitute the variables involved? One would first seek to define the intellectual parameters of the cognitive structure— the complexity, number, and quality of its concepts. However, without an open mind to the possibility of greater intellectual ability than might be immediately apparent, teachers will not search out the concepts within the structure. Of course, teachers must accept concepts as evidence of intelligence; this part of intelligence concerns what is known. But a second aspect of intelligence would be whether children use what they know, that is, whether they can profit from experience. A third factor would be the length of time it takes them to learn; a fourth, the ratio of intelligence and age quotient; and a fifth, their intellectual ceiling. For example, with what level of abstraction can they work? Finally, teachers should consider the children's ability to express or verbalize what they know and their ability to comprehend the expression of others.

Intelligence, then, may be said to consist of the complexity of the cognitive structure, the degree to which that structure may become more sophisticated, and the ability to apply that structure to the task at hand. There is danger in the fact that teachers may form premature judgments about intelligence because they are not familiar with a disadvantaged child's cognitive structure. If teachers are unfamiliar with that structure, they are patently unable to relate concepts considered essential by the school to what the children already know. Worse, they will judge such children stupid, and their judgment will probably become a self-fulfilling prophecy.

Undoubtedly, many disadvantaged children have very sophisticated cognitive structures derived from vivid experiences that remain unfathomable to teachers who are either naive or biased. These children might be dismissed as shrewd or cunning—indications of intelligence, but the "wrong kind." Skillful teachers of the disadvantaged appreciate such knowledge as evidence of intelligence. Moreover, they will search for other evidence of intelligence in their pupils. If a child is not proficient in standard American English but his cognitive structure is complex in terms of concept formation and integration, that child *is* intelligent. However, intelligence may not become evident or measurable for a long time, since at present there appears to be no convincing way to map that structure.

Children may not perform well in school because what they know is seemingly not relevant to school tasks or vice versa. It is the teacher's responsibility to learn what the children do know and to show how this knowledge can relate to the task at hand. At the least, teachers should be extremely cautious in labeling children who are linguistically different; rather, they should adopt a wait-and-see attitude. If children have formed concepts—often from experiences that might be considered rather harsh—and the concepts are clear, interrelated, stable, and capable of being expanded and brought to bear upon similar activities, these children are intelligent, although they may have immense difficulty with school tasks and little motivation to perform in school. They will not appear intelligent to the teacher who does not stimulate, search out, and accept the often unexpected concepts these children have developed.

Seven aspects of intelligence have been discussed: what is known, its application, time taken to learn, ratio with age (i.e., IQ), intellectual ceiling, linguistic expression, and comprehension. Obviously the list is incomplete. Traditionally, emphasis has been placed on time—time to learn a task and time in terms of the children's age level. These two factors ultimately appear less significant. It does not matter, really, if it takes children more time to learn, if they can eventually assimilate ideas. If children cannot learn abstract concepts, might the fault not lie in our inability to relate such concepts to what the children already know in a way they can understand? For example, many very bright people encounter unusual difficulty in mastering data analysis. It might be that the problem lies not in the nature of the statistical concepts but in the difficulty of relating the concepts to the conventional experiences of college students.

LANGUAGE LEARNING AND THE COGNITIVE STRUCTURE OF CHILDREN

Recent research has shown that the most effective ways of learning language are different for adults and for children. Adults have a sophisticated network of concepts in their native language to bring to bear upon a second-language learning task (Ausubel, 1964). Children do not have as sophisticated an intellectual structure, nor are their native language competencies as extensive. The children's naiveté, however, enables them to learn a second language with minimum interference from the first—the key factor making it possible for them to develop a perfect accent (Politzer and Weiss, 1969). Children also bring spontaneity and an eagerness to imitate, whereas older students are more inhibited, fearful of producing sounds that they think would be embarrassing.

Summary

Language serves two functions. It enables us to communicate with other people, and it also enhances our ability to operate intellectually as we learn new concepts and call previously learned concepts into play in the thinking process. For example, each new word learned other than by rote becomes an added concept in our intellectual structure. Language learning involves learning intellectual skills and motor skills, as well as developing attitudes and emotional perspectives. Effective language teaching keeps the three areas in harmonious balance.

Four learning theories, all well documented with experimentation with humans, appear relevant to language learning in these three areas. First, classical and, second, operant conditioning can be used to induce learning, with or without the pupils' awareness of the technique being employed. Third, modeling theory can be applied to increase pupils' efficiency in learning oral language skills as well as more complex skills and attitudes. Categorization and meaning acquisition—the two basic types of concept learning—usually involve operant and classical conditioning, respectively. The two types of concepts learned through categorization and meaning acquisition are almost reciprocal in that both call for some common feature and for association.

Children's intellectual development is directly dependent upon the number, quality, and discriminability of the concepts that comprise their cognitive structures. Concepts used in bilingual or bidialectal programs should meet the criteria of immediate and long-range usefulness to the children. Since each word—other than rotely learned—becomes a concept, vocabulary is a determiner of intellectual capability. The entire structure of intellectual development based upon the concept approach corresponds to a fourth learning theory, cognitive field.

Adults and children do not learn languages most effectively when taught in the same way. Current research findings indicate that adults have the mixed blessing of a well-learned native language: it facilitates language learning but at the same time causes language interference, usually preventing the acquisition of accent-free second-language skills. Children are less inhibited and benefit from techniques perhaps not appropriate for adults. Some of these techniques include modeling and pattern drills. Apparently, an important variable determining the success of bilingual or bidialectal programs is the degree to which the classroom setting approaches a natural language-learning setting; that is, the extent to which language learning may continue on a more casual basis throughout the day with a minimal amount of structured practice.

6

Language
and the Disadvantaged

Muriel R. Saville

LINGUISTS assert that spoken language is primary and that reading is a complex process of decoding writing, which symbolizes speech sounds, which in turn encode messages. Preparedness for reading includes recognition, perception, and production of speech sounds as well as knowledge of grammar and skill in comprehension. Reading requires, for example, a grasp of sentence meanings, including awareness of levels of abstraction, shifts in meaning, and idiomatic usage.

The Relationship Between
Reading Instruction and Linguistics

No reading program for disadvantaged children will be effective unless it takes into consideration the children's spoken language habits. Determining their exact nature, contrasting these habits with both the standard dialect of the school and the language used in reading, and assisting in the selection or development of appropriate instructional materials are important ways in which linguists can contribute to education.

Linguistic analysis can have a number of practical applications to reading instruction; it can, for example, provide valid material for the phonics programs. Spelling-to-sound mappings are usually made for standard pronunciation. Separate mappings of other dialects are needed to guide the presentation of written material to children who do not have the same phonological system

115

and therefore cannot learn the same sound-symbol relationships. In addition, linguistic science can contribute descriptions and contrastive analyses of the other factors of written and spoken languages and provide educators with information to help build programs of instruction and evaluate their results.

The Linguistic Method in TESOL

When someone speaks of the linguistic method in Teaching English to Speakers of Other Languages (TESOL), he is usually referring to a procedure that involves first comparing any two languages in order to predict and describe the problems that the speakers of one will have in learning the other and then ordering the various elements of the target language so that a sequential presentation may be made. Techniques and models for analysis are widely variant among linguists today, and further divergence can be expected as new developments in linguistic theory are applied to the teaching of language. To speak, therefore, of "the linguistic method" is gross oversimplification. For the moment it is probably sufficient for the teachers of English to understand the general principles that have governed linguistic study in recent years. They should, however, be aware that new methods will regularly be developed and offered to educators and be willing to evaluate their effectiveness in the classroom.

As the first step toward preparing valid material for language instruction, the linguist describes in detail the native language or dialect of the pupil and the target language, that is, the language he is to be taught. Standard American English is usually the target language for basic reading instruction in this country. These analyses should describe the phonology, syntax, vocabulary, intonation, and orthography of both languages.

A contrast must then be made between the pupil's native language or dialect and standard English in order to take into account the ways in which native speech patterns are likely to produce interference problems. Points of similarity will be found in the systems that will prove easy for the learner of English. These may be phonemes containing a nearly equal range of sounds, similar word order in grammatical constructions, cognates in vocabulary, or the use of the same symbols to represent some of the same sounds. Points of partial similarity that might be discovered include sounds that exist in both languages but have a different range in the respective phonemic systems, words that have similar form but different meanings, and similar symbols that represent different sounds. Lastly, points of dissimilarity should be noted, such as sounds that exist in one language but not in the other, different word order or grammatical categories, and the use of symbols other than those in the English alphabet.

From his contrastive analyses the linguist finds patterns of similarity and difference and then proceeds to prepare instructional material based on these comparisons. Because other languages and other dialects of English are systematic, their speakers' language habits do not lend themselves to piecemeal "correction." The portions of the target language system, standard English, that are different must be presented in an orderly fashion and in a graded sequence. In order to fix the new language behavior in automatic and habitual responses, repetitive drill and pattern practice are probably profitable at all levels of instruction.

Elements of Language to be Considered in Language Instruction

Language, as seen by a linguist, is basically a system of phonological, syntactical, and semantic features. The concept of "system" is crucial for describing and teaching languages. A speaker of standard English operates within one system, a speaker of French within another, and a speaker of Swahili within yet another. Not so obvious, however, is the fact that a speaker of a nonstandard dialect of English is actually using a quite different system (Bailey, 1965; Smith, 1968).

The complete mastery of all elements of a new language is not necessary for successful communication. Although a speaker must have nearly perfect control of the sound system in order to avoid misunderstandings, he can operate effectively with 50 to 90 percent of the grammatical structures and perhaps even less than 1 percent of the vocabulary under control (Gleason, 1961).

Many naive teachers think of language learning merely in terms of acquiring a new vocabulary. They do not consider the elements of phonology and syntax, which are acquired very early in a native language, either because the acquisition process was unconscious or because they have forgotten it. A child masters most of the distinctive sounds in his language before he is three years old and controls most of its basic grammatical patterns before he enters school (Menyuk, 1969; Stewart, 1964a; Carroll, 1961). Vocabulary development can continue throughout a person's life, and it is therefore a conscious and well-remembered process.

Because speaking precedes writing in the language learning of a native speaker, linguists assert that the same sequence should be followed in learning a second language. This view and the resultant changes in methodology proved themselves effective during the Second World War with the countless students who not only learned foreign languages more efficiently than with earlier methods but could actually communicate in them when course work was finished. A few linguists and educators have gone as far as to say that a language cannot be read until it can be understood and produced orally. The many graduate students in American universities who read a second language but are unable to understand it when spoken or to speak even one sentence in it disprove this extreme position.

The majority of linguists and educators, however, have concluded from research and observation that reading should not be introduced until some facility in the spoken language has been achieved.

PHONOLOGY

The range of sounds that can be produced by a babbling infant is determined by inherent biological factors and not by the language spoken by the child's parents (Lenneberg, 1967). An infant of six months can produce all vowel sounds and most consonant sounds—including some sounds that are not used in English. If he lives in an English-speaking household the child will learn to group and distinguish those that give contrastive meanings to words in English (the phonemes) and to disregard those that do not. A child raised in a Spanish-speaking household will distinguish sounds the English-speaker learns to ignore and will disregard some sound differences vital to English word meanings. He will, for instance, hear *share* and *chair* as the same word (Gleason, 1961), but distinguish between Spanish *pero* and *perro*, which are heard as the same word by most speakers of English.

The phonemes of a language can be identified easily by isolating minimal pairs, two words whose difference in meaning is signaled by a difference in only one segment of sound. Examples of minimal pairs in English are /Θiŋk/ *think:* /siŋk/ *sink* and /bæt/ *bat:* /mæt/ *mat*. The first pair of words shows that /Θ/ and /s/ are contrastive phonemes in English, and the second pair shows that /b/ and /m/ also contrast. Additional words, such as /miŋk/ *mink* and /sæt/ *sat*, indicate that all four of the sounds mentioned above are contrastive in English.

The ways in which sounds are articulated may also be contrasted. Differences will depend on the vibration of the vocal chords, on the passage through which the air flows, on the points of articulation, and on the manner of articulation.

Many languages have distinctive features that speakers of English learn to ignore. The /p/'s of /pay/ *pie* and /kəp/ *cup* differ phonetically: the /p/ of *pie* is aspirated and the /p/ of *cup* is not. This difference in aspiration is distinctive in several other languages. The pitch of the voice does not alter the meaning of isolated English words, but in Navajo changing from two highly pitched syllables /átʔí/ to a low-high pitch /atʔí/ changes the meaning from *he does* to *he is rich*.

All dialects of American English use a more or less common pool of phonemes, and a child learning English in any part of the United States must master most of the same sounds. The distribution of phonemes in a language (the phonotactics) must also be considered and may differ among dialects. English is one of the languages that restricts the occurrence of some phonemes to certain positions: /ž/ is restricted to medial (*azure*) and final (*rouge*) positions; /h/ to initial (*house*) and medial (*grasshopper*) positions. In addition, only certain consonants may cluster in English, and then in a restricted order (Hill, 1958).

SYNTAX

The area of syntax includes all the formal features that express meaning or relationship in language. Common examples of these formal features are word order, agreement, and inflection.

The syntactic features that can be observed in spoken or written language are language-specific and even vary from dialect to dialect. There is current speculation, however, that there may be underlying syntactic features, as well as phonological features, that are universal and inherent in the language used by all human beings (Bach and Harms, 1968; Greenberg, 1963). Languages that have a common ancestor, such as Spanish, French, and German, which are in the Indo-European family, have more syntactical features in common than unrelated languages, such as Arabic and Hopi.

The development of children's syntactic structures has been the subject of many studies in linguistics, education, and psychology. Recent research on language acquisition indicates that by the time a typical child is five or six he tends to use most of the basic sentence forms in his language (Menyuk, 1969). If this child is a speaker of English, the sentence structures used in his beginning reading material will be well below his understanding and production level. It is not this typical child who concerns us in this book, however.

Disadvantaged children have also acquired the basic syntactic forms of their language by the time they are five or six, unless they have been totally deprived of language experiences. The problem for teachers of reading is that these children have learned the syntax of another language or of a nonstandard dialect of English and not the syntax of the classroom variety of English. The basal reading material has not been prepared for them.

Although the vocabularies of developmental reading series are carefully controlled, there is very seldom any attempt at a comparable sequential presentation of sentence structures. This is because the "typical" child finds all the forms familiar. The pre-primers of one major reading series contain the following complex of syntactic patterns: nouns and noun phrases, intransitive verbs and verb phrases, transitive verb phrases, subject and predicate constructions, infinitive constructions, modal constructions, auxiliary constructions, constructions using *is*, negative constructions, and other sentence patterns. These introductory reading texts may also be considered "typical."

SEMANTICS

The third major element of language to be considered is semantics. This includes not only what we commonly call vocabulary, but an analysis of meanings in each language, selection and co-occurrence restrictions, and other factors.

Semantic structure is essentially the linguistic organization of experience. This organization is unique for each culture and language. The development of the semantic structure of any language is due in part to capricious factors, but it is influenced by other languages, the physical environment of the speakers, and their interests and way of life.

Words are usually considered the basic lexical elements of a language and are defined as minimum forms that can stand alone. English words are composed of sound segments (phonemes) and stress; minimal differences in these features can make a difference in meaning. In other languages minimal differences in such features as pitch, vowel length, and nasalization may also make differences in word meanings.

Words can often be separated into parts, such as the stems, suffixes, and prefixes of English. Sapir (1921) gives the following example from Paiute, which illustrates an extreme in word complexity: /wii-to-kuchum-punku-rugani-yugwi-va-ntu-m(u)/ *they who are going to sit and cut up with a knife a black cow (bull).* Other examples can be found in Hoijer's analysis of Apachean verbs (1945, 1946, 1948, 1949). He lists fourteen different slots in the structure of these verbs that may be filled in a specified order by the indirect object, postposition, adverbial prefixes, theme prefix, interative mode, number prefix, and so forth. Some of the slots are mutually exclusive.

Because of such wide variance in word structure, linguists find it more satisfactory to deal with morphemes, the recurring parts of words that carry meaning. The English word *boys* contains two morphemes: it can be divided into the recurring parts *boy* and *-s*. Reading teachers do not have to face all these complexities when defining a word, for in written language a word is what appears between the white spaces. Many more factors must be considered, however, when comparing languages or when preparing material for instruction. *Boy, dog, cat, boys, dogs,* and *cats* are six different words, but they contain only four morphemes that must be taught: *dog, cat, boy,* and *-s*.

The problems pupils have with English word meanings are not as easy to detect as their distortions of English phonology and syntax. Apparent meaning equivalents in other languages are often misleading. Learning the vocabulary of a new language by no means requires merely learning different sequences of sounds to express the same meanings. Experience is categorized differently in different languages. Pupils tend, however, to use the same categories into which experiences are classified in their native language, applying labels learned in the second language.

Very obvious examples of how experience is categorized differently are the color terms of different languages. For instance, the range of the color spectrum that is categorized as green and blue by English-speakers is categorized as only one distinct color by speakers of Navajo. The range of the spectrum that is categorized in English as black is divided in Navajo into two distinct categories with two labels (Haile, 1926).

Embarrassment or misunderstanding can result from the different connotations that similar or even phonetically identical words can have in different languages or dialects. Most students do not realize which words in a new language are offensive, or completely taboo, until they meet with a negative reaction from native speakers. They may in turn be shocked by the topics of conversation permitted in the new language.

The selection and distribution of morphemes are also restricted, but the restrictions vary in different languages and even within the same language. Some words cannot be put together in English, such as *flowers eat hay*. The class of verbs that contains *eat* is not allowed to occur in the same clause after the class of nouns that contains *flowers*. We tend to attribute such co-occurrence restrictions to "natural logic." The universality of these restrictions becomes doubtful when we find that the Navajo sequence that translates *the big horse* sounds just as illogical to speakers of that language. The Navajo verb denoting bigness cannot occur with the class of nouns to which *horse* belongs. When asked why not, a native speaker replied, "Because a horse is as big as he is."

It has been well established that other features of word selection are culturally determined. Word-association tests have shown, for instance, that speakers of English are most likely to choose *woman* to go with *beautiful*, whereas speakers of Navajo select *horse*. Other associations of Navajo-speakers that vary from the English pattern include *bitter:chili pepper; river:canyon;* and *whisky:it's no good* (Rosenzweig, 1961).

Dissimilarities in the associative networks of two languages might provide another area for contrastive analysis and prediction of interference that would aid in the construction of instructional material. Lambert (1963) suggests, for instance, that the presentation of vocabulary in a second language might be patterned on the network of the associations made by native speakers of the language.

Among other factors that must be considered in the semantic structures of languages are social conventions. Each of the following greetings is appropriate to speakers of some language: *How are you? Where are you from? How much money do you earn? What do you know? What is your name?* (Abercrombie, 1948). Differences in social acceptability and effect can be seen between the Spanish expression *Dios mío* and its English translation *My God*, which is much stronger, or the Spanish use of *Jesús* as a common given name and the English view that this practice is disrespectful (Lado, 1957). The teacher who laughed when a Navajo child called her *grandmother* did not understand that the title was meant to be one of honor and respect, as it is in the Navajo language. Ignorance of the cultures reflected in the native languages of the pupils can greatly reduce the effectiveness of any teacher or educational program.

ORTHOGRAPHY

An ideal system of spelling would allow a native speaker to pronounce correctly any strange string of letters he saw and to spell any strange sequence of sounds (Hill, 1967). Although the English writing system is far from perfect in this regard, it does contain spelling patterns that consistently represent patterns of sounds. It is important for teachers to understand both the regularities of English spelling and the ways in which it may differ from the writing systems used by pupils with other language backgrounds.

There are some invariant patterns in English spelling. The letters *b, f, k, m, n, v, y,* and *z* almost always have the same pronunciation regardless of their environment. The pronunciation of some letters, such as *c,* varies according to the surrounding letters. The letter *c* usually represents /s/ before *e, i,* or *y* and /k/ before *a, o, u,* any consonant except *h,* or in final positions. The position of a letter in a word can also affect its pronunciation: *a* is usually pronounced /æ/ when it occurs between consonants unless the word is a monosyllable ending in *e.* Recent listings of these and many other rules for English spelling are available and would be of considerable value to teachers and pupils (Venezky, 1967).

There cannot be a single program for teaching a symbol-sound relationship for English to speakers of all its dialects; in different dialects the same letter may represent different sounds. Therefore, beginning reading materials that depend on invariant pronunciation (such as the Initial Teaching Alphabet) do not seem appropriate for many areas of the United States. A beginning reader's confusion may be compounded when the written form of standard English he meets does not correspond to what he hears or says. Some linguists and educators think that for this reason a child should first be taught to read in his own language or dialect (Goodman, 1967).

All writing systems represent speech, but they may take different forms. English uses a morphophonemic system, in which symbols represent phonemes to some degree, but in which there are many alternatives, each appropriate to a given morpheme. Many languages, including English, Greek, and Arabic, are written in alphabetic systems. Others use syllabic systems, in which symbols represent syllables. A very interesting example of this type is the Cherokee writing system of eighty-five symbols, which was invented by one man (Foreman, 1938). In logographic systems, such as Chinese, symbols represent words or morphemes.

Pupils who have learned the writing systems of their native languages tend to transfer their writing habits to a new language. Often they will mispronounce or misspell words because they expect the same symbol to represent the same sound in the second language as it did in their native language.

Specific Language Problems

Most linguistically different children in the United States come from homes where a nonstandard dialect of English is spoken or where the primary language is Spanish, French, or one of the many American Indian languages. The particular problems that children with these language backgrounds have with English are considered below as are the reasons such problems can be predicted from linguistic analysis.

NONSTANDARD DIALECTS OF ENGLISH

Disadvantaged children in urban centers often have little opportunity at home for oral language development in the prestige dialect of the wider society. They usually live in crowded, noisy apartments and have few models of standard language usage available. Children in middle-class homes learn to speak as adults correct them, supply needed articles, verbs, auxiliaries, and so forth. Disadvantaged children often do not have this experience.

The nonstandard dialects of people in New York, Washington, D. C., and Chicago differ, according to published descriptions (Labov, 1964; McDavid, 1967; Stewart, 1964b); their variance from standard English, however, is similar in many respects. The sounds /ð/ and /θ/ are not used, but appear initially as /d/ and /t/, as in /dis/ *this* and /tin/ *thin* and elsewhere as /v/ and /f/, as in /məvə/ *mother*, /nəfin/ *nothing*, /briyv/ *breathe*, and /bref/ *breath*.

The most common variations in syntax are the omissions of the plural and possessive markers (*two boy go to school, this is the boy ball*), of the third-person singular *-s* in the present tense (*he know you*), and of the verb *to be* in various constructions (*he a big boy, they gone, the window open, I going to school*). These syntactic omissions may be due to the operation of different phonological rules. Some syntactic deviations are less likely to be phonological in nature. For instance, the person-number concord of *to be* may include *I were* or *we was* in the past, and *be* or *is* with all persons in the present instead of the differentiation of *am, is, are*. Number-concord differences also produce *I does* and *he do*. *Those* may appear as *them*, as in *I see them dogs*, or as a compound *them-there*.

Some nonstandard forms represent an extension of standard forms by analogy. The comparative and superlative inflections may appear as *she is a beautifuler girl* and *he is the wonderfulest boy*. The processes by which *my* becomes *mine* or *myself* may also generate *yourn, hisn, hern, ourn, theirn, hisself*, and *theirselves*. Double comparisons are sometimes used, such as *that is a more prettier girl* and *that is the most nicest boy*.

Statements that speakers of nonstandard dialects cannot express themselves as fully as speakers of standard dialects have not been substantiated. Many people are quite articulate in their own dialect, and disadvantaged children can communicate more effectively in their homes and neighborhoods by using their own language system than they would if they completely adopted standard forms of speech.

In the classroom many misunderstandings can arise because of different meanings given to words. A middle-class teacher may say, "Johnny, would you like to do your work now?" and be taken literally when what she really means is

"Sit down and shut up!" While teachers should serve as models of excellence in speech, they should at least realize that some translation may be necessary even within English.

Some variation in stress is possible within standard English, as in *résearch* and *reséarch*. Some variations in stress occur within regional standard dialects, as in *cemént* and *cément*. Teachers should accept such variations in standard usage and not react as did one second-grade teacher in Texas when a new pupil from California put an accent mark on the second syllable of *cement* in his reading workbook; she marked the accent mark wrong because it did not agree with her own pronunciation. Even after she was made aware of the dialect difference, she insisted that the pupil's pronunciation was "wrong" because "two things can't be right or it will confuse the children." Some variations in stress are commonly made by speakers of nonstandard dialects and are not acceptable in all language situations. One variant is the placement of primary stress on a final syllable that is weak in standard English, such as *accidént*. Another is the movement of the primary stress to the first syllable, as in *guítar* or *pólice*. A third is the omission of weakly stressed syllables before primary stress, as in *porter* for *reporter*.

A pupil, whatever his dialect, will often make spelling errors that reflect his pronunciation. When he omits inflectional affixes at the ends of words, he will also frequently omit the final *-d* or *-s* when writing them (Cook and Sharp, 1966).[1] He may not use *a* and *an* correctly in writing because he does not make a distinction between them in speech. Purely orthographic rules are inadequate as a guide, for one might then produce *a honor* or *an use* (Stewart, 1964a).

One way to correct such spelling problems may be to base the sound-symbol relationships on the pupil's own sound system. When the sounds are omitted in his speech, as in the examples above, the nonstandard speaker must be taught to hear them in the speech of others or to use at appropriate times a second, standard dialect, upon which the spelling rules are based.

The nonstandard dialects of English spoken by many disadvantaged blacks in urban centers differ in some fundamental ways from the nonstandard speech of disadvantaged whites living in the same areas (Center for Applied Linguistics, 1965; Loflin, n.d.; Pederson, 1964; Stewart, 1964b). Some of the surface features, the phonology, for example, seem to be derived from rural southern dialects and may be accounted for by past and present migration patterns. These features are reinforced by a constant flow of new migrants from the South and evidently in many cases by a desire to maintain cultural identity. Different features in the grammar of nonstandard black speech have also been found that are not derived from any other known dialects but probably reflect features of African languages spoken by the original slave population or features that developed in the creolized form of English originally learned by blacks in the Caribbean and in the American South.

---

[1] The conclusions of Cook and Sharp are based principally on writing by Navajo children.

The phonological system shows the strongest southern influence in vowel usage and in the omission of /r/ after vowels, as in /tin/ *ten*, /sət/ *soot*, /fo/ *four*, /do/ *door*, /təma·/ *tomorrow*, and /kæ·id/ *carried*. Final consonant clusters tend to be simplified, as /ditn/ *didn't*, /dentis/ *dentist*, and /hep/ *help*. Another form of simplification is the addition of a vowel between clustered consonants, as /æskiz/ for *asks*. Common substitutions are /d/ for /ð/, as in /dis/ *this*, and /b/ for /v/, as in /sebəm/ *seven*. Final /-m/ and /-n/ may be neutralized, often becoming merely a nasalization of the preceding vowel.

The most diverse variant found in nonstandard black speech is in its verbal system. Usually a verb is not inflected differently for simple past and present in this system. *He throw the ball* may mean either "he throws the ball" or "he threw the ball." A past perfect is used, for example, *I seen it*, "I have seen it," and there is a form to express action completed earlier, *I been seen it*, that has no equivalent in standard English. *I be busy* refers to habitual activity and is also unique to black speech. These variants may be at least partly phonological in nature, as mentioned above (Labov, 1967).

Other variations have been noted in the syntax of the speech of some blacks. The third-person singular verb may not end in -s, but -s may appear in forms that do not occur in standard speech: *I sees, you sees, he see*. *Done* may be used as a perfective auxiliary, as in *he done read* it, and the use of -*ed* as a past tense marker may be extended to *singed, throwed,* and *eated*.

Word-association tests show some differences in responses in white and black populations that might indicate differences in semantic structures (Entwisle, 1967). The variations in words and meanings in black speech seem to cover much the same regional and social range as in other dialects.

Although foreign-language methods are appropriate in many respects when teaching a second dialect, there are major differences in the difficulties the learner encounters. Often, a speaker of nonstandard English already has a passive knowledge of the standard forms. He may find producing them harder than will a speaker of a foreign language because his own language system is so closely related that it causes a great deal of interference.

It should also be recognized that nonstandard English encompasses many dialects, both regional and social. Each will present slightly different teaching problems. Any instructional materials prepared for disadvantaged speakers of English should be carefully evaluated for appropriateness for any particular group of children and amended as necessary to stimulate maximum language learning.

SPANISH

Disadvantaged children with Spanish-language backgrounds present a major educational challenge to many schools, particularly in New York and the Southwest. The degree of language handicap exhibited by these children in an English-language classroom setting is sufficiently great to explain much of their academic underachievement and their high dropout rate. Contrasts between English and Spanish have been well described by linguists, and Spanish-speaking children have so far received most of the attention in elementary-school programs for teaching English as a second language. More reading and oral language materials for them will be published soon.

Not all Spanish-speaking children have the same language system any more than all English-speaking children do. Some of their families have come to the United States from Puerto Rico, Cuba, and various parts of Mexico. Others have lived for generations in parts of the United States where various dialects of Spanish have developed. When one considers that there are social dialects within the regional ones, the language problem seems very complex. There has been sufficient research to show that these dialectal differences in Spanish influence the children's use of English, but no comprehensive analysis is yet available.

In general the Spanish sound system does not contrast /š/ and /č/, and substitution or interchange of these English phonemes is the most obvious error Spanish-speaking children make in pronouncing English words. They may often say /čuw/ for *shoe* or /šer/ for *chair*. Spanish has one phoneme that covers the range of both English /b/ and /v/, and it often sounds as if the children say /beriy/ for *very* and /kəvərd/ for *cupboard*. Other common substitutions are /s/, /f/, or /t/ for /θ/; and /z/, /v/, or /d/ for /ð/. Consonant clusters cause many problems, particularly when they contain a sibilant, such as /s/.

Spanish uses only five vowel phonemes; children learning English must distinguish several more. The range of Spanish /i/ includes the vowel sounds of *mit* and *meat;* /e/, those of *met* and *mate;* /u/, those of *pull* and *pool;* /o/, those of *coat* and *caught;* and /a/ covers a range that includes the vowel sounds of *cut* and *cot.*

There are several basic differences in the grammatical structures of Spanish and English that cause interference for a pupil learning English as a second language (Brengelman, 1964). The verb-noun pattern of *es un hombre* must be equated with the noun-verb-noun pattern of *this is a man.* Similarly, the interrogative-verb pattern of *¿qué es?* is patterned in English as interrogative-verb-noun, *what is that?* A difference in word order is seen in the following examples: *la mano derecha* (D-N-Adj): *the right hand* (D-Adj-N); *le da el sombrero* (IO-V-DO): *he gives him the hat* (S-V-IO-DO); *¿está abierta una ventana?* (V-Adj-N): *is a window open?* (V-N-Adj). A relationship that has been indicated by word order in *la cabeza de un perro* must be indicated by inflection in *a dog's head;* the situation is reversed in the case of *dará*, which is expressed in English as *he will give.* Many Spanish-speaking children transfer the use of double negatives from Spanish to English. It is good Spanish to say *no hay nada en la mesa*, but the sentence literally translated is *there's not nothing on the table.*

The semantic structure of English also presents a number of problems for speakers of Spanish. There are many cognates in the two languages. The most difficult new words to learn are the "false friends," words that sound the same but have different meanings. An example is the Spanish verb *asistir*, which means in English *to attend* and not *to assist*.

Teachers often comment that their Spanish-speaking pupils read without expression. To understand and correct the real problem they should first know that the Spanish intonational system has one less degree of stress than the English system, different rhythm and stress patterns, and different intonational contours. A Spanish-speaker will pronounce every syllable for about the same length of time, shorten English stressed syllables, put the stress on the wrong syllable, and not reduce vowels in unstressed syllables. He will use a rising pitch for a confirmation response and a low-mid-low pitch pattern for statements instead of the mid-high-low contour usual in English.

Improper intonation in reading English questions and exclamations may be partly a problem with symbols. If the pupil has learned to read in Spanish, he is used to the signals ¿ and ¡ at the beginning of questions and exclamations, respectively. Because the initial signals are missing in English he may get close to the end of these constructions before he realizes that they are questions or exclamations.

Most of the problems Spanish-speaking children have in learning to read and spell English words are due to the different correspondences between sounds and symbols. Vowels cause the greatest difficulty; pupils could conceivably write *cat* for *cot*, *mit* for *meat*, and *met* for *mate*. They might read *fine* as /fine/ instead of /fayn/ and *but* as /buwt/ instead of /bət/. These reading and spelling errors cannot be corrected unless the pupils can first consistently hear and use the vowel phonemes of English. The symbols can then be related to these sounds.

A similar problem may be noted in arithmetic if pupils have learned to write numerals in Mexico or one of several other countries. They will write 1 as *1* and 7 as *7*. Consequently, teachers and pupils may confuse 1's and 7's in problems and answers.

ACADIAN FRENCH

Many families in the United States speak some variety of French as a native language. The largest concentration of French-speakers is found in Louisiana; they are primarily the descendents of Acadians who were forced to leave Nova Scotia in 1755. These groups of Louisiana French, or Cajuns as they are frequently called, have been very persistent in preserving their linguistic identity. Other French-speakers came directly to Louisiana from Europe, and a sizable black population in the region developed still another variety of French. The complex of French dialects in Louisiana transcends race, social status, and geographical boundaries.

In 1960, according to the United States Bureau of the Census, Louisiana had the highest rate of illiteracy in the United States, and the illiteracy rate within this state was highest in its twenty-six predominantly French-speaking parishes.

A variety of factors contributes to this educational problem, and one of the most serious is the inability of pupils to cope with standard English in the classroom. A correlation between linguistic and economic factors was found by Bertrand and Beale (1965). They report that of the families they interviewed in the region who use predominantly French at home, 69 percent of the whites and 88 percent of the blacks had annual incomes under $1500, and 19 percent of the whites and 12 percent of the blacks had annual incomes between $1500 and $2999.

Cajuns typically have difficulties with standard English phonology, syntax, and vocabulary.[2] The phoneme /d/ is substituted for /ð/, resulting in /diy/ for *the*, /diyz/ for *these*, /doz/ for *those*, and /dæt/ for *that*. English phonemes /š/ and /č/, and /ž/ and /ǰ/ are not contrastive pairs in Cajun speech. The /č/ and /ǰ/ variants may be substituted for /š/ and /ž/ under emphatic stress. Final /-s/ is omitted in some words.

English consonant clusters are often simplified by Cajuns. The phonemes /l/ and /r/ are often dropped before a consonant, and *like to* may be pronounced without the /k/. Final /-nd/ may be reduced to /n/ in *mind*, /-bl/ to /b/ in *noble* or *terrible*, /-br/ to /b/ in *September*, /-kl/ to /k/ in *miracle*, and /-pl/ to /p/ in *simple* (Conwell and Juilland, 1963). Variant pronunciations are not uncommon; in one interview a single informant pronounced *ask* as /æks/, /æst/, and /æs/. Initial clusters may also be simplified: /pl/ to /p/, /pt/ to /t/, and /str/ to /st/. Whenever /r/ or /l/ forms part of a cluster, that phoneme is the first element deleted.

Vowels present additional problems, for variant pronunciation is allowed within Louisiana French phonemes that cross phoneme boundaries in English, making an unwanted difference in meaning in English words. The phoneme /ə/ may alternate with /e/ in emphatic speech or be deleted after a single consonant or at the ends of words. An /o/ may alternate with /u/ in unstressed syllables or with /ɔ/ in some environments. An /e/ may alternate with either /a/ or /æ/ before /r/, /l/, or /m/.

The syntactical errors made by Cajun informants include the plural inflection of mass nouns (*hairs*), the deletion of *to* in infinitive constructions (*I'm going get it*), and the omission of modals and auxiliaries in questions (*What I do?*). Other common expressions are *talking at you*, *listening at you*, and *I have you an idea*.

Some French words are used by these speakers in otherwise English sentences. The most frequent seem to be the interjections /me/ *well* and /æ/ *what?* In many sentences the words are all English, but the sequence is nonstandard. At mealtime you may hear, *Put me some potatoes, please*, or *Save the sugar*, meaning

[2] The description of Acadian French presented here draws on data collected by the author from speakers of the Lafayette region and on data collected by Marilyn Conwell in the same parish.

"store" it. Instead of being "delivered," *the mail passes*, and a Cajun may ask, *Is the mail passed?* The same verb is used for *visit: You make a pass on town.*

In some parts of Louisiana a child may go through elementary school without hearing standard English spoken because his teachers come from the same region and speak the same dialect. The language system of the textbooks is therefore kept separate from the language system he speaks and hears. This barrier to learning is hurdled by some, but it is part of the educational and economic barricade surrounding thousands of French-speaking citizens.

NAVAJO

A number of unrelated languages are spoken by the more than half a million Indians who live on reservations in the United States. Many groups have adopted some form of English as a primary language, and some continue to use the languages of their ancestors. On the Navajo reservation, forty thousand pupils are now attending schools and the number increases each year. The teaching of English is recognized there as one of the most serious problems in education and one that must be solved as part of the assault on generally low wages, high unemployment rates, and poor living conditions.

The specific problems Navajo children have with English are considered here because the Navajos are the largest tribe in the United States. Their problems, as well as those of speakers of Spanish and French, depend on the points of contrast between their language and English, and thus cannot be generalized to include all Indian languages. These points should serve to indicate, however, the types of problems that may be encountered by speakers of languages completely unrelated to English.

There are many differences between English and Navajo both in the articulation of sounds that have similar positions in the phonemic systems of the two languages and in the articulation of sounds that occur in one language but have no correspondents in the other.

Navajo-speakers do not distinguish between English /p/ and /b/ and usually substitute their own slightly different /b/ for both. This sound never occurs in syllable final position in Navajo, however, so they often substitute /ʔ/ (a glottal stop) for final /-p/ or /-b/ or reduce all final stops to the Navajo /-d/. This /d/, which sounds like the /t/ in /stap/, is also typically substituted for English /t/ or /d/ in initial position. The /ʔ/ is frequently substituted for stopped consonants and added before initial vowels, making Navajo speech sound choppy to speakers of English. In Navajo there are no correspondents to /f/, /v/, /θ/, /ð/, and /ŋ/.

The primary differences between the vowel systems are the use of vowel length and nasalization to distinguish meaning in Navajo and the greater variety of vowel sounds in English. The vowels /æ/ and /ə/ do not occur in Navajo and are the hardest for pupils to learn. Navajo-speakers must also learn to distinguish among English /o/, /u/, and /uw/.

English consonant clusters present a major problem for Navajo-speakers, who often substitute similar affricates for them. Much of the Navajos' difficulty with noun and verb inflections may be traced to their failure to hear or produce final consonant clusters (Cook and Sharp, 1966).

Tonal pitch in Navajo serves as the only distinctive feature to differentiate meaning in such words as /níłį́/ *you are*, /nilį́/ *he is*, /átʔį́/ *he does*, /atʔį́/ *he is rich*,/ azéé?/ *mouth*, and/ azee?/ *medicine*. Whereas Navajo uses fixed tones with relation to vowels and syllabic nasals to distinguish meaning, English uses a variety of sentence pitch patterns, or intonational contours. Navajo-speakers must learn to disregard the pitch of individual phonemes. On the other hand, English makes use of stress to distinguish meaning in some words, whereas stress is never distinctive in Navajo.

The use of a rising sentence inflection to indicate interrogation or the use of other types of pitch to convey, for example, the connotation of surprise is not possible in a tone language, is not used as a mechanism for this purpose, or is used in a different way. Particles in Navajo convey meanings expressed by intonation in English. For instance, /daʔ-íš/ and /-ša/ added to Navajo words signal questions, /-gaʔ/ gives emphasis, and /-ʔas/ indicates disbelief. Navajos may speak and read English without the appropriate modulations and inflections because they are unaccustomed to the use of intonation to express meaning in these situations (Young, 1961).

Other very general phonological problems that teachers of Navajo children should concentrate on are the voicing of stops, the production of most consonants in final position, and the production of glides.

Many features of English syntax are difficult for Navajo-speakers. Articles and adjectives are very troublesome because, with a few exceptions, they do not exist in Navajo. The idea of prettiness would be expressed by a verb and conjugated "I am pretty, you are pretty," and so forth. English adjectives present problems in both their word order and comparative patterns. Few Navajo nouns are inflected for plural; thus a common type of error in English is *four dog*. Possessive *-s* is also a problem, since the Navajo pattern for *the boy's book* would be *the boy his book*. English third-person pronouns are commonly confused. Navajo /bí/ translates as any of the following: *he, she, it, they, him, her, them, his, her, its, their*. This means that gender, number, and case distinctions must all be learned. Navajo makes other distinctions among third-person pronouns not found in English, however, such as distance from the subject. There are also numerous and complicated differences in the verb structure.

Even if a Navajo child has mastered the phonological and syntactic components of the English language, he is faced with a semantic system that categorizes experience in a very different way. English often uses several unrelated words to describe something that is seen as different aspects of the same action in Navajo, or one word to describe an action seen as unrelated events. For example, if the object of each action is the same, the English verbs *give*, *take*, *put*, and several others are translated by one Navajo verb stem that means roughly "to handle." Different Navajo verb stems will be used for *to handle* depending on the shape of the object.

There has been no interference from written Navajo because the language has been recorded only by linguists and missionaries. Programs are now under way to teach reading and writing to Navajos in their native language. A standardized orthography has been developed. Questions concerning its possible interference with learning the English writing system have been raised, but some leading educators agree that basing the orthography on the Navajo language itself is a far more important consideration than any interference with English that may result (Ohannessian, 1969).

Linguistic Contributions to Methodology

Linguists can contribute to the instruction of disadvantaged children by analyzing their languages and dialects, predicting which features of standard English will be problems for each group, and developing for teachers efficient teaching methods and materials for teaching English as a second language or dialect. The key to this efficiency lies in the selection of the material to be taught and in the careful ordering of language structures for sequential presentation.

Linguists are not in complete agreement as to the best methods for teaching children to write English. Suggested methods can be summarized as inductive, which present examples and let the children discover a rule, and deductive, which present a rule and examples to which the children can apply the rule. Inductive methods require more time and many children fail to solve the problem at all. Those who do, however, are probably better able to transfer what they have learned to related problems. Children who learn by deductive methods can usually apply what they have learned to specific examples, but show little ability to transfer this learning to related problems.

Probably a combination, "the eclectic method," will prove best for most classrooms. The teacher should begin with examples and let the children verbalize rules if they can. The sequence of examples and the nature of the teacher's leading hints would be crucial. Examples should possibly be given in which one sound and symbol remain constant, such as *fat*, *hat*, and *mat*. The children would then learn the rule that the symbol *a* often represents the sound /æ/. Later they could be presented with another set of examples, such as *fate*, *hate*, and *mate*, and learn a new rule. Perhaps a better method would be to present the minimal pairs *fat*:*fate*, *hat*:*hate*, and *mat*:*mate*. Children seeing and hearing these examples would learn that *a* represents both /æ/ and /ey/ and they would then discuss the environment that determines the sound. This same method might introduce *c* in *circus, cat, cite, ceiling*, and *coat* and lead the children to the rule that *c* represents /s/ before *i* and *e* and /k/ before *o* and *a*. This method takes longer but might prove more effective in terms of retention and transfer (Calfee and Venezky, 1968).

Another way the linguistic method of contrastive analysis can be used by the classroom teacher is in the construction of tests for the purpose of diagnosing language problems and evaluating language growth. Measures should be available for efficiently testing the ability of each pupil to recognize and produce the features of standard English that are likely to be a problem for speakers of his native language or dialect.

Unfortunately, most tests of language proficiency now available either are too time-consuming to be practical for general classroom use or require a trained linguist for administration and interpretation. Some are too general, lacking in features that should be tested in the specific language or dialect group to which the pupils belong while containing features that do not represent potential problems to them. Some combine all these shortcomings. Many other linguistically sound measures cannot be used to diagnose oral language ability because young children cannot follow the directions, maintain the required attention span, or perform such test-taking requirements as working from left to right on one line at a time.

It is important to remember that English proficiency tests prepared for native speakers of Spanish will not be entirely appropriate for native speakers of any other language. For maximum efficiency, each test should be concerned with only those features that a contrastive language analysis has shown to be a potential problem for the pupils to be tested.

Vocabulary tests are more abundant, easier to construct, and less important than tests of phonology and syntax because vocabulary is the feature of language most obvious to the classroom teacher in varied school activities.

Questions of Method

Linguistic principles may be applied in language teaching to challenge traditional methods as well as to offer alternatives, to note weaknesses in existing instructional materials as well as to develop new ones, and to point out the vast complexities of second-language acquisition as well as to help teachers understand the process. While linguists are generally in agreement on the benefits of initial contrastive language analyses, the presentation of all elements of language in graded sequence, and the importance of drill methods to instill language habits, they voice some differences of opinion on other language-teaching issues that concern teachers and administrators.

First, it has not been decided whether homogeneous groups are preferable to mixed classes, which may present the teacher with a wide variety of instructional problems at one time. Segregation of the disadvantaged pupils from the more "typical" children in a school district is almost completely achieved whenever there is a pre-first or similar "special" class. The children thus set apart may at best have the advantages of a teacher specifically trained to meet their unique learning problems and a curriculum designed to meet their interests and needs. At worst, such administrative divisions continue in effect on the playground and in the community and deprive the children of the motivation to learn and practice English in order to communicate with friends.

Mixing children with different instructional needs in the same classrooms is quite common. It does not mean they will get uniform instruction. Children learning standard English as a second language certainly do need different lessons in language usage than those learning more about their native language. Even so, they have many learning needs in common. All prereading pupils, for instance, need training in auditory discrimination, and exercises on the contrastive phonology of English would be of value to the whole class. In a heterogeneous class children can be grouped for separate drill on vocabulary and syntax in the same way as for any other type of instruction.

If the classroom teacher cannot teach English effectively for some reason, a special language teacher can take groups from each class for a short time each day. This is unlikely to prove as satisfactory because such language instruction has fewer possibilities for integration into the total curriculum. A special language teacher could better serve as consultant, resource teacher, and assistant in preparing drill material for the classroom teachers to use.

Another controversial question concerns when to begin teaching the second language or dialect. Although linguists agree that oral command of the language, whether native or second, should precede the introduction of reading in it, there is disagreement on which language should be taught first in school. Many believe it is easier to introduce the new language system in kindergarten, or earlier if possible, and use it as a vehicle of reading instruction. Others maintain that reading should be taught in the vernacular of the child and that no attempt should be made to modify the spoken language until basic reading skills have been acquired. There has been some research on the stages of grammatical development during which exposure to instruction is most effective and efficient (Labov, 1964), but further study on this issue is required before many conclusions are reached.

Finally, there are still some individuals who believe that the purpose of language instruction is to eradicate nonstandard English. This attitude has contributed to the resistance of many children to the speech model prescribed in school. There are those who do not wish to adopt the middle-class pattern as their language system but prefer to retain that of their friends and family. They can communicate more effectively in their neighborhoods if they use their nonstandard dialect or native language. Teachers have the best chance for success in teaching English to these children if they try to *add to* rather than replace the dialect or language of the home.

The children should be made aware of other levels of language and of the difference their use can make in occupational opportunities, but their own patterns of speech should not be rejected as "sloppy" or inferior. The goal of language instruction for disadvantaged children should be to enable them to achieve sufficient flexibility to communicate easily on more than one level and in diverse situations.

7

Language Characteristics
of Specific Groups

NATIVE WHITES

Raven I. McDavid, Jr.

IT IS a truism that the problems of the current disadvantaged groups in achieving a reasonable share of the national affluence are more poignantly intense than, but are similar in kind to, those of the other groups that preceded them into our cities—Irish, Germans, Scandinavians, Italians, Ashkenazic Jews, Hungarians, and Poles. Each of these groups began at the bottom, crowded into its ethnic enclaves, suffered discrimination and contempt from its predecessors, and came to value almost painfully its new status in the lower middle class of skilled-labor and white-collar workers.

When we discuss the disadvantaged native whites we mean those of monolingual English experience, as distinguished from whites of French, Spanish, or other non-English-speaking background. (The latter groups are treated elsewhere in this book.) For reasons of economic and cultural history, most of the disadvantaged white group are Southern rural whites.

What distinguishes the troubles of the Southern rural whites, the Negroes, and the Spanish-Americans is a change in the social environment. Though the bottom groups on the economic totem pole, they are among the oldest inhabitants of our country; they are not immigrants, but mostly native citizens.[1] Furthermore, they come into the more highly urbanized and industrialized aspects of our society at the time when automation and other developments have sharply

---

[1] One should remember, of course, that none of these groups is monolithic. For instance, the Spanish-Americans include the border groups in Texas and Southern California, the long-settled rural population in New Mexico, the recent immigrants from Mexico and Puerto Rico (some in urban enclaves, others as migratory labor), and the exiles from Communist Cuba.

constricted the number and kinds of jobs for unskilled labor, and the opportunities to rise from such jobs, that for a century and a half have provided newcomers with routes into the dominant culture.

The linguist naturally draws a sharp line between the problems of the monolingual speaker of English and those whose first language is something else—whether Puerto Rican Spanish in East Harlem, Acadian French in southwestern Louisiana, or Navajo in Arizona and New Mexico. The speaker of another language is confronted with three tasks: (1) learning to read and write his native language; (2) learning to speak a second language, that is, English; and (3) learning to read and write in this second language well enough to communicate within the American industrial society of which he has become a part.

The way in which the sequence of these operations is organized will naturally vary from place to place and from language group to language group; what is constant, however, is the need for the teacher to approach any language with respect for it as the medium through which the child has been introduced to society, as one of the child's most intimate possessions, and as a viable means of communication in its own right.

Where the native language is English but the dialect is different from that of the teacher, the same kind of compassion should be shown that is properly exhibited toward the speaker of a foreign language. In most respects the problems of the native monolingual speaker of English are the same, regardless of the race of the students, i.e., matters of pronunciation or grammar; those that can be surely assigned to Caucasian or Negro or American Indian [2] alone are very few, and their number continually decreases with the increase in our information about the varieties of English. Even where a particular feature is popularly assigned to one racial group, like the uninflected third-singular present (*he do, she have, it make*)—a shibboleth for Negro nonstandard speech in urban areas—it often turns out to be old in the British dialects, and to be widely distributed in the eastern United States among speakers of all races. It is only the accidents of cultural, economic, and educational history that have made such older linguistic features more common in the South than in the Midland and the North, and more common among Negro speakers than among whites.

If the disadvantaged Negro may suffer in the schools because he is physically conspicuous, the disadvantaged white may suffer because he is physically inconspicuous; his divergences from the teacher's dialect are likely to be ascribed to his innate ignorance, whereas the Negro's divergences are ascribed to his race. And both ascriptions are equally fallacious.

The strikingly disadvantaged Caucasian is, of course, disadvantaged primarily in terms of urban ethnocentrism, as typified by school bureaucracies and by the impersonal, pressure-cooker urban environment. Characteristically rural and small-town in upbringing, he may be far more self-sufficient than the city dwellers

---

[2] Many American Indian groups, such as the Catawba of South Carolina, have lost the tribal language.

among whom he has moved—so long as he stays in his own environment. Like many other disadvantaged groups, he has a rich tradition of oral narrative and song; but this tradition is ignored by the schools—especially when he moves to the city. His tradition of individualism is repressed or ridiculed to the point where he welcomes an opportunity to quit school altogether.

Language Characteristics

PRONUNCIATION

The disadvantaged Caucasian child comes most often from a Southern or South Midland background; translated to a Northern urban environment, he often suffers from the ignorance of the local teachers where dialect differences are concerned. Despite four decades of serious investigation of regional and social differences in American speech, some teachers still cherish the fantasy that a Boston pronunciation—say, of a Kennedy—is somehow more elegant in itself than the Missouri pronunciation of a Truman or the Texas pronunciation of a Lyndon Johnson, though the three follow with equal fidelity their local educated models. As pernicious, and even more widely spread, is the notion that there is a uniform "General American" or "consensus English" that the schools are obligated to teach—regardless of how uncomfortable and resentful children become at having their native mode of speech disparaged. In cold fact, every regional or local variety of educated American English is as good as any other. And for the student who has not moved, it would seem the part of wisdom to organize the reading program in terms of the local standard. After all, the common Southern homonymy of *pen* and *pin* is no more exotic than the Boston homonymy of *collar* and *caller;* any well ordered program can take care of both groups.

Actually the Southerner or South Midlander has nearly all of the significant pronunciation contrasts of the Northeastern and Midwestern city dweller. In fact, he may retain a number of contrasts that his new neighbors lack: he may distinguish *due, dew* /dju/ from *do* /du/; he may have a three-way distinction between *merry* /mɛri/, *marry* /mæri/, and *Mary* /meri/; he may contrast *hoarse* /hors/ and *horse* /hɔrs/, or *wails* /welz/ and *whales* /hwelz/. In fact, he may feel that the Northerner who lacks these contrasts is somehow speaking broken English. In field work in the South I have often been asked, "Why is it that the educated Northerner speaks so much like the uneducated Southerner?"

In the distribution of sound-units, the Southerner is likely to simplify consonant clusters—or more likely (since he grows up among those who practice such simplifications) to retain the traditional simplifications that in some areas have been replaced by sometimes painful spelling pronunciations. Thus *acts* and *ax* are homonyms, and *six, sixth, sixths* are alike as /sɪks/. This is particularly noticeable when base-forms of nouns and verbs end in /-sp, -st, -sk/. In the noun plural or the verb third-singular, the final consonant of the singular is dropped,

so that *wasps, posts, costs* are /wɔs, pos, kɔs/, and *wrists, risks* are both /rɪs/. A
Southerner reared with books around him will learn to make the special accom-
modations between the sound system and the spelling system; the one without
early exposure to books may have trouble in both reading and spelling.

Some of the problems of the Southerner in Northern schools come from the
inability of Northern-reared teachers to recognize phonetic contrasts the Southerner makes as a matter of course. The Northerner may confuse the Southerner's
pronunciations of *hod, hard, hide, hired* (respectively [hɑd, hɑ·əd, ha·d, ha·əd]),
which are as distinctive to the Southerner as *leak* and *lick*. There are Northern
anecdotes that Southerners confuse *rat* and *right*, *all* and *oil;* actually the phonetic differences are clear ([ræt] and [ra·t], [ɔol] and [ɔ·əl]), but the distinctions
the Southerner makes are not the ones the Northerner is accustomed to recognizing. Since the contrast is there, it creates no problem, provided the teacher
knows what he is dealing with.

It may be otherwise, though, with the widespread lack of contrast between /ɪ/
and /ɛ/ before nasals, with *pen* and *pin, winch* and *wench* being homophones.
Here, as in other instances, the extent of early exposure to books is the determining force, and the fact that library holdings and book sales in the South are far
behind the national average cannot be ignored. But, of course, there are some
children in every community who have few books at home, and the characteristic
speech-forms of other regions, such as the Utah homonymy of *card* and *cord*,
create their own problems.

STRESS

The Southerner or South Midlander, of whatever degree of education, usually
has a wider range than the Northerner between high and low pitch and between
strongest and weakest stresses. He is likely to speak more rapidly; the well-
advertised "Southern drawl" is an illusion, created by prolongation of strong-
stressed syllables and shortening of weak-stressed ones. As weak-stressed syllables are shortened, the final syllables of *borrow* and *Tuesday* appear as /ə/
and /i/ rather than the full /o/ and /e/ of many Northern speakers—pronunciations, incidentally, that often strike the Southerner as affectations.

The uneducated Southerner, more often than his counterpart farther North,
may follow the millennial tendency of English toward initial stress, yielding
pólice, guítar, éfficiency, and the like; or he may strongly stress the *-ence* and *-ent*
suffixes that usually have the reduced vowel /ə/ in educated speech, yielding
evidénce, settlemént, and the like. But that these are not the peculiar property of
the uneducated Southerner may be observed from listening to any speech by
former President Eisenhower.

GRAMMAR

The disadvantaged white is, of course, likely to use many nonstandard grammatical constructions; this is almost a tautology, since it is the advantaged who
in the long run determine what is the grammatical standard. And where the

discrepancy between educated and uneducated speech is greatest, as in the South, the incidence of such nonstandard forms will be highest. The only caution is that there are wide variations in the extent to which the various subcultures—in informal usage—tolerate deviations from the norms of formal expository prose.

The Teacher's Role

Here one may raise the possibility of not only recognizing and encouraging a variety of styles and degrees of formality, for a variety of purposes, but also initiating students into the joys of reading by using in their first books the more relaxed norms of their everyday speech. This is a question beyond the competence of the linguist. What is within his competence is the recognition that every variety of speech—*every dialect*—has a system of its own and is acquired in the same way.

While aiming at the indubitable models of formal prose, the teacher must at the same time work for greater understanding of dialect differences and greater understanding of the processes by which dialects originate and are transmitted. If normal associations prevail among students, the "newly arrived" will of their own accord shift their pronunciation and grammar in the direction of the local norms; but an effort to accelerate this change by asserting the inferiority of the variety of the language the newcomers naturally speak can only be self-defeating. With Northern-born executives moving to Nashville and Atlanta, dialectal accommodation is no longer a one-way street, and the son of a Boston Brahmin may grow up with an impeccable Richmond accent. It is the duty of the teacher to avoid forcing an external standard upon his students; he should simply adapt his techniques to the structure of the students' dialect and let the overwhelming power of the culture do its work.

BLACKS

William Labov

ONE of the most extraordinary failures in the history of American education is the failure of the public school system to teach black children in the urban ghettos to read. The fact of reading failure is so general, and so widespread, that no one school system, no one method, and no one teacher can be considered responsible. We are plainly dealing with social and cultural events of considerable magnitude, in which the linguistic factors are the focal points of trouble or centers of difficulty rather than the primary causes. Before considering specific linguistic problems, it will be helpful to look at the general reading problem of disadvantaged blacks in its cultural setting.

Since 1965, research has been conducted into the structural and functional differences between the nonstandard vernacular used by black speakers in the urban ghettos and the standard English of the classroom.[1] One of the first studies was a series of seventy-five interviews with black boys in randomly selected "Vacation Day Camps" in Harlem in the summer of 1965. These day camps were conducted in recreation centers and schools, and each child's parents had to enroll him personally in the program; there was therefore a large factor of selection for intact homes and favorable family attitudes. In these interviews we found that the great majority of these boys, aged ten to twelve, had considerable difficulty in reading second- or third-grade-level sentences such as the following:

> Last month I read five books.
> When I passed by, I read the posters.
> When I liked a story, I read every word.

In the course of the next two years, the language and behavior of a number of preadolescent and adolescent peer groups in South Central Harlem were systematically investigated. The researchers avoided contact with the home and the school, the adult-dominated environments; instead, they worked through participant-observers in the area to reach the boys on the streets, in their own territories, in environments dominated by peer-group interaction. In the same areas, marginal members of the groups and isolated individuals were studied. The latter included boys from the Vacation Day Camps and boys from the immediate neighborhood of the peer groups, who were "lames"—definitely not participants in the vernacular street culture. Reading tests showed that reading skills were very low for most boys—close to zero for many. More important, reading was truly irrelevant to the daily life of these boys. For, example, two

---

[1] The research reported here was supported by the United States Office of Education as Cooperative Research Projects 3091 and 3288. The most complete report is provided in W. Labov, P. Cohen, C. Robins, and J. Lewis, *A Study of the Non-Standard English of Negro and Puerto Rican Speakers in New York City*, Final Report on Cooperative Research Project 3288 (Washington, D. C., 1968; available through ERIC, Center for Applied Linguistics, Washington, D. C.). The sections of this chapter entitled "The Problem of Black Dialect," "Relevant Patterns of Black Speech," "Some Phonological Variables and Their Grammatical Consequences," "Changes in the Shapes of Words," "Grammatical Correlates of the Phonological Variables," and "Consequences for the Teaching of Reading" were adapted from William Labov, "Some Sources of Reading Problems for Negro Speakers of Nonstandard English," in A. Frazier, ed., *New Directions in Elementary English* (Champaign, Ill.: N.C.T.E., 1967), pp. 140–67, and are used by permission of the National Council of Teachers of English. Some of the treatment in this chapter is derived from William Labov, "A Note on the Relation of Reading Failure to Peer Group Status," *Teachers College Record*, Vol. 70 (1969), pp. 395–405.

boys who were best friends and saw each other every day had very different read-ing abilities. One could read the last page in Gray's Oral Reading Test, and the other could not read the second-grade-level sentences; the first was astonished to find that his friend could not read, and the second was even more surprised to find that the first boy could read so well.

With the cooperation of the New York City Board of Education, the school records were examined for most of the individuals studied.[2] Figure 7–1 shows the relation of reading level to grade level for thirty-two isolated individuals. The horizontal axis is the actual grade at the time the investigators were in con-tact with the boys; the vertical axis is the average Metropolitan Achievement Test score. The central diagonal, from lower left to upper right, represents read-ing on grade: the pair of symbols at the upper right of the diagram, for example, shows two boys in the eighth grade reading at the eighth-grade level.

In Figure 7–1, we see that most of the children studied from South Central Harlem are indeed below grade in reading, though there are some who are doing quite well. The general movement of the population from lower left to upper right indicates that learning is taking place.

We can contrast Figure 7–1 with Figure 7–2, which shows the same relations for forty-six children who are members of various gangs, clubs, or hang-out groups—fully participating members of the street cultures. The overall pattern is very different from Figure 7–1: only one person is reading on grade, and the great majority are not learning to read at all. Year by year, the boys belonging to these groups fall further below grade—four, five, or six years, until they finally drop out.

The sharp difference between these two figures represents information that could not have been gathered by research within the schools, since teachers have no means of knowing which children are indeed fully identified with the street culture. The linguistic differences between the two groups are minor, but the difference in acceptance or rejection of school as an institution is very great indeed.

These figures make it fairly evident that there are factors operating that are more important than native intelligence or verbal ability—culturally-determined values and attitudes that interfere with the process of learning to read. The funda-mental problem revealed in Figures 7–1 and 7–2 should be kept in mind so that the relative importance of functional and structural problems is not obscured. At the present time we can give a number of concrete suggestions on linguistic problems and some of these are presented in the following pages. As helpful as these may be, it should be clear that they deal with only one (and certainly not the major) problem interfering with the learning of reading.

---

[2] Data given here are based on a relatively small sample of seventy-five boys, since many had moved or been transferred, suspended, or discharged during this period.

FIGURE 7-1

Grade and Reading Achievement of Thirty-two Nonmembers
of Street Groups in South Central Harlem

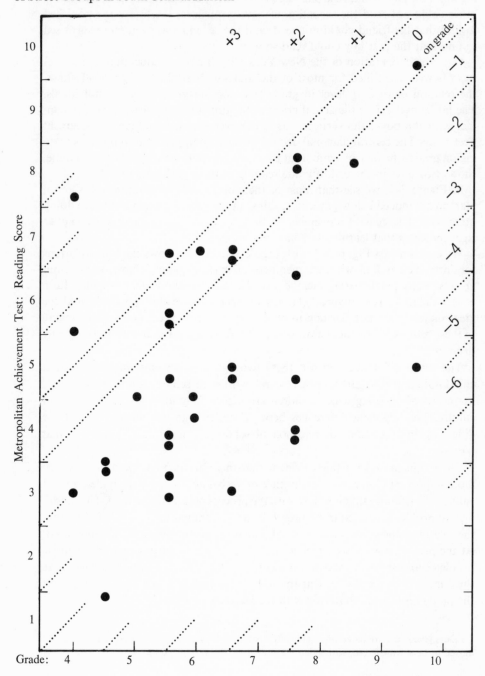

FIGURE 7-2

Grade and Reading Achievement of Forty-six Members
of Street Groups in Harlem

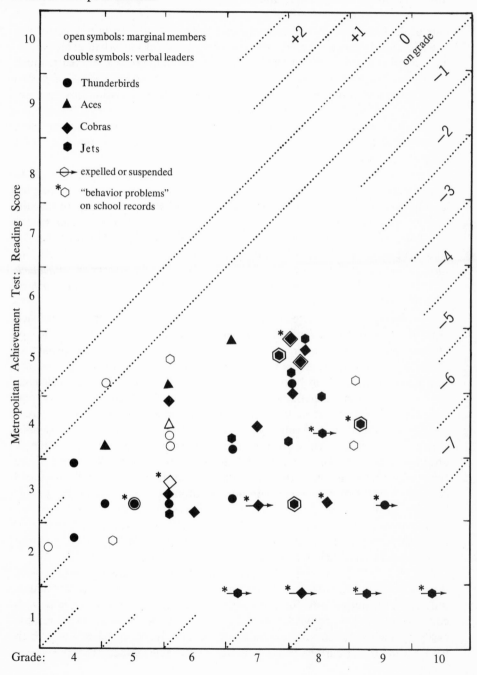

The Problem of Black Dialect

One of the first questions to which we must address ourselves is whether or not there is a single definite pattern of speech used by blacks in urban ghetto areas. This question has provoked a great deal of discussion in the last few years, much more than it deserves. At many meetings on educational problems of ghetto areas, time that could have been spent in constructive discussion has been devoted to arguing the question as to whether black dialect exists. The debates have not been conducted with any large body of factual information in view, but rather in terms of what the speakers wish to be so, or what they fear might follow in the political arena.

For those who have not participated in such debates, it may be difficult to imagine how great are the pressures against the recognition, description, or even mention of black speech patterns. For various reasons, many teachers, principals, and civil rights leaders wish to deny that the existence of patterns of black speech is a linguistic and social reality in the United States today. The most careful statement of the situation as it actually exists might read as follows: *Many features of pronunciation, grammar, and lexicon are closely associated with black speakers—so closely as to identify the great majority of black people in the northern cities by their speech alone.*

The correspondence between this speech pattern and membership in the black ethnic group is of course far from complete. Many black speakers have none—or almost none—of these features. Many northern whites, living in close proximity to blacks, have these features in their own speech. But this overlap does not prevent the features from being identified with black speech by most listeners: we are dealing with a stereotype that provides correct identification in the great majority of cases, and therefore with a firm base in social reality. Such stereotypes are the social basis of language perception; this is merely one of many cases where listeners generalize from the variable data to categorical perception in absolute terms. Someone who uses a stigmatized form 20 to 30 percent of the time will be heard as using this form all the time. It may be socially useful to correct these stereotypes in a certain number of individual cases, so that people learn to limit their generalizations to the precise degree that their experience warrants; but the overall tendency is based upon very regular principles of human behavior, and people will continue to identify as black speech the pattern that they hear from the great majority of the black people they meet.

The existence of a black speech pattern must not be confused of course with the myth of a biologically, racially, exclusively black speech. The idea that dialect differences are due to some form of laziness or carelessness must be rejected with equal firmness. Anyone who continues to endorse such myths can be refuted easily by such subjective-reaction tests as the Family Background Test, which we are using in our current research in Harlem. Sizable extracts from the speech of fourteen individuals are played in sequence for listeners who are asked to identify the family backgrounds of each. So far, we find no one who can even come close to a correct identification of black and white speakers. This result does not contradict the statement that there exists a socially based black speech pattern; it supports everything that I have said above on this point. The voices heard on the test are the exceptional cases: blacks raised without any black friends in solidly white areas; whites raised in areas dominated by black cultural values; white southerners raised in predominantly black areas; blacks from small northern communities untouched by recent migrations; college-educated blacks who reject the northern ghetto and the South alike. The speech of these individuals does not identify them as black or white because they do not use the speech patterns that are characteristically black or white for northern listeners. The identifications made by these listeners, often in violation of actual ethnic membership categories, show that they respond to black speech patterns as a social reality.

Relevant Patterns of Black Speech

One approach to the study of nonstandard black speech is to attempt a complete description of this form of language without direct reference to standard English. This approach can be quite revealing, and can save us from many pitfalls in the easy identification of forms that are only apparently similar. But as an overall plan, it is not realistic. We are far from achieving a complete description of standard English, to begin with; the differences between nonstandard black speech and standard English are slight compared to their similarities; and finally, some of these differences are far more relevant to reading problems than others. Let us therefore consider some of the most relevant patterns of black speech from the point of view of reading problems.

Some black-white differences are plainly marked and easy for any observer to note. In the following examples, the black forms are patterns that frequently occur in our recordings of individual and group sessions with boys from ten to seventeen years old—ranging from careful speech in face-to-face interaction with adults to the most excited and spontaneous activity within the primary (closed network) group:

Black	*White*
It don't all be her fault.	It isn't always her fault.
Hit him upside the head.	Hit him in the head.
The rock say "Shhh!"	The rock went "Shhh!"
I'm a shoot you.	I'm g'na shoot you.
I wanna be a police.	I wanna be a policeman.
Ah 'on' know. [a o no]	I d'know. [a^{I}dno^U]

Now consider the following examples, in which black-white differences are less plainly marked and very difficult for most people to hear:

Black	*White*
He [pæsɪm] yesterday.	He [pæsdɪm] yesterday.
Give him [ðeˡ] book.	Give him [ðɛə:] book.
This [jɔ:ɭ] place?	This [jɔ:ˀ] place?
[ðæs] Nick boy.	[ðæˡs] Nick's boy.
He say, [kæ:ˀɭ] is.	He says, [kærəl] is.
My name is [bu].	My name is [buʔ].

This second series represents a set of slight phonetic differences, sometimes prominent, but more often unnoticed by the casual listener. These differences are much more significant than the first set in terms of learning and reading standard English. In truth, the differences are so significant that they will be the focus of our attention. The slight phonetic signals observed here indicate systematic differences that can lead to reading problems and problems of being understood.

Corresponding to the phonetic transcriptions on the left, we can and do infer such grammatical constructions and lexical forms as

> He pass him yesterday.
> Give him they book.
> This you-all place?
> That's Nick boy.
> He say, Ca'ol is.
> My name is Boo.

Each of these sentences is representative of a large class of phonological and grammatical differences that distinguish nonstandard black speech from standard English. The most important are those in which large-scale phonological differences coincide with important grammatical differences. The result of this coincidence is the existence of a large number of homonyms in the speech of black children that are different from the set of homonyms in the speech system used by the teacher. If the teacher knows about this different set of homonyms, no serious problems in the teaching of reading need occur; but if the teacher does not know about it, there are bound to be difficulties.

The simplest way to organize this information seems to be under the headings of the important rules of the sound system that are affected. By using lists of homonyms as examples, it will be possible to avoid a great deal of phonetic notation and to stay with the essential linguistic facts. In many cases, the actual phonetic form is irrelevant: it is the presence or absence of a distinction that is relevant. Thus, for example, it makes no difference whether a child says [pɪn] or [pɪˀn] or [pe:ˀn] or [pɛn] for the word *pen;* what counts is whether or not this word is distinct from *pin*. The linguistic fact of interest is the existence of contrast, not the particular phonetic forms that are heard from one time to another. A child might seem to distinguish [pɪn] and [pɛn] in northern style in one pair of sentences, but if the basic phonemic contrast is not present, the same child might reverse the forms in the next sentence, and say [pɪn] for *ink pen* and [pɛn] for *safety pin*. A linguistic orientation will not supply teachers with a battery of phonetic symbols, but rather encourage them to observe what words can or cannot be distinguished by the children they are teaching.

Some Phonological Variables and Their Grammatical Consequences

R-LESSNESS

There are three major dialect areas in the eastern United States where the *r* of spelling is not pronounced as a consonant before other consonants or at the ends of words: eastern New England, New York City, and the South (upper and lower). Thus white speakers from Boston, New York, Richmond, Charleston, or Atlanta will show only a lengthened vowel in *car, guard, for,* and usually an obscure centering glide [schwa] in place of *r* in *fear, feared, care, cared, moor, moored, bore, bored,* and so on. This is what we mean by *r*-less pronunciation. Most of these areas have been strongly influenced in recent years by the *r*-pronouncing pattern that is predominant in broadcasting, so that educated speakers, especially young people, will show a mixed pattern in their careful speech. When the original *r*-less pattern is preserved, we can obtain such homonyms as the following:

guard	= god	par	= pa
nor	= gnaw	fort	= fought
sore	= saw	court	= caught

and we find that *yeah* can rhyme with *fair, idea* with *fear*.

Black speakers show an even higher degree of *r*-lessness than white New Yorkers or Bostonians. The *r* of spelling becomes a schwa or disappears before vowels as well as before consonants and pauses. Thus in the speech of most white New Yorkers, *r* is pronounced when a vowel follows, as in *four o'clock;* even though the *r* is found at the end of a word, if the next word begins with a vowel, it is pronounced as a consonantal [r]. For most black speakers, *r* is still not pronounced in this position, and so never heard at the end of the word *four*. The white speaker is helped in his reading or spelling by the existence of the alternation in which the underlying *r* comes out before a vowel, as in *four o'clock*, but the black speaker has no such clue to the underlying (spelling) form of the word *four*. Furthermore, the same black speaker will often not pronounce intervocalic *r* in the middle of a word, as indicated in the dialect spelling *inte'ested*,

Ca'ol. He has no clue, in his own speech, to the correct spelling form of such words, and may have another set of homonyms besides those listed above:

    Carol = Cal
    Paris = pass
    terrace = test

L-LESSNESS

The consonant *l* is a liquid very similar to *r* in its phonetic nature. The chief difference is that with *l* the center of the tongue is up and the sides are down, whereas with *r* the sides are up but the center does not touch the roof of the mouth. The pattern of *l*-dropping is very similar to that of *r*, except that it has never affected entire dialect areas in the same sweeping style. When *l* disappears, it is often replaced by a back unrounded glide, sometimes symbolized [ł], instead of the center glide that replaces *r;* in many cases, *l* disappears entirely, especially after the back rounded vowels. The loss of *l* is much more marked among the black speakers we have interviewed than among whites in northern cities, and one therefore finds much greater tendencies toward such homonyms as

    toll = toe   all   = awe
    help = hep   Saul = saw
    tool = too   fault = fought

SIMPLIFICATION OF CONSONANT CLUSTERS

One of the most complex variables appearing in black speech is the genera tendency toward the simplification of consonant clusters at the ends of words. A great many clusters are involved, primarily those ending in /-t/ or /-d/, /-s/ or /-z/.[3] We are actually dealing with two distinct tendencies: (1) a general tendency to reduce clusters of consonants at the ends of words to single consonants, and (2) a more general process of reducing the amount of information provided after stressed vowels, so that individual final consonants are affected as well. The first process is more regular and requires more intensive study in order to understand the conditioning factors involved.

The chief /-t, -d/ clusters that are affected are (roughly in order of frequency)

---

[3] When the /-t/ or /-d/ represents a grammatical inflection these consonants are usually automatic alternants of the same abstract form *-ed*. Phonetic rules delete the vowel (except after stems ending in /-t/ or /-d/), and we then have [t] following voiceless consonants such as /p, s, t, k/ and [d] in all other cases. In the same way, [s] and [z] are coupled as voiceless and voiced alternants of the same *-s* inflections, but in clusters that are a part of the root word we do not have such automatic alternations.

/-st, -ft, -nt, -nd, -ld, -zd, -md/. Here they are given in phonemic notation; in conventional spelling we have words such as *past, passed, lift, laughed, bent, bend, fined, hold, poled, old, called, raised, aimed.* In all these cases, if the cluster is simplified, it is the last element that is dropped. Thus we have homonyms such as

past	= pass	mend	= men
rift	= riff	wind	= wine
meant	= men	hold	= hole

If we combine the effect of *-ld* simplification, loss of *-l*, and monophthongization of /av/ and /aw/, we obtain

[ši wa: ɬ]   She wow! = She wild!

and this equivalence has in fact been found in our data. It is important to bear in mind that the combined effect of several rules will add to the total number of homonyms, and even more, to the unexpected character of the final result:

told = toll = toe

The /-s, -z/ clusters that are often simplified occur in such words as *axe* /æks/, *six* /siks/, *box* /baks/, *parts* /parts/, *aims* /eymz/, *rolls* /rowlz/, *leads* /liydz/, *besides* /bisaydz/, *John's* /džanz/, *that's* /ðæts/, *it's* /its/, *its* /its/. The situation here is more complex than with the /-t, -d/ clusters, since in some cases the first element of the cluster is lost, and in other cases the second element.[4]

In one sense, there are a great many homonyms produced by this form of consonant-cluster simplification, as we shall see when we consider grammatical consequences. But many of these can also be considered grammatical differences rather than changes in the shapes of words. The /-t, -d/ simplification gives us a great many irreducible homonyms, so that a child has no clue to the standard spelling differences from his own speech pattern. Though this is less common in the case of /-s, -z/ clusters, we can occasionally have

six	= sick	Max	= Mack
box	= bock	mix	= Mick

as possible homonyms in the speech of many black children.

WEAKENING OF FINAL CONSONANTS

It was noted above that the simplification of final consonant clusters was part of a more general tendency to produce less information after stressed vowels, so that final consonants, unstressed final vowels, and weak syllables show fewer

---

[4] The loss of the first element—that is, assimilation to the following *s*—is most common in forms where the *-s* represents the verb *is* or the pronoun *us* in *it's, that's* and *let's*. In none of these cases is there a problem of homonymy.

distinctions and more reduced phonetic forms than initial consonants and stressed vowels. This is a perfectly natural process in terms of the amount of information required for effective communication, since the number of possible words that must be distinguished declines sharply after we select the first consonant and vowel. German and Russian, for example, do not distinguish voiced and voiceless consonants at the ends of words. However, when this tendency is carried to extremes (and a nonstandard dialect differs radically from the standard language in this respect), it may produce serious problems in learning to read and spell.

This weakening of final consonants is by no means as regular as the other phonological variables described above. Some individuals appear to have generalized the process to the point where most of their syllables are of the CV type, that is, consonant plus vowel, and those we have interviewed in this category seem to have the most serious reading problems of all. In general, final /-t/ and /-d/ are the most affected by the process. Final /-d/ may be devoiced to a [t]-like form or disappear entirely. Final /-t/ is often realized as glottal stop, as in many English dialects, but more often disappears entirely. Less often, final /-g/ and /-k/ follow the same route as /-d/ and /-t/: /-g/ is devoiced or disappears, and /-k/ is replaced by glottal stop or disappears. Final /-m/ and /-n/ usually remain in the form of various degrees of nasalization of the preceding vowel. Rarely, sibilants /-s/ and /-z/ are weakened after vowels to the point where no consonant is heard at all. As a result of these processes, it is possible to have such homonyms as

Boot = Boo		seat	= seed	= see
road = row		poor	= poke	= pope
feed = feet		bit	= bid	= big

It is evident that the loss of final /-l/ and /-r/, discussed above, is another aspect of this general weakening of final consonants, though of a much more regular nature than the cases considered in this section.

OTHER PHONOLOGICAL VARIABLES

In addition to the types of homonymy singled out in the preceding discussion, there are a great many others that may be mentioned. They are of less importance for reading problems in general, since they have little impact on inflectional rules, but they do affect the shapes of words in the speech of black children. There is no distinction between /i/ and /e/ before nasals in the great majority of cases. In the parallel case before /-r/, and sometimes /-l/, we frequently find no distinction between the vowels /ih/ and /eh/. The corresponding pair of back vowels before /-r/ are seldom distinguished; that is, /uh/ and /oh/ fall together. The diphthongs /ay/ and /aw/ are often monophthongized, so that they are not distinguished from /ah/. The diphthong /oy/ is often a monophthong, especially before /-l/, and sometimes cannot be distinguished from the vowel /oh/, so that *oil* = *all*.

Among other consonant variables, we find the final fricative /-θ/ is frequently merged with /f/, and similarly final /-ð/ with /v/. Less frequently, /θ/ and /ð/ become /f/ and /v/ in intervocalic position. Initial consonant clusters that involve /r/ show considerable variation: /str/ is often heard as /skr/; /ʃr/ as [sw, sr, sɸ]. In a more complex series of shifts, /r/ is frequently lost as the final element of an initial cluster.

As a result of these various phonological processes, we find that the following series of possible homonyms are characteristic of the speech of many black children:

pin = pen	beer = bear		poor = pour
tin = ten	cheer = chair		sure = shore
since = cents	steer = stair		moor = more
	peel = pail		
Ruth = roof	stream = scream		boil = ball
death = deaf	strap = scrap		oil = all
find = found = fond			
time = Tom			
pound = pond			

Changes in the Shapes of Words

The series of potential homonyms given in the preceding sections indicate that black children may have difficulty in recognizing many words in their standard spellings. They may look up words under the wrong spellings in dictionaries and be unable to distinguish words that are plainly different for the teacher. If the teacher is aware of these sources of confusion, he may be able to anticipate a great many of the children's difficulties. But if neither the teacher nor the children are aware of the great differences in their sets of homonyms, it is obvious that confusion will occur in every reading assignment.

However, the existence of homonyms on the level of a phonetic output does not prove that the speakers have the same sets of mergers on the more abstract level that corresponds to the spelling system. For instance, many white New Yorkers merge *guard* and *god* in casual speech, but in reading style they have no difficulty in pronouncing the /r/ where it belongs. Since the /r/ in *car* reappears before a following vowel, it is evident that an abstract *r* occurs in their lexical understanding of the word. Thus the standard spelling system finds support in the learned patterns of careful speech and in the alternations that exist within any given style of speech.

The phonetic processes discussed above are often considered to be "low level" rules—that is, they do not affect the underlying or abstract representations of words. One piece of evidence for this view is that the deletable final /-r, -l, -s, -z, -t, -d/ tend to be retained when a vowel follows at the beginning of the next word. This effect of a following vowel would seem to be a phonetic factor, restricting the operation of a phonetic rule; in any case, it is plain that the final consonant must "be there" in some abstract sense if it appears in this prevocalic position. If this were not the case, we would find a variety of odd final consonants appearing, with no fixed relation to the standard form.

For all major variables that we have considered, there is a definite and pronounced effect of a following vowel in realizing the standard form.

The same argument, however, can be applied to show that black speakers have underlying forms considerably different from those of white speakers. The white speakers showed almost as much overall simplification of the clusters before a following consonant, but none at all before a following vowel; in other words, their abstract forms were effectively equivalent to the spelling forms. The black speakers showed only a limited reduction in the degree of simplification when a vowel followed.

Grammatical Correlates
of the Phonological Variables

As we examine the various final consonants affected by the phonological processes, we find that these are the same consonants that represent the principal English inflections. The shifts in the sound system therefore often coincide with grammatical differences between nonstandard and standard English, and it is usually difficult to decide whether we are dealing with a grammatical or a phonological rule. In any case, we can add a great number of homonyms to the lists given above when we consider the consequences of deleting final /-r, -l, -s, -z, -t, -d/.

THE POSSESSIVE

In many cases, the absence of the possessive *s* can be interpreted as a reduction of consonant clusters, although this is not the most likely interpretation. The *-s* is absent just as frequently after vowels as after consonants for many speakers. Nevertheless, we can say that the overall simplification pattern is favored by the absence of the *-s* inflection. In the case of *-r*, we find more direct phonological influence: two possessive pronouns that end in /-r/ have become identical with the personal pronoun:

[ðeɪ] book   not [ðɛːə] book

In rapid speech, one can not distinguish *you* from *your* from *you-all*. This seems to be a shift in grammatical forms, but the relation to the phonological variables is plain when we consider that *my*, *his*, *her*, and *our* remain as possessive pronouns. Only in areas under strong Creole influence will one hear *I book*, *she book*, or *we book*, for there is no phonological process that would bring the possessives into near-identity with the personal pronouns.

THE FUTURE

The loss of final /-l/ has a serious effect on the realization of future forms:

you'll = you	he'll = he
they'll = they	she'll = she

In many cases, therefore, the colloquial future is identical with the colloquial present. The form *will* is still used in its emphatic or full form, and various reductions of *going to* are frequent, so there is no question about the grammatical category of the future. One contracted form of the future heard only among black speakers is in the first person, *I'm a shoot you;* there is no general process for the deletion of this *m*.

THE COPULA

The finite verb forms of *be* are frequently not realized in sentences such as *you tired* and *he in the way*. If we examine the paradigm as a whole, we find that phonological processes have obviously been at work. In the first person, we find that either the full or contracted form is normal; such forms as *I here* or *I is here* are extremely rare except perhaps among very young children, but because they are so striking many casual observers have reported them as common. The third-person form *is* represents a true variable for all vernacular speakers. We have found that the deletion of *is* ranges from 20 or 30 percent to 70 or 80 percent, but it is never absent entirely even in the most casual speech. On the other hand, the second-person singular and plural form *are* is deleted much more frequently and is almost completely absent for many speakers. It is evident that the phonological processes that affect *are* are much stronger than those that affect *is*.

It may seem strange at first to speak of phonological processes operating to effect the deletion of a whole word. However, our recent studies of the copula have revealed that in every situation in which standard English cannot contract to *'s*, the nonstandard vernacular does not permit deletion of *is*.[5] Thus contraction precedes deletion in the rules operating here; the rules of consonant-cluster simplification, discussed above, apply in part to this situation.

[5] Thus in *He is here*, *He ain't here, is he? Yes he is, I'm smarter than he is, That's what it is*, and many other cases we find that *is* can neither be contracted or deleted. See William Labov, "Contraction, Deletion and Inherent Variability of the English Copula," *Language*, Vol. 44 (1969), pp. 718–22.

THE PAST

Again, there is no doubt that phonological processes are active in reducing the frequency of occurrence of the /-t, -d/ inflection.

pass = past = passed   pick = picked
miss = mist = missed   loan = loaned
fine = find = fined   raise = raised

At the same time, there is no question about the existence of a past tense category. The irregular past tense forms, which are very frequent in ordinary conversation, are plainly marked as past no matter what final simplification takes place.

I told him   [atoɪm]   he kept mine   [hikɛpmaɪn]

The problem that confronts us concerns the form of the regular suffix *-ed*. Is there such an abstract form in the structure of the nonstandard English spoken by black children? The answer will make a considerable difference both to teaching strategy and to our understanding of the reading problems that children face. We have carried out a number of quantitative studies of consonant clusters and the *-ed* suffix on this point.[6] The behavior of speakers in spontaneous group interaction has been studied, as well as their ability to recognize *-ed* in reading as a past tense signal and to detect nonstandard forms in printed material. Our conclusion is that there are many black children who do not have enough support in their linguistic system to identify *-ed* as a past tense signal, and they must be taught the meaning of this form from the outset. There are many others who have no difficulty in *reading -ed* even though they do not pronounce it. In our investigations, we use test sentences such as

1. Tom read all the time.
2. Last month I read five books.
3. Now I read and write better than my brother.
4. When I passed by, I read the sign.

The unique homograph *read* helps us to discover the status of the *-ed* suffix for the reader. If he correctly reads aloud sentences 1 and 2 with the past tense form [rɛd], and sentence 3 in the present tense form [riːd], then we know that he can interpret this homograph in a standard manner depending on whether it is placed in a past or present context. Then in sentence 4, he should give us the pronunciation [rɛd] *if* he deciphers the *-ed* in *passed* as a signal of the past tense, whether or not he pronounces it.

[6] See "Some Sources of Reading Problems" cited in note 1 and Cooperative Research Report 3288 for quantitative data.

AN OVERVIEW OF THE NONSTANDARD VERNACULAR

We have contrasted the casual speech of peer groups of ten- to twelve-year-olds with that of groups of fourteen- to sixteen-year-olds. We find that the rules for the basic vernacular become more consistent and regular rather than more mixed with standard English. Some phonological conditions become more consistent, and the spelling forms of individual words, such as *box*, come closer to the standard forms. But the basic grammatical patterns (no third-person singular *-s*, no possessive *-s*, weak *-ed* suffix, stylistic deletion of the copula, and so on) remain well fixed. Whereas the dropping of the plural *-s* is never more than an occasional feature, the third-person singular *-s* has no more support among sixteen-year-olds than among twelve-year-olds.

The most striking evidence of these underlying grammatical facts is the effect of a following vowel on the consonant cluster concerned. When a vowel follows *-ed*, as in *messed up*, the percentage of simplified forms drops moderately. When a vowel follows clusters that are a part of a word, as in *act* or *box*, we see a regular decrease in simplification. This effect becomes stronger with the increasing age of the speakers; and when a vowel follows plural clusters, as in *books*, there is a marked decrease in simplification as well. But when a vowel follows the third-person singular *-s*, as in *works*, or possessive *-s*, as in *John's*, we do not find the *-s* remaining more often. On the contrary, it appears *less* often than when a consonant follows. For this reason, we can argue that there is no phonological process involved here at all. In the underlying grammar, there simply is no morpheme *-s* representing the third-person singular of the verb, and no morpheme *-s* representing the possessive. To be sure, there is a possessive category in *my*, *our*, *his*, and *mine*, and so on, but the particular use of *-s* to mean the possessive after nouns must be taught from the beginning.

Consequences for the Teaching of Reading

Let us consider the problem of teaching a youngster to read who has the general phonological and grammatical characteristics just described. The most immediate way of analyzing his difficulties is through the interpretation of his oral reading. As we have seen, there are many phonological rules that affect his pronunciation, but not necessarily his understanding of the grammatical signals or his grasp of the underlying lexical forms. The two questions are distinct: the relations between grammar and pronunciation are complex and require careful interpretation.

If a pupil is given a certain sentence to read, say *He passed by both of them*, he may say [hi pæs ba^I bof ə dɛm]. The teacher may wish to correct this bad reading, perhaps by saying, "No, it isn't [hi pæs baᴵ bof ə dɛm], it's [hi pæst baᴵ boθ əv ðɛm]." One difficulty is that these two utterances may sound the same to many children—both the reader and those listening—and they may be utterly confused by the correction. Others may be able to hear the difference, but have no idea of the significance of the extra [t] and the interdental forms of *th-*. The most embarrassing fact is that the child who first read the sentence may have performed his reading task correctly, and understood the *-ed* suffix just as it was intended. In that case, the teacher's correction is completely beside the point.

We have two distinct cases to consider. In one case, the deviation in reading may be only a difference in pronunciation on the part of a child who has a different set of homonyms from the teacher. Here, correction might be quite unnecessary. In the second case, we may be dealing with a child who has no concept of *-ed* as a past tense marker, who considers the *-ed* a meaningless set of silent letters. Obviously the correct teaching strategy would involve distinguishing between these two cases and treating them quite differently.

How such a strategy might be put into practice is a problem that educators may be able to solve by using information provided by linguists. As a linguist, I can suggest several basic principles derived from our work that may be helpful in further curriculum research and application.

1. In the analysis and correction of oral reading, teachers must begin to make the basic distinction between differences in pronunciation and mistakes in reading. Information on the dialect patterns of black children should be helpful toward this end.

2. In the early stages of teaching reading and spelling it may be necessary to spend much more time on the grammatical function of certain inflections that may have no function in the dialect of some of the children. In the same way, it may be necessary to treat the final elements of certain clusters with the special attention given to silent letters such as *b* in *lamb*.

3. A certain amount of attention given to perception training in the first few years of school may be extremely helpful in teaching children to hear and make standard English distinctions. But perception training need not be complete in order to teach children to read. On the contrary, most of the differences between standard and nonstandard English described here can be taken as differences in the sets of homonyms that must be accepted in reading patterns. On the face of it, there is no reason why a person cannot learn to read standard English texts quite well in a nonstandard pronunciation. Eventually, the school may wish to teach the child an alternative system of pronunciation. But the key to the situation in the early grades is for the teacher to know the system of homonyms of nonstandard English and to know the grammatical differences that separate her own speech from that of the child. The teacher must be prepared to accept the system of homonyms for the moment if this will advance the basic process of learning to read, but not the grammatical differences. Thus the task of teaching the child to read *-ed* is clearly that of getting him to recognize the graphic symbols

as a marker of the past tense, quite distinct from the task of getting him to say [pæst] for *passed.*

If the teacher has no understanding of the child's grammar and set of hom-onyms, she may be arguing with him at cross purposes. Over and over again, the teacher may insist that *cold* and *coal* are different, without realizing that the child perceives this as only a difference in meaning, not in sound. She will not be able to understand why he makes so many odd mistakes in reading, and he will experience only a vague confusion, somehow connected with the ends of words. Eventually, he may stop trying to analyze the shapes of letters that follow the vowel and guess wildly at each word after he deciphers the first few letters. Or he may completely lose confidence in the alphabetic principle and try to recognize each word as a whole. This loss of confidence seems to occur fre-quently in the third and fourth grades, and it is characteristic of many children who are effectively nonreaders.

The sources of reading problems discussed here are only a few of the causes of poor reading in black ghetto schools. But they are quite specific and easily isolated. The information provided here may have immediate application in the overall program of improving the teaching of reading to children in these urban areas.

SPANISH–SPEAKERS

Albar A. Peña

"THERE IS nothing inherent or God-given in wanting to learn to read. One does so because one sees reasons for reading or is expected to learn to read" (Hicker-son, 1966). Middle-class children usually see reasons for reading because environ-mental factors have encouraged them to read or have at least pointed them in the right direction. Unfortunately, this is not the case for the millions of eco-nomically deprived children of Spanish or Mexican descent. Most youngsters from such poor environments rarely learn to read beyond a third- or fourth-grade level. Obviously, some children from poor families do learn to read, and read well. But there are more who do *not* than do.

There are many factors that contribute to the deficiencies of disadvantaged Spanish-speaking children in reading—physical and economic deprivation, lack of motivation, lack of experiential background conducive to learning to read, lack of trained personnel, lack of adequate materials and teaching techniques, and, in some instances, actual discrimination, either overt or subtle. In addition, there is another factor involved—and it is a major one—commonly identified as the language barrier. As long as public schools insist on assuming that all these children can be treated as native speakers of English, and therefore are ready to read in that language, teaching them to read will continue to be a problem. The language barrier is directly related to the high rate of failure these children experience in reading. In order to arrive at some possible remedy, we must delve into the language characteristics of disadvantaged children whose first language is Spanish.

Language Characteristics

It is often contended that disadvantaged children are nonverbal or have verbal inadequacies (Riessman, 1962). They seem to have enormous difficulty expressing themselves verbally in many situations. This difficulty of expression becomes evident when these children first enter school. Consequently, there has arisen a rather firm belief that disadvantaged children are basically inarticulate, that they lack the verbal ability so important in reading and eventual school success. This belief cannot be well supported in the case of Spanish-speaking children, as we can see when we analyze the language characteristics of these children in order to specify the exact nature of their verbal functioning.

Most Spanish-speaking children are essentially nonverbal in English in their early school years. However, they come to school with considerable knowledge of their native language, and though the language they speak is sometimes limited due to their age and background, it is and has been a useful form of communication for them. Peña (1967) made a study to ascertain what basic sentence patterns and fundamental transformations disadvantaged Spanish-speaking first-graders possess in both Spanish and English; the findings suggest that their native language is more developed than most educators would expect. Educators generally consider their language so substandard that they sometimes refer to these children as alingual. In most instances, when the children were asked to respond spontaneously to an object or given situation pertinent to their experiential background, they responded in complete and correct grammatical constructions. It was also evident that even though the children possessed "complete grammatical constructions" in their native language, the noun and verb slots were often filled with words borrowed from English or English words they had hispanicized. For example, they might say, "Es una *cap*" (instead of *gorra*) or "Yo la sé quechar" (hispanicizing the verb *catch*).

In general their oral language in Spanish lacks the vocabulary refinement to overcome so-called Americanisms, nonstandard words and forms that they find necessary to include in their vocabulary in order to express themselves in the dominant culture they are entering (Haugen, 1956). They have been forced to adopt these words in order to find useful devices for extending their vocabulary in Spanish. If the appropriateness of language is to be judged on the basis of standard American Spanish or the particular English dialect used in the classroom situation, Spanish-speaking children appear to be somewhat deficient. But in assessing such deficiencies, one must bear in mind the age level and maturity of these children and also the background that has engendered the language they now possess.

If Spanish-speaking children bring to school with them a limited knowledge of their native language, they bring, more often than not, an even more limited knowledge of English. Their oral language in English often is fragmentary and when they manage to state what would be considered a complete sentence, it is frequently bungled, lacking both subject-verb agreement and correct word order. They are likely to intersperse their sentences with words borrowed from their native language, for example, "This is a *lápiz*." Their pronunciation will be highly accented due to interference caused by at least five consecutive years of speaking Spanish and very little English or none at all. This will be more evident when they try to pronounce English phonemes that are nonexistent in their native language. When it comes to English, Spanish-speaking children seem to understand more than they speak: their "receptive" linguistic ability is much better than their "expressive" language.

Dialect

Disadvantaged Spanish-speakers, by virtue of their general deprivation and, in some cases, ghetto-like environment, far removed from their homelands, have created their own social dialect. This social dialect is rich in its use of slang and words they have coined in order to have a feeling of belonging to a group. Nevertheless, the basic grammatical construction of their utterances will be correct. The deviation of this type of dialect from the so-called standard language will stem from the fact that these constructions will be filled with Spanish barbarisms and neologisms, old Spanish words that have taken on new meanings. Also, such dialects will differ depending upon the geographical location of these disadvantaged groups. In the case of Mexican-Americans in the Southwest, many have been able to maintain control of their dialect because of their proximity to Mexico. Their dialect, although somewhat corrupted, more closely resembles standard American Spanish than the dialect of Puerto Ricans in East Harlem, who are further removed from their homeland; the Spanish that Puerto Ricans speak probably suffers more from having had to acquire an acculturation vocabulary. Under the present conditions, the Cubans now residing in the United

States probably find themselves in the same situation as the Puerto Ricans. The situation will create a semantic problem in view of their having to learn and assimilate new connotations of words and concepts.

Some Effective Teaching Methods

It is critical that the full potential of disadvantaged Spanish-speaking children be realized in spite of their formal language deficiencies. The forms of communication characteristic of Spanish-speaking children raise important educational problems. The acquisition of knowledge obviously requires some degree of facility with formal language. These children are capable of utilizing language in a rich and free fashion in their environment and have well-developed, if sometimes corrupted, ways of expressing themselves, but they are sorely lacking in advanced linguistic form. The problem, then, is how to help them attain this formal level of language so that their creative potential can be realized.

In a recent language research study (Horn, 1964–68) conducted in San Antonio, Texas, special procedures and techniques were utilized in an attempt to achieve such a goal. In order to develop a standard oral language in these disadvantaged children, a series of lesson plans, based on science material, was written using audio-lingual techniques to teach these children basic sentence patterns in English. The teacher served as a model and the children repeated a particular sentence pattern until it became habitual. Later, through activities, suggested in the lesson plans, that were rich in concrete experiences, the children had a chance to express themselves freely with the language they had acquired. Since research has pointed out that disadvantaged children are apt to learn better through physical and visual means (Riessman, 1962), every opportunity was afforded them to see and manipulate the particular object or situation they learned to talk about during the language drills. In addition to the linguistic build-up they received in English, some of them also used the same lesson plans with a linguistic buildup in Spanish. This procedure not only minimized the language barrier, but also afforded the children an opportunity to improve what has been termed their deficient vocabulary in their native language.

Thus, it would seem essential that methods of teaching formal language to disadvantaged children take advantage of their communication style by employing teaching techniques that stress the visual, the physical, and the active as much as possible. These techniques are in essence the procedures used in teaching English as a second language. However, one must bear in mind that there is no exclusively "correct" approach. It is suggested only that various techniques and procedures be applied to the situation and that the school make sure that these children learn at least to understand its formal language before embarking on any reading program.

AMERICAN INDIANS

Robert W. Young

A HALF-CENTURY ago, the reservation Indian schools were unusual on the American educational scene in that they were the only segment of the national school system wherein a primary concern was the teaching of English as a second language and Anglo-American culture as a second way of life to a student body composed *entirely* of children from a different cultural-linguistic background—from as many such different backgrounds as there were tribes, in fact.

The scene has undergone many changes since that time, but the special problems involved in Indian education have not disappeared on all reservations. They remain important factors in some Alaskan villages and in some Indian communities in western states. In fact, the problem of teaching English as a second language and Anglo-American culture as a second way of life to Indian children who enter school with little or no previous experience in those subject areas remains a focal point of the education program serving America's largest Indian tribe—the Navajo.

Although in the past, the peculiar complex of problems involved was present to some extent in other school systems serving the children of European immigrants and those of national linguistic minority groups—the Spanish-speakers of the Southwest, for example—its closest modern parallel in the United States is probably the situation that has developed in recent years in certain urban centers with the influx of Cuban refugees, Puerto Ricans, and members of subcultural groups from regions where the language, although English, diverges significantly from standard American speech. The resulting crisis in education, coming as it has within the especially favorable social climate of the mid-twentieth century, has attracted the attention of a host of trained technicians, who have brought the specialized knowledge of many disciplines to bear on the peculiar problems of educating cultural-linguistic minorities.

Educators, linguists, psychologists, anthropologists, and sociologists have played a prominent role in developing the modern techniques of language teaching and induced cultural change that are presently an integral part of many school programs. The same techniques are rapidly being adapted to the requirements of reservation Indian schools, supplementing and reinforcing those methods that Indian education had developed, from its own resources, in the past. Not only have modern methods of teaching English as a second language (ESL) become part of the teaching program in Indian schools, but universities, foundations, and specialists from many parts of the country are collaborating in the training of teachers for Indian schools and in the production of instructional materials adapted to local Indian needs. The University of California at Los Angeles and the University of California at Berkeley both operated special training sessions during the summer of 1967 for teachers of Navajo Indian children, and the Alaska Rural Teachers Project was established in 1966, financed primarily by the Ford Foundation, at the University of Alaska. In addition, a number of universities and colleges in New Mexico and Arizona, as well as in other states, have incorporated into their curriculum courses designed to meet the unique training needs of teachers of Indian children. To no small extent these developments represent a continuation of efforts begun by the Bureau of Indian Affairs in the early 1940's.

The Relationship Between Language and Culture

Cuban refugees, Puerto Rican immigrants, Mexican-Americans, speakers of regional dialects of American English, and non-English-speaking Indians and Eskimos share the need to learn standard American English as a second language; to this extent they are similar. However, upon analysis of the circumstances surrounding each such group, it becomes obvious that the similarity is superficial. In accomplishing his objective, each student of English as a second language is confronted by a set of obstacles stemming from divergent features peculiar to his first language and first cultural environment.

In the case of an educated Cuban refugee, the learning of English, although a problem of significant proportions, is primarily one of acquiring the ability to think and express himself in a new, but generically related, language, within the framework of a set of cultural concepts, most of which already form part of his past experience. Not only can he relate elements of American culture to counterparts in the system in which he was reared, and thus transfer them to the new cultural-linguistic situation, but also, to further simplify the problem, he finds a wealth of lexical elements in English that are cognate with familiar terms in his own native Spanish—*language/lenguaje; system/sistema; member/miembro; second/segundo; different/diferente; school/escuela; mountain/montaña*, to list a few. In addition, although there are many phonological and grammatical differences between Spanish and English there is, at the same time, a large area in which they overlap, even in these aspects of the two speech systems—far more than is the case between either English or Spanish and Navajo, Eskimo, or Mandarin.

Language is an aspect of culture, and culture, including its related speech system, is made up of a complex set of habitual modes of behavior, perception, and reaction to the world. Together, culture and language establish the frame of reference within which a society lives and functions, but the cultural-linguistic framework of one social group may diverge radically from that of another and different community.[1] All languages share certain universal concepts that are not culture related (for example, sky, hand, man, fire, cloud, eat, walk), but obviously they do not share those ideas and peculiar features that constitute the areas of difference between speech communities (for example, acre, millionaire, banker, vaccinate, edit).

The Interference of Cultural
and Linguistic Differences in Language Learning

Once firmly established, customary modes of speech and behavior, as with other types of habits, are difficult to modify. Such preformed habits interfere with the process of learning to participate in another culture and of acquiring the ability to communicate in its speech system. Confronted with the unfamiliar features of a different language and culture, our first inclination is to seek counterparts corresponding to familiar elements in our own system on the mistaken premise that all features important in our own experience must be universal; we tend to relate and explain the unfamiliar in terms of the familiar. When J. H. Beadle (1873) inquired into Navajo language and culture nearly a century ago, he proceeded on the premise that such concepts as that of a Supreme Being were universal. The misinterpreted response to his inquiry led Beadle to the erroneous conclusion that Navajos knew little about the attributes of God, rather than to the more accurate conclusion that the concept of a Supreme Being was not a feature of Navajo culture. He recorded what his Navajo informant said, *whaillahay*, as the Navajo name for God. He would have been astonished and chagrined had he realized that the Navajo term he recorded for God was probably nothing more than *xólahéi*, roughly translatable as "Damned if I know!"

Seeking familiar patterns in unfamiliar situations, speakers of English and Spanish are likely to substitute such linguistic features as their own peculiar /r/ phoneme for those of the other language—an English-speaker may pronounce the /r/ of Spanish *ron* as though it were the English phoneme in cognate *rum*, and the Spanish-speaker may pronounce English *rum* as though it were the initial phoneme in Spanish *ron*. A pupil's substitutions become even less valid as approximations when the phoneme involved in the new language has no approximate correspondent in his own speech system, or when substitution fails to take

[1] See *Language, Thought and Reality*, by Benjamin Lee Whorf, Massachusetts Institute of Technology, 1956; *Language and Environment*, by Edward Sapir, reprinted in *Selected Writings of Edward Sapir*, Berkeley, 1949; "Cultural Implications of Some Navajo Linguistic Categories," by Harry Hoijer, *Language*, Vol. 27 (1951); "An American Indian Model of the Universe," by Benjamin Lee Whorf, *International Journal of American Linguistics*, Vol. 16, No. 2 (1950); *Psycholinguistics*, Supplement to *International Journal of American Linguistics*, Vol. 20, No. 4 (October, 1954).

into account phonemic distinctions that are used by native speakers to mark differences in meaning. The Navajo pupil who pronounces English *big* as *pig* by indiscriminate substitution of his own bilabial stop /b/ (like /p/ in English s*p*ot) for the distinctive English phonemes written /b/ and /p/ may not be understood. And by the same token, although there may be some remote acoustic similarity, the English-speaking person who pronounces Navajo *tl'aaí* (left-handed) as *cly* may be understood by a native speaker only if the context leads the latter to guess correctly.

Not only do pupils attempt to find phonological correspondents between their native language and the new speech system they are learning, but they look for corresponding grammatical features as well. Familiar distinctions in tense, mode, aspect, gender, and number seem indispensable if they are features of the native language, and pupils may search in vain for similar distinctions in a speech system to which these distinctions are entirely foreign. The idea that the Navajo pronoun *bí* can represent *he, she, it,* or *they* without indication of gender or number seems to reflect a glaring deficiency in a set of semantic distinctions essential to English-speakers. The English practice of suffixing a morpheme /-'s/ to the noun representing the possessor instead of to the noun possessed (for example, *boy's*) seems to be backwards to Navajo-speakers who prefix a possessive pronominal element to the noun representing the object possessed (*ashkii bimá*, "the boy's mother," that is, "boy his-mother").

Although any language-learning situation presents problems, the fact remains that learning a second language that relates more or less closely to our own familiar cultural background is generally easier than learning a new language that relates to a radically different culture; and if the second language is closely related to our own native speech form, the difficulty is further minimized. This is true because fewer of our previously formed habits require modification. As speakers of English, we learn French or Spanish with comparative ease, but Navajo or Mandarin pose many problems; by the same token a native speaker of Navajo would be expected to learn Jicarilla Apache, a related language, much more readily than English; and a speaker of Mandarin Chinese would be expected to learn one of the other more or less closely related Chinese languages with a minimum of difficulty. The same factors are involved in the relatively simple process of *translating* shared cultural concepts between two languages in contrast to the comparatively difficult problem of *interpreting* nonshared concepts between two distinct cultural-linguistic systems.

Cultural-Linguistic Diversity Among American Indians

The basic principles underlying modern ESL programs are applicable generally in language-teaching situations, irrespective of whether the learner is a participant in one of the regional forms of Western European-American culture or a member of a different cultural system, but their application is likely to be most effective if the content of the ESL program is closely adapted to the peculiar requirements of each learning situation. (Instructional materials and other program elements that have proven to be effective in teaching English as a second language to Spanish-speaking people may not be equally productive when applied for the same purpose to learners whose first language is Navajo, Apache, or Eskimo.)

Adaptation of such materials, however, requires careful identification of the areas of major divergence between the target language and culture on the one hand, and the learners' native language and culture on the other. On the premise that such differences will constitute predictable problem areas for learners in any ESL program, they will become focal points in the development of planned instructional materials. The identification of areas of cultural and linguistic divergence, in turn, requires a carefully detailed process of contrastive analysis.

A basic ESL program designed for the teaching of English to Spanish-speaking people has wide application with minimum need for regional adaptation to meet special local requirements within the broad Spanish-speaking community. Not so, however, with reference to the speakers of American Indian languages. In the first place, Indian cultures do not all share, with regional variations, in a broad common cultural system comparable to the Western European-American pattern. There is no general "Indian culture"—there are many *Indian cultures*, and their divergence from one another can be extreme depending, in part, on the regional environments in which they developed. Not only is there no "Indian culture," but there is no "Indian language"—there are many Indian languages. True, many of the tribal groups that were adapted culturally to the requirements of life in such geographical regions as the American Southwest, the eastern woodlands, and the Great Plains shared a number of cultural elements, and many groups of Indian languages are interrelated after the fashion of English-Spanish-French-German-Russian-Greek. At the same time, however, such tribes as the Iroquois were as different culturally from the Pueblos as, perhaps, they were from the Mayas or the Kurds; and the several families into which Indian languages are grouped seem to be as unrelated to one another as Indo-European and Sino-Tibetan.

In the American Southwest alone the languages of the neighboring Navajo, Zuñi, and Hopi Indians are as dissimilar as English, Finnish, and Mandarin. There is not even a common language spoken by the culturally interrelated Pueblo Indians in New Mexico. Some speak Keresan; some speak one of the languages of the Tanoan group (Tiwa, Tewa, Towa), which, although related to one another in the sense that Spanish, Rumanian, and French are interrelated, are nonetheless not mutually intelligible; and the members of one Pueblo group, the Zuñi, speak a language that is not demonstrably relatable to any other Indian language.

As Hoijer (1946) points out, there is greater linguistic diversity among the aboriginal languages of the Americas than in any other part of the world, and "furthermore, this diversity is found in grammatical structure and phonology, as well as in historical origin. There are no structural or phonemic features peculiar to all or a majority of American languages which set them off in comparison to other groups. In brief, then, the term American Indian languages is only a geographical designation, it has neither historical nor a-historical classificatory significance."

Hoijer lists fifty-four linguistic groupings, each comprising a number of specific languages, for North America north of Mexico alone, an additional twenty-three for Mexico and Central America, and at least twenty for South America, though little is known as yet about the interrelationship of South American aboriginal languages.

On the basis of cultural-linguistic divergence then, the development and adaptation of ESL materials and instructional programs for American Indians pose many problems. Language-teaching materials cannot be built around the contrastive analysis of a common Indian language or culture, but must be constructed on the basis of analysis of many Indian languages and cultures for use with specific Indian groups. Materials designed for use among the Navajo are not equally adaptable to the requirements of the Zuñi, the Sioux, or the Eskimo.

One teacher, whose method was described in a 1904 publication of the Bureau of Indian Affairs entitled *Teaching Indian Pupils to Speak English*, observed that "the work will be greatly enhanced if the method is varied to suit the needs *of the particular class*." Had she pursued this line of reasoning further to conclude that the method would be most efficacious if it were adapted to suit the peculiar needs of each *particular tribal group* involved, and had she then proceeded to analyze the language and culture of the Indian community with which she worked as the basis upon which to develop her instructional program, she might have launched a highly effective ESL program over sixty years ago. But it was not until the 1940's that ESL principles and modern knowledge of the factors involved in cultural change became available to educators and began to find their way into the reservation schools. Since that time Indian education has contributed a generous share of the foundation upon which modern ESL programs rest.

III

Implications for Teachers

8

Nursery School and Kindergarten

Clyde I. Martin
Alberta M. Castaneda

THE PURPOSE of this chapter is to ferret out from the work of sociologists, psychologists, and linguists those findings or suggestions that have implications for the teaching of reading in programs designed for disadvantaged children from about age two through five. First, however, to provide a framework for this discussion, let us clarify the place of reading in early childhood education.

The Role of Reading
in Nursery School and Kindergarten

A primary concern of teachers and parents is the maximal development of all aspects of children's growth. The question must then follow, What is the contribution of reading to the education of children under six? In trying to answer this query, we will examine the well-known assumption that reading is a facet of the total language development of human beings.

READING AS A FACET OF LANGUAGE DEVELOPMENT

Although the acts of speaking-listening and reading have some common aspects, they also have differences. Many books have been written about reading, but few have enlightened us very much about the interrelationships of the speaking-listening and reading aspects of language use. Certainly, we entertain a host of questions about the age at which children are developmentally ready to read, even though in practice the time for beginning reading instruction is fairly well established as age six.

As a result of findings from studies of the relationships between the oral language and the intellectual development of young children, our present knowledge concerning the development of oral language seems to be on a firmer basis than our knowledge about reading. For example, according to Jensen (1967), children spend the first two years of their lives trying to gain sensory control of their environment and attempting to interconnect learnings from all the senses. They must acquire more connections in the first two years than they will ever have to again in their entire formal education. With the development of speech comes the crucial development of the verbal control of learning.

Young children may name objects; however, they probably think of the names as characteristics of the objects. Soon afterward in the process of learning development, the labels facilitate learning. In other words, verbal responses begin to control the learning process. Advanced human learning consists of linking verbal responses, whereas the learning of very young children and of animals is a process of linking stimuli with overt motor reactions (Jensen, 1967). It is here that we find agreement between Montessori and Piaget. According to Gardner (1968), they point out that a child is capable of manipulating transformations and other mental operations "only when he manipulates the object concretely." It seems reasonable, then, to infer that intellectual development is taking place in nursery-school children when they see, hear, say, and do, all more or less at the same time.

The continuing growth of learning in kindergarten children consists of the elaboration of verbal linking chains. Two examples of ways in which elaboration may be accomplished will be discussed here: (1) children who live in an environment rich in sensory stimulation and who are guided in language they understand by persons who care will, we can assume, develop many spontaneous concepts, "bits of knowledge that can be greatly expanded"; (2) in kindergarten, to insure the elaboration of verbal linking chains, children are introduced in a well-planned, structured manner to basic or elemental concepts from the physical and cultural environment that are selected because of generic value. These particular concepts have been referred to as scientific concepts. The introduction of concepts through the use of concrete objects makes possible the extension of verbal chains through the many relationships of these concepts to other ideas. Children might learn spontaneously that apples, oranges, and bananas are fruits, but such concepts as market, custom, law, and transportation must be structured by the teacher.

Therefore, the choice of generic concepts to be taught in the kindergarten program is crucial. Equally important are the processes through which children are guided in exploring the concepts. "If every concept is a generalization, then the relationship between concepts is a generality" (Vygotsky, 1962). Hence, each selected concept is placed in a position of generality that makes possible many relationships to other ideas, which children seem to work through under their own power.

The child who, through dramatic play, reconstructs in his own way experiences from the real world is probably able to do so because verbal processes, through generalization, have enabled him to formulate the aims and means for such complex behavior (Luria and Yudovich, 1968). The same kind of verbal responses may be responsible for the re-creation of experiences through drawing and painting, building with blocks, constructing in wood, and sculpting in clay or paper. In addition to providing direct experiences with concepts, and equally important, the kindergarten makes provision for the clarification and extension of concepts through dramatic play, movement, painting, sculpting, and music. It seems reasonable that these "direct" and "indirect" experiences with concepts are closely related and indispensable parts of the learning process.

READING INSTRUCTION AT THE PRESCHOOL LEVEL

Again we must examine the question, What is the role of reading in the intellectual development of preschool children? Although there may be differences in the semantic and linguistic learning of individual children, there is generally a lag between a child's ability to speak and his ability to express the same ideas in writing. This seems to offer some insight into the nature of reading. Writing is speech in thought and image only, requiring symbolization of the sound image in written signs (Vygotsky, 1962). Reading requires that children translate written symbols into appropriate sounds and also bring meanings to the symbols; thus, the abstract quality of both reading and writing appears obvious.

This does not mean, however, that the teaching and learning of reading do not begin with children under six years of age. A rather common practice in kindergarten is the labeling of objects after the meanings are grasped. The teacher supplies labels; children attach them to objects. Stories are written as children tell them. Poetic expressions are recorded. Records of experiences dictated by the children are made into books or charts. Children extend concepts by "talking through" an informational book with the teacher. Games, puzzles, and plastic alphabets are a common part of the kindergarten environment. In these ways the child is initiated into reading on his own. Whether or not the complex aspects of reading should receive a more direct kind of instruction is an unanswered question.

Few experienced persons in the field of early childhood education would question the value of literature in school programs. A love of, and positive attitude toward, reading are usually exhibited by children who from a very early age have had parents and teachers read aloud to them. The books that are available to American children are characterized by excellent illustrations and themes well chosen and presented. A child who values books and seeks them may be well on the road to becoming a reader. It is through imaginative literature read to them that preschool children participate in reading long before they are concerned about reading for themselves. However, this experience is a rarity with disadvantaged children.

In terms of the position that has been set forth in this section, the implications of Parts I and II for the teaching of reading to disadvantaged preschool children will be discussed.

Suggestions for Preschool Reading Programs for Disadvantaged Children

SOCIOLOGY AND PSYCHOLOGY: IMPLICATIONS

According to the profile sketched in Chapters 1–3, disadvantaged children (1) are economically poor; (2) are experientially impoverished; (3) live in an environment that is not education oriented; (4) lack a tradition of literacy; (5) feel rejected by the major cultural groups; (6) suffer from poor self-concepts; and/or (7) have difficulties with the English language considered acceptable by the school.

For many years research in the field of reading has pointed out that any one of these disadvantages might adversely affect a child in learning to read. A family that is constantly concerned with "maintenance needs"—food, clothing, and shelter—probably has little time, energy, or money left for other pursuits. It cannot provide a stimulating home environment or out-of-school experiences that may relate to the school culture.

Possibly, a culture of affluence, by its nature, supports in the disadvantaged feelings of rejection by the major groups as well as a personal sense of unworthiness. The common observation is that difficulty in learning to read is often symptomatic of much larger personality problems. Valuing self, family, and school are fundamental aids to learning that middle-class children often bring to their first school experience; teachers may fail to recognize the part that these values play in their success in teaching. Adequate feelings about oneself are surely more likely to develop in an environment in which a child knows he is accepted and valued. However, acceptance is not enough; children must have encounters with learning that demand growth of personal powers. To determine what these encounters should be and which will work in terms of children's capacities are crucial factors in teaching reading to any child. Failure of the school to recognize these variables often reinforces negative feelings.

A reasonable assumption based on studies of the disadvantaged is that they are deprived in terms of experiences that affect the "communication modes and cognitive structure" (Hess, 1964). Possibly, this is the area in which excellent programs for disadvantaged young children can make their greatest contribution to reading. If conceptual development progresses as children explore new meanings through seeing, hearing, saying, and doing, then the kindergarten and nursery school do "teach reading" as new objects are explored and their names learned, and as these experiences are related to other experiences through oral language. An extensive storehouse of meanings that can be handled orally may be one of the greatest resources a first-grade child brings to reading.

The fact that some children can be taught to read earlier than the age of six is fairly well known and accepted, but the question of general practice remains. Should teachers of these children be concerned with the printed symbol, the abstract aspect of reading; should they extend children's understandings of the physical and cultural world as they solve problems through concrete, immediate situations; or is there some effective combination of the two? Despite findings that have been projected about how young children learn language, many teachers continue to work with all children under the assumption that no one learns unless he reads from printed materials. This situation pinpoints one of the crucial needs in the nation today, that of the adequate preparation of teachers for young children.

Children from disadvantaged groups lack a tradition of literacy. Within this statement lies a clear implication for the teaching of reading to these children. The field of children's literature is extensive, replete with excellent books illustrated by well-known artists. From a very early age children can identify with experiences from literature; sometimes meaning is grasped through illustrations; at other times, their receptive vocabulary enables them to understand the story. A love of reading can begin early in a child's experience and be nourished throughout his preschool days. It follows that attitudes toward reading would then be positive when the child first reads for himself.

Many children from the culture of poverty have difficulty with English considered acceptable by the school. Of course, the acceptable language, standard American English, predominates in basic readers (although typical primers do not represent standard everyday language) and other reading materials that are introduced in the primary grades. Kindergartens and nursery schools are in a unique position to deal effectively with—or prevent—some of the problems that black, Indian, and Spanish-speaking children encounter in their initial reading experiences. For example, in their work with conceptual development involving meaning and oral language, teachers can provide models that assist black children in adding to their speech phonological and structural characteristics that will probably insure success in reading. There is also the possibility that black children might never develop these characterisitics unless effective language experiences are provided early in their lives.

If Indian and Spanish-speaking children who come from homes in which English is not spoken are to be introduced to reading English in the first grade, the readiness with which very young children learn a new language should not be overlooked in their preschool experience. Meanings from concrete experience and their appropriate symbols in oral English should permeate the early school experience. Drill or practice in English to which children bring no meaning is not to be confused with learning language in the sense that is described here. The reasons for the use of English in nursery school and kindergarten should be explained to the parents of these children, in particular those parents who may feel that their native language is being threatened. They are probably interested in successful school experiences for their children and should realize that school success depends on learning English.

LINGUISTICS: IMPLICATIONS

It is clear from the discussions in Chapters 6 and 7 that the oral language of at least several groups of American schoolchildren can be described and contrasted with the standard American English spoken by most American schoolchildren and by most American teachers. These children who come to school speaking a language or dialect other than standard American English encounter noticeable difficulty in learning to read. There are two possible solutions to the problem: change the child who approaches the task, or change the task. The final goal of reading standard American English is determined by the necessity of functioning within a society in which printed material is written in standard American English. The initial task, however, is open to change. That is, what is asked of children in beginning reading instruction can be varied in an attempt to fit the task to the particular child.

It is also true that as a group these children experience failure in learning to read more often than do children who come to school speaking standard American English. Is it, then, indicated that a way to change such children to make them better able to learn to read is to change their oral language to bring it closer to standard American English? If such a change is indicated, how can a preschool program contribute to that change?

Linguistic differences are quantifiable, and change in linguistic behavior is demonstrable. Such data are attractive. However, language is not the only characteristic in which disadvantaged children differ from the general population, and linguistic descriptions of their oral speech do not indicate their only language handicap. Most of these children are not middle-class children whose speech varies from the accepted standard. They are poor children from cultural backgrounds different from the dominant culture. They are children whose ethnic identification and poverty have brought them rebuffs, negatively influenced their motivation for school achievement, and perhaps damaged their self-esteem. Their parents' poverty has kept them from many experiences that might have resulted in rich conceptual development. In addition, they have been denied an interested, attentive adult to help them put their experiences into language. They have not been encouraged to speak nor rewarded for a precise or poetic quality of speech, for humor based on accidental word usage or sound substitutions, or for verbal invention. These, too, are language limitations and undoubtedly more basic to a child's cognitive functioning than are linguistic deviations from standard American English.

Beginning reading for many first-grade children is a process of decoding words and then speaking them and immediately perceiving their meaning. The printed symbol is being learned for the first time, but the meaning or image was acquired much earlier in the child's experience. For most children under six, however, and especially for disadvantaged children of this age, the preoccupation is with gaining meanings of many concepts and learning to speak their names or symbols.

Building the child's storehouse of meanings and developing his skills of inquiry are absolute necessities, for with the spoken words and meanings already acquired for the written symbols, learning to read becomes a problem of code breaking. It is important to remember that the code-breaking process of learning to read requires the seeking out and using of information, and that skills of information processing may be as vital to decoding as the parallel between the learner's oral speech and the printed word.

Is it possible for preschools to provide programs that will allow disadvantaged children to broaden their base of concepts, refine and extend concepts that they already have, sharpen their inquiry skills and at the same time increase their facility with language, their command of standard English, and their eagerness to communicate? The interrelation between these processes is complex, but perhaps that very complexity makes it possible to foster growth in all areas at the same time. If children are provided with objects, processes, and events to observe, and if, as they observe or otherwise perceive this display, *they report their observations, state or demonstrate their conclusions*, they are developing concepts, using inquiry techniques, and increasing their language abilities at the same time. The teacher's task is to be aware of the deficiencies that exist in all areas and tailor her lessons to fit the children involved.

What material will provide the child with some contradiction to his past experiences? What questions will allow him to respond verbally or otherwise and include that apparent contradiction in *his* mental constructs? What questions will allow the child to use his perception as a source of authority for the accuracy or appropriateness of his response? What perceptions and manipulations will allow the child to form his own concepts, uncontaminated by the teacher's perceptions or misconceptions, and his own abstractions from the material presented? Attempting to answer these questions presents the really great tasks of early childhood education—the aim being to build the child's confidence in his own perception and cognition at the same time as his ability to use language.

The phonological component of language used for this purpose is not as important as are the syntactical and semantic components. In observing pupils' language, teachers must remember the ages of these children. All young children struggle to make themselves understood. Every teacher of young children has sat patiently while a child started, stopped, began again, rethought, and tried again to state an idea, and then has indicated by some comment or action that she understood what he said, that he has *communicated*. No greater compliment can be paid to a child, no greater indication of his worth can be given to him, than that a teacher (or any caring person) valued his thoughts highly enough to wait, and to attend to him, while he put them into words; and no greater encouragement to try another time can be offered him than the knowledge that he has communicated.

The instructional aim is to provide materials, problems, and questions that will lead a child into a need to use language for clarification of concepts, and to provide an atmosphere of supportive inquiry that will encourage him to venture observations and conclusions.

A program attempting to build oral language in this way is sometimes called an experiential program. Critics contend that it attacks only the vocabulary or semantic aspect of language, and that only a sequential, directed program can produce the changes in phonology and syntax that are needed if the child is to break the code between oral and written English. This might be true if a label for a class or names for classes of objects, processes, or events were the only language given him or used by him in the experiential program. However, just in arriving at the class criterion, the child must inquire or conjecture about relevant information. This often cannot be done with a single word. Also, it is frequently noticed that children's conversation, dramatic play, and art work reflect their experiences vividly, and in these language may play a role.

Oral language is intrinsic to the child's learning and personal development. It must not be considered primarily a vehicle for learning to read. The quality of oral language must be judged not just in terms of the adequacy of sound production and word order but also in terms of the ideas that the learner has to communicate, his efficiency and power in communication, and his willingness or desire to communicate.

But if changes in phonology and syntax are deemed essential, can an instructional plan aimed at changing specific oral language patterns, phonology and syntax, be fitted into a preschool program? Perhaps the defensibility of structured, language instruction in a preschool might depend upon the primacy afforded to the goal of oral language change within the total program.

If the goal of oral language change dominates the program at the expense of the development of inquiry skills, at the expense of the child's eagerness and satisfaction with his own role in school, at the expense of broadening and refining concepts, at the expense of the use of language as a means of communication, then its value must be questioned. Learning to read, as a problem in information processing, requires effort and desire on the part of the learner. Any program hoping to prepare a child to learn to read cannot be concerned only with linguistic characteristics of the child's oral language but must also be concerned with other language characteristics, inquiry skills, self-image, and motivation.

This is not to say, however, that teachers should ignore the information now available regarding the speech of the specific groups of disadvantaged school-children. Just as there is the possibility of overemphasizing the importance of this information, there is also the possibility of making no use of it. The effectiveness of any language program will depend on the classroom teacher's knowledge of the role of language in intellectual and personal development as well as her knowledge of the elements of contrast between the speech of the children and standard American English.

In summary, then, a realistic reading program for disadvantaged children seems to require teachers who understand the needs of their pupils—both linguistic and cultural—and who view reading as a part of total language development on the principle that children involved in experiences planned for concept learning must work with the language necessary to handle the ideas.

9

Primary Level: Grades 1-3

L. Jean York
Dorothy Ebert

ALMOST every parent sends his child to elementary school hoping that he will learn to read during that first magic year in school. For thousands of parents and children, disadvantaged children in particular, the first year of school is a frustrating experience because the child does not make satisfactory progress in reading.

It is apparent from Parts I and II that schools have an opportunity and a responsibility to aid disadvantaged children by (1) translating the values of the home in such a way that the children continue to respect and appreciate their homes and families as they learn the values of the school and the majority of society; (2) providing an atmosphere that is conducive to building a healthy self-concept; and (3) adjusting the curriculum to the needs of disadvantaged children by starting with development in language and vocabulary before attempting to teach reading. This chapter is devoted to the identification of methods that can be used by primary-school teachers to adjust the language-arts curriculum to the needs of disadvantaged children in order to achieve these objectives.

Preserving Old Values and Teaching New

CHANGING LANGUAGE PATTERNS

By the time children enter school, they have learned to live in their home environment, and they have become identifiable members of a particular culture—a culture sometimes different from, but not inferior to, the culture of the middle

179

class. They use the dialect or language that is used in the home and with it readily communicate their needs and thoughts. Their language is part of their unique pattern of behavior, is representative of their culture, and is essential to their self-concept; hence, it must be accepted with understanding and empathy. A child's use of a pattern that differs from standard American English can be an opportunity to teach a substitute or alternate pattern to express his needs at school. By teaching alternative, acceptable, and appropriate forms rather than being critical of those used in the home, the teacher is helping the child to live in two worlds—his home and his school.

One of the most important implications for teachers is found in Chapters 6 and 7, which identify the language characteristics of disadvantaged white, black, Spanish-speaking, and American Indian children. Since language is a body of sound and meanings held in common by a linguistic group (Strickland, 1957), it is entirely predictable that a variety of speech structures would be apparent in different groups. However, in our society, standard American English, as defined through usage by the majority culture, is the speech for formal usage. Texts in reading and other content areas are almost without exception written in standard American English. Reasonable command of standard American English is also necessary if children are to gain social acceptance and ultimately economic independence. Consequently, teachers must teach the structure and system of standard American English. But, in the process, teachers should help children understand that their own dialects are acceptable in the family group and in any other informal situations. They should help children have pride in their home, culture, and language, but they must also provide them with the skills to develop, as Strickland (1957) puts it, a "wardrobe of language" that is appropriate for different occasions.

McDavid (1969) has said that each language has its own system and structure —thus standard American English is new content for disadvantaged children. In the methodology for teaching this new content, teachers should be sensitive to each child's feelings and constantly aware of his need for consonance with his cultural group. When dissonance occurs and he becomes alienated from his group, he is, indeed, a lonely wayfarer and a more likely future dropout.

Much initial attention should be given to two of the basic language skills: listening and speaking. Disadvantaged children need to be trained both to hear and to reproduce the language with which they must perform throughout their academic life. While intensive language training is going on in the primary grades, their own language—that of the home environment, whether it be a dialect of English or another language such as Spanish—should not be rejected or held up to ridicule by the teacher.

The various disadvantaged groups do not share language structure or systems of speech, but they do share some language problems. With the information available in Part II, primary-school reading teachers can proceed to the problem of helping individual children.

As a first step in the attempt to teach the standard language prior to beginning reading, teachers should determine as precisely as possible the range and degree of language differences that may be expected in the classroom. They should determine each child's "pattern of error" (Manning, 1969) in order to make a status profile of the individual pupil's instructional need. The extensive individual and group use of the tape recorder, the use of dialogues in small and large groups, and the provision for informal oral language experiences are useful in accomplishing this task. Teachers who seriously attempt to overcome language handicaps must, first of all, create a *talking* and *listening* classroom. The emphasis must be on getting children to experiment with language—never on keeping them quiet!

Furthermore, correct language models should be supplied readily and repeatedly for children struggling to acquire language facility. Ruddell (1966) states that "the teacher's model and that of other children could also exert a positive influence on children's language development in the classroom." Primary teachers of language should be constantly alert to the need for appropriate language models. Allowing a child with adequate language development to "express himself freely" is one thing, but leaving a non-English-speaker or a child with restricted language development to flounder helplessly for grammatical constructs or experiential concepts that he does not possess is quite another. The presentation of appropriate language models should be an on-going activity in the classroom where disadvantaged children are struggling to elaborate and expand language skills. Ample opportunity must be given for each child to interact verbally with his teacher and his peer group. Such practice may be provided during well-planned, structured language sessions, with emphasis on strengthening specific skills or patterns, and in a variety of informal ways throughout the school day.

Role playing, story telling, language experience charts recorded by the teacher from pupil dictation, group discussions, and planning of all classroom activities are examples of such language enrichment (Kane, 1964; Edman, 1967; Ching, 1965; Strickland, 1963). Metfessel points out in Chapter 4 the need to build a fund of experiences along with the related vocabulary for nonnative speakers. Extra care should be taken to give the children concrete illustrations whenever possible and to check often for comprehension. Careful teachers of the disadvantaged take nothing for granted as new words and concepts are developed; instead, they spend considerable time relating known to unknown and developing precise meanings.

When extensive individual use of the tape recorder is employed, the teacher has an opportunity to identify each child's gross language deviations and to plan specific remediation. In this regard, there is considerable help today from the linguists who have amply illustrated many of the specific language problems of various ethnic groups within the disadvantaged community. With more abundant and precise diagnostic information becoming available concerning the language needs of the disadvantaged, it is reasonable to expect improved teaching.

In summary, Smith (1969) states that improved oral language makes possible a specific kind of classroom situation: "(1) a social setting which stimulates constant practice in the use of language; (2) an environment rich in the things, the experience, and the ideas, for which words stand; and (3) adult example and assistance in the clearly motivated maturing of language skills."

CHANGING SOCIAL VALUES

Competition, individual excellence, and material wealth are less valued by certain other cultures than by the American middle class. For example, Indians and Latin Americans value group membership more than personal competition. It is important that teachers help children to understand the strengths of their respective cultures rather than simply stressing the superiority of middle-class culture.

Many disadvantaged children are not competitive about grades nor about excelling in their class; they tend to accept little responsibility for their own learning. Yet, learning is one of the most important means for the child to become self-realizing, to become mobile in society, and to become a member of a different economic group. Therefore, it should be organized in such a way that children can pursue some of their own real interests. It needs to be organized in such a way that they feel free enough to experiment yet secure enough to fail on an occasional attempt at learning without being punished (Bruner, 1961). The learning environment must provide outlets for frustration and good-natured exuberance, for children thrive on movement, activity, and projects. Disadvantaged children are accustomed to the physical expression of emotions and ideas. Indeed, they are "action oriented" and often express what they are unable to verbalize by bodily movements or by acting out. Teachers who stifle this natural outlet for self-expression risk not only the pupil's loss of enthusiasm for learning but also the loss of an extremely valuable vehicle for language development.

Reading satisfies many of the requirements of an effective school program, since literature abounds with tales of excitement and adventure, stories of humorous events, stories containing funny, make-believe language, and stories about a young child's desire for a better future. The creative teacher who makes good children's literature come alive in the classroom can encourage disadvantaged children to expand their world of experience and imagination. As they identify with fictional or real characters from the world of books, they may increase their range of possibilities for living and learning.

Building a Positive Self-Concept

Warm acceptance of disadvantaged children and identification of their strengths are especially important in the primary grades. Such acceptance should include whatever language the children bring to school. Typically, a disadvantaged child comes to school with a positive self-concept (Soares and Soares, 1969). If from the outset the teacher focuses on his lack of knowledge in the areas related to middle-class experiences and pointedly rejects his language, the pattern of defeat and alienation is fairly well assured, for the child is very likely to develop a poor self-concept.

A highly motivated, concerned teacher, able to see past the "problems" to the "potential" of such children, refuses to despair of them. Instead, she sets about providing the intensive oral-language foundation that must precede success in most academic tasks and takes pains to provide these experiences in a creative, flexible, and happy classroom situation where the children can feel accepted and worthwhile.

The home language of the children should be respected and might be used as a basis for extended and expanded language learning. Some of the most exciting and rewarding language experiences, both oral and written, occur in the classroom where these children and an appreciative and sensitive teacher meet. Kohl, in his excellent book entitled *Teaching the "Unteachable"* (1967), provides many rich examples of what can happen when the life experiences and language of disadvantaged children are treated with respect and appreciation in the classroom. Some exciting and promising experiments with bilingual teaching in the primary grades with populations of disadvantaged Mexican-American, black, and white children indicate how easily most young children take to language learning and point the way to building bridges of understanding between cultural groups (Arnold, 1968a).

There are so many rich possibilities for using children's life experiences to promote language growth that it would be impossible to list them here. One enthusiastic and perceptive young teacher constructed an eye-level, freestanding bulletin board for her classroom and labeled it simply "Class News." Each morning simple one- or two-sentence news items supplied by the children were quickly printed and placed on the newsboard. A typical day's headlines might include: Dan has a brown puppy; Mary wore a new yellow slicker; Tommy is eight today; Angela skinned her knee; Manuel's father has a new blue truck; today we will visit the bakery. Many primary teachers have found that the use of a large-print typewriter in the classroom to type out what the children say right before their eyes is a very satisfying experience for children just beginning to discover the magic of communication. Often a holiday, field trip, or class project can lead to a pupil-made book that can be read so that the experience can be shared by the class over and over again. Using the children's own language and common experience to produce teacher-pupil-made reading material has a number of obvious advantages. Not only does it promote a desire to read, but it also bolsters the child's self-image and sense of worth, since it is his *own* language that is being recorded for the class to read.

It is especially important in the primary grades that disadvantaged children be met with respect and acceptance. Riessman (1962) states repeatedly that the disadvantaged child does not so much need love as he needs *respect* in the classroom. As Havighurst and others point out elsewhere in this book, the mere fact that a child lives in a slum, belongs to a minority group, or comes from a home where the income is below the poverty level does not mean that this child, even though suffering some language and concept deficiencies, is necessarily seriously disadvantaged if family ties are strong and there is emotional security and ethnic pride. If middle-class teachers can meet such children with genuine respect, assess objectively both their strengths and weaknesses, and then create a learning atmosphere in which they can find repeated, steady success, the primary years will be rewarding for them. Building a positive self-concept and a feeling of "it is fun" and "I can do it" are crucial ingredients in the primary years. An atmosphere of positive expectation must permeate the school if disadvantaged children are to overcome their handicaps to learning.

Meeting Special Needs

HEALTH NEEDS

Many disadvantaged children come to school suffering from chronic colds, aching teeth and ears, poor eyesight, and in some cases actual pangs of hunger. Hence, their attendance at school may be irregular because of their illnesses. Inasmuch as a child cannot be expected to concentrate on instruction when physical problems are distracting him, it behooves the school to alleviate these if possible.

Most schools have a hot lunch program that can provide a free noontime meal and some now provide a low-cost breakfast using surplus foods. When breakfast is not available, however, an interested teacher can sometimes obtain a carton of milk and a slice of bread for the child who is in discomfort because he had no breakfast. In addition, in many school districts, philanthropic service clubs will pay for the treatment of vision and hearing problems of disadvantaged children. However, someone must initially refer the needy children to the philanthropic groups.

Teachers can also give academic assistance to children who are frequently absent because of illness by offering them individual attention before, during, or after school. A one- or two-week absence probably means that a child has missed considerable instruction in reading skills and that he is seriously handicapped in his knowledge of the phonology that has been inductively presented through first-hand experiences. The tutoring offered by the teacher can be the key to the child's continued progress in reading and language arts. Some retentions of first-year children could be avoided if this kind of individual instruction were available for all children.

It is quite true that many disadvantaged children come to school with severe social, emotional, and physical problems that interfere with learning. These problems are often acute, and the children will not make satisfactory academic progress unless some attempt is made to relieve them. For this reason, it is vital that the modern elementary school that hopes to meet the needs of children of poverty have adequate health, psychological, and social services available within the school.

A school nurse, trained counselor, and school social worker or visiting teacher are essential. In addition, direct referral channels to community agencies that are equipped to meet the specialized physical and mental health needs of the children are a must. When broad supportive services of this kind are made available to classroom teachers, teachers may be trained to observe children carefully and take advantage of the special services available to meet their needs. Primary teachers play a key role here; the earlier a child's special physical or mental health needs are discovered and treatment is begun, the better are his chances for normal school progress. Although these problems may not be directly related to his language differences, it is obvious to any experienced classroom teacher that a child who is suffering from severe emotional disturbance or serious physical neglect cannot hope to make much academic progress until these basic needs are met.

FINANCIAL NEEDS

A definition of poverty depends not only on total income, but on the amount of necessary family expenditures, which vary with the size of the family and the location of residence. This means that depending on whether the family is urban or rural, there are accompanying variables of space and recreational facilities, and there may be supplementary sources of food, such as gardens and livestock.

Some children may come from a family whose income averages over $6000 a year and still be considered needy if that income is insufficient to provide the common necessities of food, clothing, and shelter for the numerous members of their household. Young children are very sensitive to the implied criticism when the teacher must ask for their funds day after day. Hence, it may be necessary to provide an installment plan if a family is to pay for the school books needed for their eight or ten children. Or, it may be necessary to compute the charges for school supplies according to a family's ability to pay. A plan should be devised so that no child sits in school six to eight weeks in the fall without supplies because his parents could not pay for them on the day funds were due.

PAUCITY OF VERBAL AND COGNITIVE SKILLS

For a long time educators and others concerned with education have given at least lip service to the close association between language development and academic success. One obstacle, lack of skill in the use of standard American English, has increasingly been recognized as a major contributing factor to the success of a child beginning his formal education. Furthermore, many years of research in reading have underscored the necessity for adequate oral language development prior to success in reading. Loban (1966) points out that children who do not possess adequate language simply do not learn to read, to comprehend, or to enjoy and appreciate what the school is trying to teach.

Linguistically different learners, even if not seriously handicapped in other ways, still present primary teachers with a formidable task; for as long as their speech remains stunted or nonstandard, they will be socially and educationally marked and will generally find academic achievement to be limited. It would seem obvious, then, that particularly in the primary years children should be given every opportunity to overcome their language deficiencies and to learn to use standard American English with ease and agility. It is not enough for them to acquire an enriched vocabulary in a socially unmarked dialect alone. They must learn to manipulate language in meaningful and efficient ways. In other words, the structure of language, the use of movables and subordinate elements, is of equal importance. Children should constantly be encouraged to listen for and to respond in sentences with increasing elaboration and variety. Reading success for disadvantaged children must entail the cognitive uses of language.

Special attention, moreover, should be given to special words that give precise meaning to language. Prepositions, conjunctions, modifiers—the words that make language "hang together" and give it precise and subtle meanings—these usually need to be taught to children who use restricted language. For example, an enterprising first-grade teacher of Mexican-American children (who typically have great difficulty with prepositions) spends a few minutes each day playing the preposition game. She simply uses some common classroom object, such as a book or pencil, and lets the children check to see if the child who is "it" can correctly place the book *behind* the record player, *under* the round table, *beside* the acquarium, *over* the sink, *between* two yellow books, and so on.

Making a game of language learning in this manner provides spontaneous, informal motivation and at the same time gives concrete illustration to expression and word meanings. Once the game is understood and several of the prepositions learned, letting a child give the verbal directions provides a further reinforcement of language learning.

The school curriculum is usually planned for children who are ready for reading, who, for example, have more verbal skills in standard English than disadvantaged children have. Most teachers teach reading to children in the primary grades by utilizing a good basal series that includes a teacher's guide and accompanying materials. Some educators say that disadvantaged children cannot learn to read from traditional books because they cannot relate the activities of the children in the books to their own lives. This may or may not be true. Loban's study (1966) indicates a correlation between a child's general language ability at the kindergarten level, as determined by vocabulary scores and by language ratings by his teacher, and his reading ability in the primary grades. He concludes that language ability is necessary for competence in reading. Thus the problem may well be the children's paucity of verbal skills rather than the content of the reading book. In this situation, language skills should be established before the reading program commences. Furthermore, speaking and listening should be an integral part of the whole language-arts curriculum.

Teachers might evaluate the content and format of the reading book and select another vehicle for instruction for children who cannot meet success with the traditional material. For example, teachers might develop oral language and reading by using content-based experiences presented in the classroom (Arnold, 1968b). Today when publishers have provided teachers with a wide variety of excellent tools for teaching reading, teachers must decide which combination of materials will best help their pupils.

It seems rather imprudent to discard a sequential reading program that is successful with twenty-five children because five children cannot relate to the story or are having difficulty with phonic analysis skills. The twenty-five children making satisfactory progress might continue in their reading program, and other materials and methods might be selected for the five children who are not succeeding. A good many instances of children making little progress in reading can be related to the fact that the teacher was trying to take children with little language experience and motivation for learning to read through a fixed number of books at each grade level.

Since disadvantaged children generally have had a minimal range of stimuli at home, teachers should expand their knowledge by using a wide variety of traditional and innovative materials in the classroom. Children can expand their knowledge by listening to tapes of favorite stories, by listening to records, and by manipulating objects. Language is learned as it is heard and used to express thought; furthermore, language is facilitated as the learner has an opportunity to see a relationship between a concrete object and its label or its function. An example of this is the primary-grade child who plays with a bar magnet, a scrap of paper, a number of pins and paper clips, iron filings, a piece of cotton, and a pair of scissors. During the process of manipulation he needs to be able both to name the objects and to communicate the function or classification of the objects. Through such processes he is learning both the phonology and grammatical structure of language as it relates to reading, or content. He is also extending his critical thinking skills.

A second example is the child who plays "store" with objects in the classroom. The presence of empty boxes and containers for items commonly purchased by more advantaged families may provide an opportunity for the child to learn about such vegetables as asparagus, Brussels sprouts, broccoli, and avocados; about such fruits as pineapples, pomegranates, and grapefruit; or about such household supplies as floor wax, fly spray, and paper napkins. These experiences, once again, expand language and thinking skills necessary for competence in reading, mathematics, and other areas of the curriculum.

Reading requires that children bring meaning to the written symbols on the page. Part of the task of teaching the disadvantaged is expanding the number and quality of experiences these children have. Teachers can assist in this process by providing a curriculum filled with exciting learning experiences, such as field trips, motion pictures, film strips, and interesting experiences in the classroom in which the children are actively involved. Teachers must expand the vocabulary and understanding of the children beyond what they have learned at home.

During instructional activities in the classroom the teacher can extend the child's understanding by the use of thoughtful questions. As Havighurst points out in Chapter 1, parents of disadvantaged children tend to speak to their children in a restricted language, whereas middle-class parents use an elaborated language. Consequently, disadvantaged children need help in seeing relationships, in recognizing causal factors, in comparing, in classifying, contrasting, and categorizing, and in sequencing and generalizing. Teachers must teach thinking skills that are of a higher order than rote recall of fact.

Teachers should also help disadvantaged children correlate concepts learned in language arts, mathematics, science, health, music, and art. Some common vocabulary appears in each of the content fields; in other instances, a child can unlock the familiar word using his reading skills but must be taught an expanded or different meaning for the word in the new content area. Such words as *set*, *bridge*, *regroup*, and *observe* have a variety of different and appropriate meanings in the various disciplines. Jacobs (1964) explained that a word is a label: "It is not the experience itself, but it is an identification tag for an experience. It is a verbal sign, signal or symbol. . . . the label is useful only to the extent that it 'calls up' an experience for both the speaker and listener or writer and reader. . . ." The teacher can help children to expand their knowledge by providing instructional experiences with words where alternate meanings for words are clarified.

In order to achieve the objective of expanding vocabulary meaning, primary teachers must carefully and prudently plan prior to the class period. It is necessary that they know what specific skills they are going to teach each child, what activities they are going to use, what learning materials are needed, and how they will evaluate the child's changed behavior, since learning is evidenced in changed behavior. They should make frequent written anecdotal records of each child's performance as he reads, for no teacher can remember precisely the numerous correct and incorrect responses made by each child if she waits until the end of the day to make such an evaluation.

Jackson (1967) states that a teacher may have as many as one thousand interactions with children per day that are unrelated to her teaching plans. The implication is that anecdotal recording—of reading errors, for example—should be done while the child is reading. Recording such data may seem unimportant to some teachers until they realize that the diagnosis of today's errors provides the basis for the next day's diagnostic teaching techniques. Teachers should take prompt action specific to their diagnoses rather than merely reiterating the time-honored phrase "meeting individual needs."

This process will enable teachers to provide an individualized sequential task for the child that is related to his present needs for learning. An analysis of the daily errors of each child gives teachers an opportunity to structure their teaching or reteaching of a concept or skill. This analysis also affords teachers an objective tool for a dialogue or meaningful discussion with the pupil concerning his personal progress. Like all children, disadvantaged pupils benefit from the teacher's personal interest in their problems. Many teachers have compassion and sympathy for the social and economic needs of the child, but are unaware that, by itself, this empathy is insufficient to help the child. When teachers complement their empathy and understanding with improved diagnostic teaching procedures for each child, they are effectively assisting their pupils.

NEED FOR INDIVIDUAL ACCEPTANCE AND POSITIVE SELF-CONCEPT

Each school has some families that immediately signal the teacher's attention because the past performance of the older children has caused the staff much difficulty. However, teachers need to be aware that each child within a given family is different. Teachers must assess each child's talents and capabilities individually and without reference to previous experience with older brothers and sisters. Children from the same family may have a wide variety of learning and coping styles; hence, each must have a chance to learn to read, utilizing his unique personal traits without being compared to those who have preceded him.

Children who drop out tend to have a lower self-concept, less skill in reading, and fewer interpersonal associations indicating a lack of peer acceptance and of "belonging." Ideally, the school organization should provide an opportunity for each child to obtain an education without the humiliation or boredom of repeating a particular grade with limited and unnecessarily repetitious learning experiences. Children need success and recognition; yet devastating numbers of disadvantaged children are "retained" each year because they have not mastered the same content as have children from more affluent homes. Research has indicated for years that children seldom benefit academically from retention in the same grade and that retention is psychologically damaging to the child's self-concept and negatively affects motivation: the child's desire to continue in school decreases until he reaches the legal age to drop out (Peyton, 1968).

The discussions in preceding chapters indicate that children who are not accepted, who do not read well, and who become alienated from their home and friends are the dropouts of tomorrow. Reading is a key to yearly promotion; reading is a key to building self-esteem; and reading is a key to learning other areas of the curriculum. Hence, primary teachers should provide reading instruction each day that will enable each child to learn something new in reading skills, something new in important ideas, something exciting about life, and something related to his important sequential development in the language arts. Teachers should analyze their instructional procedures accordingly. When the child in the primary grades, subjected to the so-called reading circle, reads a sentence or a paragraph and then "drops out" for the rest of the twenty-minute reading period while the other children read aloud, much of his learning time is wasted. Similarly wasteful is the interminable coloring and completion of unrelated mimeograph work that some teachers use to keep children busy while they manage three or four reading groups. Instead, teachers should encourage more productive activities so that children are actively involved with learning—activities such as reading library books, working in programmed learning, reading children's magazines, utilizing reading or writing laboratories, playing educational language-arts games, listening to tapes, making tapes of speech or reading, and viewing filmstrips.

Alternative instructional procedures such as these allow for further reinforcement and enrichment in reading, speaking, and thinking, and they also provide children with an opportunity to be responsible for some of their own instruction. A variety of reading and language-arts materials will stave off boredom and allow for self-pacing and self-selection while retaining a sequential developmental program in the group situation in which the teacher plans the sequence. Such instructional procedures also give children an opportunity to work and play with a greater number of classmates. This contact is helpful in assisting children to make new friends and to feel that they belong in the group. Furthermore, it gives them valuable practice using language relevant to academic content.

Perhaps the key words for teachers of disadvantaged children are *respect* and *expectation*. Often the problems these children bring to school seem, especially to beginning teachers, quite overwhelming. If teachers can meet them with *respect* for their worth as human beings and with genuine positive *expectations* for their success in learning, a positive learning environment will have been established. Over and over in the writings of sociologists, psychologists, and educators concerned with knowing and understanding disadvantaged children, one finds the notion that success comes in small steps, but each small success may represent a giant step to an individual child. The most effective teachers of disadvantaged children we have observed are those who make sure that each child experiences daily success in many small ways in the classroom. Each small achievement is noted and praised; each genuine effort is encouraged until the child develops the habit of success and the self-confidence that must precede sustained effort. No other task is more important, especially in the primary years, than that of giving a child the feeling that he is important and that he can achieve success! Much of this feeling of worth and achievement can be accomplished, moreover, by simply giving the child the opportunity to develop the language with which to express his wonder, curiosity, discovery, and feelings.

10

Intermediate Level: Grades 4-6

William R. Harmer

IF IT IS important to place emphasis on speaking, listening, and vocabulary development preceding and during the teaching of reading in the primary grades, it is even more important in the intermediate grades. There are three factors that create the need for this continued emphasis: (1) the greatly increased general, nontechnical vocabulary used in most basal readers and in most commercially prepared companion or enrichment materials, which requires of pupils greater skill in word recognition and vocabulary usage; (2) the use of materials with ever increasing numbers of words whose greatest pertinency is to a single subject-matter area; and (3) a continued and pressing need to present reading not only as a necessity in reaching desired goals but as an intrinsically enjoyable activity.

Meeting these needs is a considerably different task for teachers of disadvantaged children than for the teachers of the majority of children. Whereas the latter may often assume with justification that their children can add new listening, speaking, and reading vocabulary by relating it to what they already possess and use, the former may not. Teachers whose pupils are not disadvantaged may with minimal direct attention foster the development and correct use of all three vocabularies and reinforce this acquisition through their use in context. Although efforts in concept development must accompany these direct and indirect vocabulary activities, the background experience that the majority of these children have acquired in extraschool activities permits them to assimilate vocabularies with concepts. Thus each type of development contributes to the other.

Language and Reading

These assumptions clearly cannot be made about disadvantaged children. Earlier chapters in this book have treated various factors that must be taken into consideration when attempting to build a school program that is realistic in its requirements and attainable in its goals. Neither the development of concepts nor the development of vocabularies—both of which are necessary if the standard instructional materials of the intermediate grades are to be used with anything approaching interest and comprehension—may be taken for granted. One spokesman after another has pointed out different aspects of the problems faced by disadvantaged pupils: differences in culture and cultural expectations, differences in motivation within a school setting, differences in facility with the English language, and difficulties in trying to relate to the typical curriculum of American schools. Since no one advocates curriculum revisions that would place emphasis on maintaining the status quo for these children, or worse, on enabling them to become "better" at being disadvantaged, it would appear that teachers of intermediate-grade pupils must do several things if any of the present curricula are to be profitably pursued.

First, introductory or preparatory activities should be continued until in the teacher's judgment adequate oral language, vocabulary, concept development, and other prerequisites of reading skills are acquired. Second, to minimize the difficulties of having children deal with total abstractions, direct attention should always be given to cognitive development and to relating studies to what may be familiar to the children. This should be done for all children in all content areas, but it is vital for children with a limited range of experiences, vicarious or real, that are related to the school culture. A third general recommendation is that the practice of "covering" an entire course of study or "finishing" a reader or other text in a rigidly prescribed period of time be abolished. This practice is the plague of children whose homes and communities generally *do* support academic endeavor. It is an outright penalty when demanded of disadvantaged children, whose homes and communities are not oriented to an "everything done on time" and a "we'll help you finish it at home" approach to education or to life in general.

The question may be raised whether to employ these recommendations throughout the standard curriculum of the intermediate grades in an effort to achieve some progress in all areas or to reduce the areas of the curriculum and institute a concentrated effort in the areas that remain. As Bereiter and Engelmann (1966) stated, "The main concern is not with what disadvantaged children can do but do not, but what they cannot do but should be able to do if they are to succeed in school." The main question, then, is *what* constitutes success in school.

While there are many contributors to success, foremost are the communication skills: listening with comprehension (auding), adequate oral expression, effective reading, and adequate spelling. Without the possession of these skills, progress is drastically limited in other areas of the curriculum, such as science and social studies. Arithmetic too is adversely affected by the absence or underdevelopment of the communication skills.

The admonitions of Bereiter and Engelmann concerning the selection of experiences that will best enable disadvantaged preschool children to overcome their language handicaps pertain to programs for older pupils as well, but with an increased emphasis on reading skills. Labov suggests in Chapter 7 that underdeveloped auditory-discrimination abilities of black ghetto children may result in a nonstandard system of homonyms and that if teachers do not recognize this system for what it is, they may incorrectly assume that children do not recognize the difference in meaning between words such as *cold* and *coal* when in reality they simply do not "hear" the difference. Labov's judgment is that children can learn to read standard English quite well in a nonstandard pronunciation and that in the early grades, teachers' first concerns should be with the process of learning to read and not with the correction of nonstandard pronunciations.

Baratz (1968) concurs, pointing out that on the basis of "the success of vernacular teaching around the world, it appears imperative that we teach the inner city Negro child to read using his own language as the basis for initial readers. In other words, first teach the child to read (in his native dialect) then teach him to read in standard English."

There are, however, many educators who take exception to this view. In their opinion oral command of standard American English is a prerequisite for success in reading. The resolution of this conflict of judgments lies in differentiating between children with second-language gaps and interferences and children with nonstandard-dialect problems. As York and Ebert point out in Chapter 9, it is one thing for a child with a nonstandard dialect to read with understanding; it is another for a child to struggle with unfamiliar concepts, syntax, vocabulary, and/or phonology. Therefore, emphasis on standard pronunciation and syntax should be maintained.

During the earliest—and probably the most difficult—stages of learning to read, the children should not be immediately compelled to cope with the additional problem of drastic alteration of their own dialects. Although they are not required to exchange their dialects for the standard language as a part of their school experiences, they will be acquiring new vocabulary—both individual words and phrases or sentences—in the standard language and will be regularly exposed to the standard language of their teacher. If this kind of training has taken place during the early grades and if some attention has been given to the development of auditory-discrimination abilities, the children's base in terms of listening, speaking, and reading should be broad enough to permit an intensive program of standard English to be included in the reading program.

It is important that the reading-speaking-listening activities be thoroughly intertwined: the activities should reinforce one another as well as what has already been learned. Thus, work on phonics as a word-recognition technique in reading should be directly related to auditory-discrimination skills in listening and to standard pronunciation in speaking. If it is risky to assume that advantaged children will make their own analytical generalizations in regard to standard English listening-speaking-reading activities, the same assumption can be disastrous in relation to children who have neither the advantage of a long-standing proficiency in standard language nor, often, a cultural background that encourages perseverance in academic tasks.

The relationships between the spoken and written word, from individual letters to variant word endings to root words, must be taught directly, using as a vehicle any subject or material in which the children are interested. A deductive technique of teaching relationships and generalizations will probably be more effective than an inductive one, at least in the early stages of the program, since the children are still acquiring the standard language in which the rules being taught will apply. This is not to say that an inductive learning method should not be used. It remains a most valuable tool and can and should be employed whenever it is judged that the children possess the knowledge and experience with words to produce, consciously or unconsciously, the correct rules to explain differences in standard pronunciation as in *rat:rate* or *cut:cute*.

Motivation and Self-Concept

The following characteristics of background and of learning behavior observed in many—not all—disadvantaged children are likely to affect their school performance.

1. Their school failure experiences have far outnumbered their success experiences, hence their lack of familiarity with success lessens its value as a goal and its effect as a motivator.
2. Their capacity for delayed reward or delayed utility of a skill is very limited.
3. They are more successful in learnings which move from part to whole than in learnings which move from whole to part.
4. They persevere longer in single activity tasks than in multiactivity tasks.
5. They misinterpret praise for academic success as an extension of evaluation rather than as a reward.
6. They learn less from what they hear than do the majority of children.

Although these characteristics and others cited in preceding chapters contribute to some degree to the school difficulties of many disadvantaged children, they cannot all be directly countered by the school. No matter how desirable it may be to provide enriched life experiences for these children, the school's first responsibility lies in equipping them with the basic tools necessary for success both in school and in life in general. It is this success that builds self-confidence that in turn often leads to perseverance in task completion and to a broadening of interests. Increased time and emphasis on the communication skills of language and reading must, therefore, serve as a vehicle for increasing motivation and for developing concepts and individual enrichment.

In implementing these language activities with disadvantaged children, however, teachers should make sure pupils regularly experience real success. This admonition is made to all teachers, but it is of particular importance to teachers of the disadvantaged. As the reading program is expanded in the intermediate grades, organizing the work into simplified and, if possible, single tasks becomes increasingly important.

An additional factor in academic success is a positive self-concept. The effect of repeated academic failure or the withholding of social approval by school personnel, possibly because of nonstandard language, may be the development of a negative or at best a deflated self-concept. The role self-concept plays in motivation, in curiosity, in perseverance, and in all aspects of success or failure has already been amply described by authors representing several disciplines. At the intermediate-grade level many children have almost literally been taught to think of themselves as poor academic learners. This lesson has been learned directly through their self-observed difficulties in reading and other portions of the curriculum—difficulties that often result from inappropriate teaching methods rather than from their own intellectual limitations. Baratz (1968) points out:

> Because the educational system has been ineffective in coping with teaching inner city children to read, the system treats the reading failure (in terms of grading, ranking, etc.) as if the failure were due to intellectual deficits of the child rather than to methodological inadequacies in the teaching procedures. Thus the system is unable to teach the child to read, but very quickly teaches him to regard himself as intellectually inadequate, and therefore, of low self worth and low social value.

Children often experience difficulties because they sense the more subtle rejection of their language patterns by their teachers. According to Furst and Mattleman (1968), "The most successful teachers, those in whose classes student achievement is greatest, are the ones who accept their students as worthwhile individuals and make the students conscious of this acceptance." Flint (1968) concurs:

> A child's concept of himself as a learner is very dependent on the attitudes that you, his teacher, display. There is also strong evidence that his achievement is affected by the way you regard his learning attempts. The child looks to you for clues that he is on the right track—that he is understood, accepted, respected, trusted and loved. He finds these clues in your behavior. He sees acceptance or rejection in words, facial expressions, gestures and general mood.

What Can Be Done?

The conclusions of the amassed literature of several disciplines for teachers of disadvantaged intermediate-grade-level children are fairly straightforward. They do not generally represent great departures from accepted teaching procedures that take into consideration the developmental-psychological factors of learning. They do, however, represent decided changes in breadth of curriculum, teaching style, and subject emphasis.

PACING

Because of their slower rate of learning, disadvantaged children need a slower rate of pacing as they acquire the various skills that are an integral part of reading. This slower rate, of course, is required because teachers should break down skills into their component parts and teach each part directly. Assumptions of prior knowledge of concepts and of the meaning, use, and standard pronunciation of words cannot be made, and this fact will necessarily lengthen the time spent in introductory activities for a given study or series of lessons.

In addition, more time is required because, as Metfessel and Seng point out in Chapter 4, even when disadvantaged children do know fact A they frequently do not know closely related fact B. Thus in remedying lack of knowledge or experience, as well as in providing a more minute breakdown and direct instruction of all reading skills, more time will be required for teaching and for reinforcement of the teaching.

The case for more time to be spent in teaching reading to these children is not overstated and is not a mere hopeful generalization that increased amounts of time will heal the ills of the standard reading program. The need for more time to cope with gaps in or lack of knowledge or experience plus the need for a more carefully organized presentation of the skills of recognition are also evident in the fact that disadvantaged children often learn less from what they hear than do advantaged children. Stated simply, this means that there needs to be more talking with children and less talking to (or at) them. It also means that there will be a greater need to have the children make immediate and direct use of the skills they are being taught. The more abstract the skill, the greater will be the need to reinforce it through use. The concept of the word segment -*tion*, for example, may be unfamiliar in isolation but a few words in which it is used will probably be known, and others can be learned by *using* those familiar words.

ADAPTING TEACHING STYLE AND SUBJECT EMPHASIS

The teaching style used with these children, then, should place less emphasis on learning by listening to teacher admonitions and should capitalize on the strengths of visual and kinesthetic procedures, though auditory discrimination remains a basic skill.

From the standpoint of sheer maintenance of attention or involvement of the children, visual-kinesthetic methods are recommended and are readily implemented through the use of appropriate films, filmstrips, and audio-visual devices that require manipulation by the pupil. The use of language-listening posts that record written or spoken responses for comparison with correct responses can also be profitable: while they place learning intake emphasis on listening, they require manipulation of equipment and some form of learning output as a direct reinforcement. It is this output, either written or spoken, that provides teachers with diagnostic evidence whether or not pupils have correctly assimilated what is being taught.

The fundamental point in teaching reading to disadvantaged children in the intermediate grades is first making the decision whether or not learning to read is the goal of prime importance in the curriculum and, if it is, adapting all materials and procedures to the needs and the *present* level of competency of the children. Once this decision has been made, all activities and all subject matter areas become vehicles for reading instruction or, more basically, vehicles for language-reading instruction. Likewise, language serves as a vehicle for cognitive development.

If the earliest grades have concentrated on teaching reading in the children's own vernacular, a transition to reading in standard English should be begun in the intermediate grades if it is not already under way. This does not mean that every child *must* be launched into the transition at a given grade level or at the same time. Disadvantaged children have their share of individual differences too.

Planning a Program

The reading teacher of the intermediate grades, then, needs to retain the diagnostic, task-analysis approach of the primary-grade teacher for use in the development of word recognition skills. It is through this mechanistic assessment of the reading competencies and deficiencies of each child that the teacher can specifically identify their instructional needs and just as specifically set about teaching them. Surely the knowledge that a child cannot regularly isolate and identify the consonant blends of /str, sl, sk, sw/ is of more value to a teacher than a general feeling that he is "weak in phonics." Similarly, recognizing that a given pupil is able to read well enough to note details but often has difficulty identifying the main idea is of more value than being generally aware that he sometimes has trouble with comprehension.

Once they have assessed the pupils' specific needs, teachers should follow a specific teaching program. Prescriptive teaching would probably be a better way of describing the program because different exercises or activities are given to individual pupils or small groups. Two pages dealing with the consonant blends of /str, sl, sw/ may be torn from a phonics workbook and given to one pupil while another pupil is given a phonics word wheel dealing with the same elements. Other pupils may be using hand-held tachistoscopic devices to further develop sight vocabulary while still others are matching words with word meaning. The teacher may at the same time be working with a small group of children on one or more dictionary skills.

A prescriptive program of reading instruction requires a wide variety of materials. Basal readers may well be used if their interest and difficulty levels are appropriate for the children. Supplementary materials of every sort are needed for many purposes, ranging from word recognition practice to appreciation of literature. Individualized reading and spelling kits can also be valuable aids as can games, filmstrip projectors, and tape recorders. No enumeration of needed materials would be complete without including materials to be read for pleasure. Paperbacks, hardbacks, magazines, pamphlets, newspapers, and anything else of interest should be available, representing as many difficulty levels as are needed. This is not a restatement of the idea that by placing the child in a lush environment of reading materials he will learn to read. It is the next logical step.

After teachers have given children both general and specific reading instruction and have followed through with appropriate exercises and activities, children need to *use* their reading skills for their own purposes. True, teachers may have a hand in helping the children develop these purposes, but when skillfully developed they *are* the children's purposes, and these purposes include reading for pleasure. Reading for one's own purposes, including pleasure—that's the ultimate goal, isn't it? And the achievement of that goal requires of teachers specific knowledge of the component skills of reading, competence in teaching these skills to children, and the provision of plenty of materials with which children can and will practice their learned skills.

There is no cookbook recipe for teaching reading to disadvantaged children— indeed there is no cookbook for teaching reading to anyone! The fundamental requirements of the task are (1) well-trained teachers who know the component skills of reading and language and constantly appraise them in the performance of their pupils; (2) teachers who are sensitive to pupils—are skilled in P.R. ("pupil reading"); and (3) teachers who are capable of choosing and/or creating reading materials for their pupils and are free to do so and who are skilled enough to choose a pace that permits children to develop a taste for success in learning.

11

Junior High School Level: Grades 7-9

James L. Kinneavy
William L. Rutherford

POSSIBLY even more than the other levels of the academic staircase, the junior high school suffers from a paucity of research and practical programs in teaching reading to disadvantaged pupils. Many of the general points discussed in Parts I and II of this book have crucial relevance to junior high school pupils. And some of the practical suggestions made in Part III for teaching in other grades can also be directly applied to the seventh, eighth, and ninth grades. This seems particularly true of many of the recommendations made by Cohen in the following chapter. Nonetheless, the problems of disadvantaged junior-high-schoolers are often specifically different and may call for distinctive solutions. Before attempting to identify the various levels of the junior high school pupil's reading problems and suggest a sequence to meet them, let us consider what research tells or does not tell us about these specific differences, as far as reading is concerned, and also take a brief look at a few attempts to meet these problems in practical situations.

Research on Reading and the Disadvantaged

Research evidence that relates specifically to reading instruction for disadvantaged junior high school pupils is quite limited. The evidence that is available is lacking in continuity and sequence and is certainly inconclusive. If the various studies that are pertinent have any relationship, it is more likely to be the result of coincidence than intent. To claim, however, that we have only limited knowledge about the disadvantaged pupil would be erroneous, for we actually have a great deal of information about him, particularly about his personality and language characteristics. Yet, most of the information has been secured through investigation and observation of preschool and primary-grade children. The perplexing fact is that the findings of a number of these studies would appear to have important implications for junior high school teachers and pupils, but there is no way other than by inference to assess the validity of these implications.

Three studies will serve as examples of the point in question. Deutsch (1964) investigated the relationship between auditory discrimination and learning and social factors. Subjects in the study were children in grades one, three, and five who came from lower-class homes. Her study and the studies of others, such as Raph (1965) and Katz (1967), support the contention that young children from such homes are deficient in the auditory modality. But for junior high school teachers a more important finding came from Deutsch's study. She found that by the fifth grade, auditory discrimination seemed not to be highly correlated with reading and verbal skills. This led Deutsch to suggest that perhaps the auditory-discrimination skills of the fifth-graders had reached a level sufficient for adequate development of reading and verbal skills, but development of these skills was not commensurate with the growth of the auditory-discrimination skills. From the findings of this study it might be inferred that disadvantaged junior high school pupils will have acquired a minimum level of auditory-discrimination skill essential to the development of reading and general verbal skills. But in a matter as important as this one, teachers should not have to rely on inference; they need positive research evidence.

Katz (1967) investigated the verbal-discrimination performance of disadvantaged children. To do this she compared normal and retarded readers in grades two, four, and six as they responded to certain verbal-discrimination tasks. Significant differences in performance on the discrimination tasks were observed between good and poor readers at each grade level. It is important for junior high school teachers to know that the magnitude of the difference decreased as the children got older. On the basis of these findings Katz suggested that deficiencies in perceptual skills, such as discrimination and attention, may be major contributors to reading disability in the earlier school grades; whereas deficiencies in cognitive abilities, such as problem-solving, may be more significant factors in the middle elementary grades. One wonders, but can only wonder, what implications, if any, these findings may have for junior high school teachers and pupils.

In a third study Katz and Deutsch (1963) investigated the relationship of auditory-visual shifting to reading achievement in forty-eight black boys in grades one, three, and five in New York City. They found that shifting between auditory and visual stimuli was more difficult for retarded readers than for good readers. However, with older children, the difference in reaction time between good and poor readers was reduced. The authors felt that their findings supported the notion that ability to shift readily from one modality to another is a perceptual skill basic to reading performance. It would be most helpful to junior high school teachers if research evidence were available to establish clearly whether retarded readers are deficient in this shifting skill when they enter junior high school or whether they have acquired it by that time.

It is obvious that researchers have not focused their efforts on the reading problems and needs of disadvantaged junior high school pupils.

Past Programs

Junior high school teachers who turn to the experiences of others as a means of seeking guidance for teaching reading to disadvantaged pupils may find themselves frustrated. The frustration does not stem from a lack of information; rather, the problem lies in organizing the masses of information into some useful form. Throughout the country there are numerous compensatory-education programs, but usually there have been no attempts to evaluate them objectively, or the evaluation has produced findings that are difficult to interpret and are of limited usefulness (Wilkerson, 1965).

A comparison of the reports from two similar compensatory programs indicates the confusion that reigns in this area. In the Demonstration Guidance Project in New York City (forerunner of the Higher Horizons program), a compensatory program for secondary-school pupils was developed with a number of special features, including (1) an expanded counseling staff to provide an intensive guidance and individual counseling program; (2) an intensive parent-education program; (3) clinical services for individual pupils; (4) remedial classes in the major subjects of English (and reading), mathematics, and foreign language; and (5) a wide variety of cultural activities both on and off campus (Wrightstone, 1960). In October, 1956, a group of eighth-graders in the program attained a mean reading-grade-placement score of 5.5 on the Stanford Achievement Test. When this group was tested as tenth-graders in April, 1959, their mean reading-grade placement had risen to 9.45. This mean gain of 3.95 was larger than that of any pre-project group in the same school.

The New York City program was replicated in part in a southern junior high school. Features of the New York City program that were not included were (1) the expansion of counseling staff (for it already approximated the New York City ratio); (2) the addition of remedial-reading and math specialists; (3) commercially sponsored cultural programs; (4) the addition of a part-time psychologist and a social worker; and (5) the addition of a supervisor of the cultural enrichment program (Brazziel and Gordon, 1963). From September, 1961, to May, 1962, a group of 301 seventh-graders in this program had a mean gain of 1.5 in reading-grade placement. This gain appears to be generally equivalent to the gain made by the New York City pupils even though in this program some seemingly important features of the New York City program were eliminated or modified.

Results from these two programs are encouraging, for they show that disadvantaged junior high school pupils who are retarded in reading can, under certain conditions, make significant gains in reading achievement. Yet, the usefulness of the findings is limited in terms of application to other situations, for obviously not all aspects of the programs are essential to reading improvement, but it is impossible to know which features are necessary and which are not.

Planning a Program for the Classroom

Most compensatory-education programs involve a number of special personnel and resources. Junior high school teachers who seek guidance in the development of a program for their own classrooms in the absence of broader school programs may well feel there is no hope for the individual teacher and give up in despair.

DEVELOPING APPROPRIATE METHODS AND MATERIALS

Teachers should not surrender before reading the articles by Strang (1967), Stout (1964), and Saine (1964). Each of these reports offers excellent practical suggestions for diagnosing and teaching the disadvantaged readers in junior high school. Teachers can find out how to use an informal test to assess pupils' reading needs. Accounts of actual situations involving pupils show how a teacher can teach a pupil to read a sentence, or use stories about personal experiences and dialogue as means of improving oral language and reading, or motivate the most reluctant reader to read. Stout offers some valuable examples of how tape recorders, written directions, appealing pictures, and classroom plays can be used to expand vocabulary and encourage use of oral language. Methods as basic as the kinesthetic method of finger tracing, plus others, are described for use in instruction and practice in word recognition. All the suggestions are based on materials and activities that are immediately meaningful to the pupil.

Teachers who work with disadvantaged pupils in junior high school certainly must recognize and accommodate in the instructional program the particular language and learning characteristics that influence progress in reading. Surely there should be an awareness that success in reading is dependent to a certain degree on facility in the spoken language and that class differences in language increase with age (Deutsch, 1963). Therefore, opportunities for use of oral language and for improvement continue to be important in the junior high school. Closely related to this need is the need for vocabulary enrichment. Using the

Thorndike basic word list as the criterion, Figurel (1964) found that disadvantaged sixth-graders have a vocabulary no greater than that of first- and second-graders who are not disadvantaged. Ironically, a task force for the National Council of English Teachers found in 1965 that in secondary schools very little work was being done in oral language development and the teaching of writing, but there was extensive work in traditional schoolroom grammar, which is generally unrelated to oral speech or vocabulary growth (Corbin and Crosby, 1965). There is no evidence that this situation has changed since 1965.

Teachers in the junior high school should know that many so-called errors in oral reading result from mispronunciation rather than faulty recognition, and this is basically a language problem, not a reading problem. This does not make the problem any less important, but it does suggest a different teaching approach. Junior high school teachers should also recognize that disadvantaged pupils are frequently less flexible in the learning process than the majority of pupils. They perform better when they can continue with a task for a period of time instead of switching from one task to another. Also it should be noted that their reasoning processes are typically inductive rather than deductive (Riessman, 1962), and that they have difficulty developing abstract concepts and making generalizations (Bloom, Davis, and Hess, 1965).

Implicit in all this knowledge is the fact that junior high school pupils who are disadvantaged have a variety of deficiencies in language and reading skills, and to overcome these, carefully planned and consistent classroom instruction is necessary. To begin the instructional program, teachers should first discover their pupils' present performance levels and immediate needs in language development and reading. When this is done a plan must be developed that will provide for daily instruction in the deficient areas.

The bases of the instruction must be materials and activities that are immediately interesting and useful to the students and that provide for instruction in a maximum number of areas. For example, a pupil might be encouraged to describe a personal experience as a means of encouraging oral expression. As he speaks, the story can be recorded on a tape recorder and the teacher can write it down on the blackboard or on a chart. This written transcription can then be used as material for teaching reading skills. When he can read the story easily and correctly, he can then record the story on the tape recorder as he reads it and then compare his initial story with the story he read as one step in recognizing differences between the two types of oral performance and the need to reconcile these differences. Thus, one activity can serve as a means of developing oral expression, teaching reading skills, and providing auditory-discrimination training, as well as making it possible for the pupil to evaluate his own needs in reading and oral language.

Whatever the nature of the instructional program, teachers must be ever cognizant of the fact that the motivation level of these pupils and their aspirations for academic and vocational achievement are generally relatively low. They do have goals, but they tend to be self-centered, immediate, utilitarian, and often inconsistent with the goals and demands of formal education (Gordon and Wilkerson, 1966).

IDENTIFYING LEVELS OF PROBLEMS IN TEACHING READING

It is precisely the motivation level of disadvantaged pupils at this age that is crucial to the present issue. If the individual pupil does not feel any urgency to improve his reading abilities, if he cannot see any vital relationship between such skills and the immediate, utilitarian situation in which he finds himself, the reading-dominated school world to which he makes unpleasant excursions may finally seem so unreal that he turns his back on it in favor of what he considers "really real."

This immediate situation is always an individual, existential, often a very private concern. But it is out of this private situational context that motivation must issue. Motivation results from a personal decision, though it may be prodded from without. Indeed the relevance of the whole educational process begins psychologically with the individual in his own situational context. It is for this reason that the sequence arrow in Figure 11–1 begins in the situational context and works outward to the cultural and subcultural context and inward to concerns that actually are the means language provides to allow an individual to achieve his own personal goals. The cultural context is also just another means an individual can use to achieve his own personal goals. Martin and Castaneda, in Chapter 8, exemplify the priority of the individual in his own situational context in their approach to the reading problem. This priority must be respected at all levels of the curriculum.

Consider how an infant learns language. He does not begin his language processes by first perfecting his physiological fund of prelinguistic abilities, such as hearing and physical articulation, then adapt these to a meaningless grammar, then impose meanings on a syntax, then start to discourse in speech, and finally perceive that speech can be relevant to his own personal needs. Such a procedure is patently ridiculous. Rather he perceives that language seems to be an efficient tool for others in their situations and might be for him in his own personal situation, and he wants to use it as an instrument: he has something to say. To accomplish this he masters what meanings and grammar he can from his culture and uses his physiological apparatus to articulate "what he has to say" or "what he finds useful to listen to." In this very important sense the primary problem of reading or any other language skill is not linguistic or even prelinguistic, nor is it cultural or subcultural. The primary focus of any language process is the relevance of the discourse to the life situation of the speaker or writer or listener.

The cultural or subcultural context in which the situational context is located provides many of the values that act as attractions to the individual and prompt his motivations. Many of the writers represented in this volume have focused

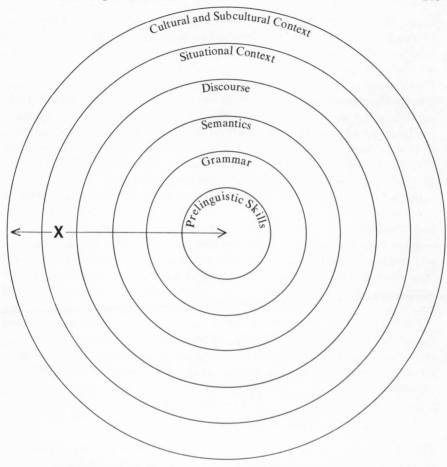

FIGURE 11-1

Identification of Levels of Problems

their attention on this level of the reading problem, analyzing the various sub-cultures of disadvantaged groups. Even more of this sort of analysis is needed, for the average teacher of disadvantaged junior high school pupils often knows very little or nothing of their subculture or sub-subculture. Yet it is only this knowledge that will provide examples of discourse that are actually meaningful to them. In Chapter 4 Metfessel and Seng emphasize, as does Cohen in Chapter 12, the typical irrelevance of school readings to the street or agrarian cultures of these pupils.

Meaningful discourses are a function of a situational context located in a cultural and subcultural context; the next level of the reading problem is the actual discourses themselves. These discourses involve skills in listening or speaking or reading or writing—the so-called language arts. But more important than the skills are the aims of the discourse. Except in some learning situations, no one speaks just to speak or listens just to listen, or even reads just to read. People speak in order to say something or listen to find out something. Consequently, the aims of discourse are much more important than the skills of speaking or reading—if discourse is to be meaningful. To these aims more attention will be devoted below. Most of the writers in language arts pay little attention to these aims, except perhaps to the literary aim. But literature is really a luxury aim of discourse. There are more bread-and-butter aims to which much more attention should be paid for both disadvantaged and other pupils.

Below the level of discourse is the level of semantics. At this level, differences in meaning and levels of usage, as well as problems of vocabulary, denotation and connotation, literal and figurative terms, and the like are studied.

Below the semantic level is the level of pure grammar, which includes phonemic and graphemic, morphemic, and syntactic concerns. They are important, but it must never be forgotten that in a meaningful life situation, grammar is only a subordinate tool. To elevate the tool to a position of primacy is to deprive it of meaning.

Finally, for the adequate articulation or reception of phonemic utterances and the adequate decoding of graphemic symbols certain basic neurological and physiological skills are prerequisites.[1] These prelinguistic skills are sometimes a crucial concern of the reading teacher, as the research of Deutsch (1964) has suggested.

TEACHING THE FOUR AIMS OF DISCOURSE

This brief survey of levels of the language (and reading) process underscores the necessity of being aware of all levels. No level can be ignored without courting failure. Since the other levels have received much attention elsewhere in this book and since the aims of discourse have been somewhat neglected, this level of the reading problem will be given a careful scrutiny in the remainder of this chapter.

What are the basic aims of discourse? Philosophers, psychologists, linguists, and others who have studied this problem arrive at a rather surprising consensus when they answer this question. All agree that language is used to impart information, to explore problems, and to systematize and prove something. These three uses have sometimes been called the informative, the exploratory, and the scientific uses of language. Together they can be called the referential uses of discourse. It is also clear that language is used as an instrument of persuasion and propaganda; many call this the persuasive use of discourse. Thirdly, lan-

[1] For a more thorough survey of these levels and a complete discussion of the aims of discourse, which are analyzed in brief below, see James L. Kinneavy, *A Theory of Discourse* (Englewood Cliffs, N. J.: Prentice-Hall, forthcoming).

guage is often used to entertain; this is often called the literary use of language. Finally, language is often used as an instrument of emotional discharge or personal expression; this is frequently called the expressive use of language.

It would be hazardous to say which of these aims of discourse is the most important, even in a given culture or subculture or at a given age level. However, in the black street culture of New York City or the agrarian subculture of the Mexican-American teenager in the lower Rio Grande valley in Texas, there are significant examples of each aim of discourse. Teenagers do use language to acquire information, to explore their own problems, to persuade their peers or others, to entertain or be entertained, and to express and to find themselves. Primarily these uses of language involve the speaking and listening arts more than reading or writing. And the media of such arts of language may be the meetings of the street gang or television rather than the literate media of academia or the sophisticated motions of parliamentary procedure. But the members of the subculture achieve the same aims of discourse as members of other subcultures, though there may be differences in sophistication or variant emphases in arts or media.

By entering into the teen-age subculture, teachers can find out what kinds of information teenagers actually are interested in acquiring, or what kinds of problems they are attempting to solve, or what issues they are being persuaded of, or what kinds of discourse actually entertain them, or what personal or social aspirations they are really attempting to express. The information may strike a teacher as trivial or even harmful, the problems may seem unimportant, the entertainment may be repugnant to an outsider, and the aspirations may appear unreal or dangerous. But if teachers are to find examples of discourses meaningful to the cultural and situational context of their pupils, they must begin here. For a teacher to impose his own value systems would be for him to move out of the world of the student and to alienate himself.

Information. What information might be meaningful? Teachers might find that information about sports is important to junior high school pupils. In this case, the sports page of the daily newspaper would be a proper medium to begin with. According to the Gunning index of difficulty, the level of typical articles on the sports page is considerably below the sixth-grade level at which many news stories in newspapers are written. Other informative reading materials might include hobby magazines of all sorts, movie magazines, business letters, and the like. If current events in some areas appeal to the pupils, there are several magazines published for school use, including *Scope* and other magazines of Scholastic Publications, that are informative and respect the intellectual interests of the pupils, but that are written at a reading level below that of most junior high school pupils. Some textbooks, written for lower grade levels, may also provide information that junior high school pupils will find interesting. Finally, biographies, autobiographies, histories, and other informative books on many topics are available at reading levels that are comfortable for disadvantaged junior high school readers.[2]

Critical reading skills in informative reading center mainly on three fundamental notions. Information, to be information, must be factual; it must be surprising; and it must be comprehensive. Factuality is tested by examining the sources of the information and assessing the reliability of the author, the journal or medium, the primary sources of the author's information, and so on. A reader can test surprise value by asking himself if this material is "news" to him. What is "news" to the pupils may be old hat to teachers, and conversely. Reading material may be very factual but not surprising; the result is that it is not really "informative." Finally, informative reading must be comprehensive: it must measure up to the fair expectancies of the average reader for whom it is intended and it must treat the subject fully enough to avoid distortion. Reading material may be both factual and surprising but distorted; in this case it is misleading and misinformative. These three norms can be applied, for instance, to a simple informative article in *Consumer's Report* on washing machines, record players, automobiles, or anything the students may be interested in. Comprehensiveness can be judged by comparing informative reports on the same event, for example, two articles on a football game from the newspapers of competitive schools or cities.

Persuasion. The second important aim of discourse is persuasion. That members of minority groups, for example, are exposed to persuasive uses of language hardly needs demonstration. They themselves are very aware of their exploitation by others. And the defensive motivation that this awareness can stimulate is not difficult to arouse. Unfortunately, school and trade books written for the intermediate level—a comfortable reading level for many disadvantaged junior-high-schoolers—and embodying examples of persuasion that they can read and analyze hardly exist at all. Teachers are forced back again to the media of the culture or subculture for meaningful materials. And they abound. Further, since they are often addressed to youngsters and adults with reading abilities at the fourth- to sixth-grade levels, they are of precisely the reading difficulty often desired. Billboards, transcripts of radio and television ads, local newspaper ads and flyers, many business letters, local grocery or automobile ads, magazine ads of all types, transcripts of local political speeches and of religious sermons—all of these are only a few of the persuasive discourses surrounding most adolescents. It is true that in the Indian subculture there are fewer of some of these kinds of

<hr/>

[2] A useful textbook series, more than usually information-oriented and intended for a relatively low junior high school reading level, is Richard H. Turner, *The Turner-Livingston Reading Series* (Chicago, 1964). Some reading lists intended for use with disadvantaged readers include the sort of informative material that is being discussed here. See Allen C. Ornstein, "101 Books for Teaching the Disadvantaged," *Journal of Reading*, Vol. 10, No. 8 (May, 1967), pp. 546–51.

discourse than in the other subcultures. But not even the Indian subculture is impervious to the assaults of commercial advertisers, political propagandists, and religious missionaries.

It is undoubtedly true that the language of persuasive discourse is not that of the formal written dialect or the oral prestige dialect. It really is a more integral part of the dialect of many of these subcultures than is the language of the typical junior high school textbook. For this reason it has a distinct bridging value that is often overlooked between subcultures and the dominant culture. In addition, it enables teachers to make some important linguistic points about levels of formality in all geographic and social dialects. Persuasive discourse often embodies some of the most dynamic features of grammatical and semantic change.

Critical reading skills involved in analyzing persuasive discourse should include an awareness of the use of personality or character appeals, such as pitches by sports heroes selling razor blades, the use of emotional appeals, and the use of seemingly logical techniques. These three rhetorical proofs have been a part of the analysis of persuasion since Antiquity.[3]

Entertainment. The most common aim of discourse, as far as reading classes and, later, English classes are concerned, is the literary aim. Reading a story or a poem for delight is one of the great benefits of an education. And "delight" is precisely the point. Any literature program that forgets that literature is primarily intended for pleasure has prostituted literature. The study of plot, theme, characterization, and setting, of rhyme and rhythm, and of other aspects of language aims ultimately to heighten the delight we receive from literature. The delight may be from a great epic or tragedy, or it may be from a simple pun or limerick.

These simpler forms of literature are especially useful for disadvantaged junior high school pupils, who are unable to read the classics. Many anthropologists and some literary critics properly distinguish between folk literature, popular literature, and classical literature. A disadvantaged seventh-, eighth-, or ninth-grader is much more likely to be delighted by some kinds of folk literature and "pop" literature than by watered-down versions of the classics. Indeed, even the sophisticated university professor of English often dips into folk and pop literature in some of his leisure moments when he indulges in simple jokes or watches a spy or western television program.

Unfortunately, much of the folk literature of every subculture is oral and unrecorded. What a diligent teacher may be able to discover can be invaluable. But "pop" literature at the level of comfortable reading by disadvantaged junior-high-schoolers does exist. Cohen, in the next chapter of this book, indicates some sources for this kind of material. Several lists of such readings have been compiled, including those by Dodds (1968) and Ornstein (1967).

---

[3] Any edition or commentary on Aristotle's *Rhetoric* can be consulted for a coverage of these points. A useful introduction is Edward P. J. Corbett, *Classical Rhetoric for the Modern Student* (New York: Oxford University Press, 1965), pp. 38–94.

Expression. The final aim of discourse is expression. In expressive discourse an individual or a group uses language to articulate personal or social aspirations. Most expressive discourse is spontaneous and oral, though written forms also exist. Much ordinary conversation ("I just wanted to get it off my mind"), some counseling interviews, cursing, many prayers, demonstrations, declarations of independence, diaries, journals, and autobiographies are all heavily expressive in aim.

The written forms of expressive discourse are very important in teaching reading to disadvantaged groups. In studying the expressed aspirations of their own subcultures or even of other cultures, pupils can see how other individuals or social minorities achieved selfhood and learn to make such adaptations themselves. They should be introduced to the expressive aspirations of individuals or groups from their own cultures or subcultures as early as possible. And, of course, in speaking situations they should be encouraged to express their own aspirations with as few restraints as possible. Of all the aims of discourse, expression may well be the most important, though it is very difficult to obtain adequate reading materials for pupils from some subcultures. The Hunter College reading materials for urban junior high school readers do include a goodly number of such readings.[4] They have been criticized as not being of a high literary quality; but these critics have failed to distinguish between expression and literature. The religious prayers of a minority group can hardly be criticized for not being literary, and they make valuable reading materials for expressive discourse. Another rich source of expressive discourses can be found in many of the simple songs of a culture. It is really much more valid to view these songs as expressive products of a culture than as literature.

Much remains to be done in the area of teaching reading to disadvantaged junior high school pupils. But if it is not done, they will be next year's dropouts. This is the critical age.

[4] Fourteen separate publications of the Hunter College materials, intended for estimated reading levels of fifth through eighth grade, are available from Macmillan Company. Teacher and pupil manuals, transparencies, tests, and record albums are also available.

12

Senior High School Level: Grades 10-12

S. Alan Cohen

BY GRADE ten a number of disadvantaged adolescents are still hanging on despite the American school's systematic programs (albeit insidiously unconscious) to eliminate "undesirables." In many high schools these "undesirables" are nonwhite or linguistically different and are victims of ethnic or social class prejudice.

Survivors of the System

Nationwide, about 83 percent of white seventeen-year-olds reach their high school senior year compared to only 62 percent of nonwhites. About 89 percent of whites, sixteen to seventeen years of age, are in high school compared to 74 percent blacks and 61 percent Puerto Rican Americans. These blacks and Puerto Ricans who do survive in school learn to achieve in spite of the same psychosocial factors found in those who drop out (Coleman, 1966).

As a group, of course, their IQ's and reading achievement scores are lower than white children's as measured by available tests. But some *finish* high school, which is an admired social value among urban ghetto children no matter how it is masked by adolescent rebellion.

What amazes some observers is that the five or six out of ten young men and women who make it come from the same disadvantaged neighborhoods and even the very homes that produce the four or five dropouts. Most of the "stay-ins," particularly those who are reading two or more years below grade placement, tend to retain dialect patterns such as "muvver" for *mother* and "he walk" for *he walks*. Many of these black urban stay-ins do not have fathers at home. Many do not have adequate food or clothing, "healthy" identity figures, or informal reading matter in the home. Many have no privacy, no place to study, no bed of their own. Yet they survive while their brothers and sisters do not. They have all the linguistic and psychosocial "diseases" needed to be legitimate school drop-outs, but they lack the symptom—they don't drop out. One begins to suspect that the psychosocial and linguistic factors educators use to explain mass failures among these adolescents may *in fact* be scapegoats for poor pedagogy (Cohen, 1968a; Mueser, 1969).

Three groups of urban ghetto children survive as far as high school. The first group of survivors is composed of the 10 percent who are high achievers. They will outlast the typical high school curriculum, which is at best mediocre, and will not be considered at length in this chapter. Whatever one *ought* to do to high achievers ought to be done to this 10 percent also. For example, at fourteen years of age, Mike had a Wechsler Intelligence Scale score of 132 IQ. By grade eight he had read every major American author and most English authors, also a liberal sample of non-English writers (including Dostoyevsky) in translation. He was a straight *A* student in his junior high school, where he was sent as a token of desegregation. Mike is black. And Mike was his school's showcase—the living example of northern "progress." But Mike was bored, not only with his curriculum but with his handlers as well. By accident he met a college professor who sent him to *A Better Chance* summer program for academically promising ghetto youngsters at Williams College. From there he attended a leading New England prep school where Mike, previously a reticent youngster, became a class president and a top student. Mike came from Harlem, where he and seven siblings of an unwed mother on welfare lived in a four-room tenement. In spite of these circumstances, Mike survived the WASP world; he stumbled upon a school experience that challenged him, which is what bright high achievers, disadvantaged or not, need.

A second group is functionally literate. They read from grade six to grade eight levels when they enter high school. They conform. They come to school on time; they avoid serious confrontations with the system; and they learn to tolerate the endless busy work, the drab texts, and the annual salutes to George Washington Carver and Martin Luther King. But many of these will drop out by grade eleven. One who did not drop out was Wayne, a sixteen-year-old serviced by a high-intensity learning program conducted by two students from Yeshiva University Reading Center in a vocational high school where the median reading level for incoming tenth-graders was grade 5.4. The median gain in reading in ten weeks for this group was 1.4 years. Wayne gained three grade levels in this program.

A third group rarely reaches grade ten—the nonreaders. Yet, some of them avoid the principal or guidance department for nine years and arrive one sunny

September in grade ten. They languish in the back row or run errands reliably for the teacher or assistant principal. Bobby was one such errandboy. This Puerto Rican youngster ran errands so well that he survived twelve years in the New York City schools. He "earned" his diploma. Three years later, he was part of a narcotics gang that subjected themselves to a detoxification and rehabilitation experiment on New York City's Lower East Side. Eleven gang members lived and worked together through the program. Ten were high school dropouts, all with IQ's above 105 and reading scores at adult levels. They were so literate that one of their favorite pastimes was group dramatic readings of Shakespeare. Ironically, the only member too illiterate to participate was the only member with a high school diploma—Bobby.

The rest of this chapter describes how reading was taught to Wayne and to Bobby.

The basic pedagogical problem in teaching reading to underachievers is how to *intensify* the instructional sequence so that the content or skill that needs to be learned and the level and rate at which it can be learned are adjusted to each individual. The second problem is how to use material and curriculum goals that are relevant to the individual. This is the problem of methodology.

Intensifying
the Instructional Sequence

THE MEANING OF DIAGNOSIS

Precisely what skill or behavior does the individual need to learn? This is the problem of diagnosis. In education, to diagnose means to describe for an individual *not* the cause of a problem but the specific behavior he must be able to perform in order to learn to read or to develop his reading further. Two misconceptions about diagnosis relevant to reading instruction persist in education.

The first misconception concerns the functional definition of diagnosis in education and psychology. That misconception describes diagnosis as an analysis of cause or as a statement of a diagnostic category or as an explanation of etiology. This is a holdover from medicine. For many medical pathologies the key to treatment is the diagnostic label. Once the cause or the name of the pathology is known, the treatment is more or less prescribed. In human behavior this is rarely if ever the case (Cohen, 1967). Knowledge of the etiology of a behavioral learning problem is rarely the key to changing that behavior. What is more useful to the teacher is an exact description of the specific behaviors an individual can perform and those that he cannot perform. The principles of bridging the gap between these two sets of behaviors are the very principles of learning that apply to all human beings regardless of the psychosocial and even physical facts that many people consider relevant. Only in the most extreme cases do the physical or psychosocial factors cancel out these principles of learning.

Perhaps it is time for school people to stop blaming psychosocial or psychophysical factors generally associated with the disadvantaged condition for the results of poor pedagogy. These conditions may exist, but they are not the reason that disadvantaged children are low achievers (Cohen, 1966, 1968a, 1968b; Mueser, 1969). A diagnosis describes not these irrelevancies, but the specific reading behaviors that can and cannot be performed by the children who are being taught.

The second misconception stems from the tradition that diagnosis is associated with remediation which is associated with underachievement or learning disability. Some educators still think of diagnosis as something specialists do to special cases. In this chapter, however, the term "diagnosis" is used to mean a *method of determining the behaviors that must be learned by each individual.* That determination is made by analyzing the individual's repertoire of skills and attitudes. This analysis includes the possible strategies and materials that can be used to engineer those behaviors the individual is unable to perform. The diagnosis specifies what each pupil needs to learn and what methods and materials will probably assist him. This is certainly a specialist's role—that specialist is the teacher. In other words, being able to diagnose what children need to learn and how to teach it is the unique specialty practiced by those in a profession called "teaching." And that applies equally to teachers of developmental skills as well as remedial skills.

THE SO-WHAT DIAGNOSIS

At the high school level the So-What Diagnosis has been found the most useful in planning a reading program for each student. One version of that form is shown in Figure 12–1. A series of group administered tests are used to gather the information needed to complete the So-What Diagnosis. One is the Diagnostic Test of Word Attack Skills (DTWAS), a series of ten tests, each one lasting four minutes or less (Cohen and Cloward, 1965). Each test taps a word attack skill (primarily phonic skills) as outlined in the DTWAS profile sheet shown in Figure 12–2. This test was developed and validated specifically with urban disadvantaged children and adolescents. Schools or school systems can easily develop their own, concentrating on the specific decoding skills the school staff feels are most important in mastering code-busting. The DTWAS profile sheet simply reports on bar graphs the percentage correct for each decoding skill measured. In high school, the test is administered to those reading at approximately grade-level five or below on the assumption that such minimal readers are still having code-busting problems. The percentage correct histogram (Figure 12–2) tells us which skills need improvement. About 40 percent of the adolescents who take this test battery are further diagnosed individually because they are so deficient

FIGURE 12-1

The So-What Diagnosis

DIAGNOSTIC PATTERN ————————————— FORM ————

Name ————————————————————————

Age ——————— Date of Birth ——————— Date of Test ———

SKILL	Grade Level	% Correct	SO WHAT?

Vocabulary
  General
  Science
  Math
  Social studies			

Follows Directions
  Definitions
  Simple choice
  Math directions
  Map directions			

Reference Skills
  Part of book
  Newspaper
  Dictionary
  Index
  Contents
  Graph
  Classification
  References
  Maps
  Organizes topics			

Comprehension
  States facts
  Inference
  Central idea
  Sequence of events			

Word Attack			

SOURCE:
Reading and Language Arts Center, Ferkauf Graduate School, Yeshiva University.

that the DTWAS gives very little explanation of the specific perceptual skill deficiencies underlying their low scores.

About 85 percent of all retarded readers who take the DTWAS score low on matching short vowel sounds with their graphemes. About 80 percent of all retarded readers who take the test, score highest in the structural analysis items (inflected endings, simple affixes, compound words). In all grades, the urban disadvantaged tend to have greater difficulty with phonic tests that involve auditory components than they do with basic reading skill tests that deal with "purely" visual decoding skills (visual matching of words or letters). Ironically, structural analysis skills and other visual tasks consume more pages of published workbooks than other code-busting skills because they lend themselves to pencil and paper exercises. Yet, these are skills we find least deficient among retarded readers in disadvantaged populations.

Usually the DTWAS is not used with those reading at approximately grade-level six or above on the assumption that a sixth-grade reading level represents strong functional literacy. While such readers may still lack specific phonic skills, they have more than enough compensatory higher-level skills. And so it is in *those* areas that the So-What Diagnosis concentrates—in reading vocabulary, interpretive comprehension skills, and in work-study skills. The version of the So-What Diagnosis report form shown in Figure 12–1 is derived from the California Reading Test at all levels, elementary through secondary (Tiegs and Clark, 1963). However, a So-What Diagnosis report form can be constructed from almost any comprehensive, standardized reading test.

NORMS VERSUS BEHAVIORS

The first thing to establish in using standardized group tests for individual diagnosis is to recognize that the test norms are the least important factors in diagnosis. What the teacher needs to know are the specific types of reading behaviors an individual can and cannot perform. In other words, the diagnostician is asking the question, What things can the individual do and not do in reading? A standardized test for tenth-graders given to a tenth-grader reading at approximately a fifth-grade level will *not* answer this question. Chances are that such a test pattern will show this tenth-grader severely retarded in reading and hitting the floor of the test on every skill. In this case all the test has told us is that this youngster is a very poor reader—something the teacher already knows.

What the teacher needs to know is not how this youngster compares to ten thousand others, but, instead, the specific reading behaviors in which the youngster is relatively weak or strong. For this purpose the teacher should use a lower-level standardized test to help diagnose this youngster's reading skills, for example, the upper elementary form of the California Reading Test (grade norms 4–6). For this youngster, then, the norms are invalidated—*they cannot be used*. The test items rather than the test itself are being used.

FIGURE 12-2

DTWAS Profile Sheet

Name _____

Skill	Test	10%	20%	30%	40%	50%	60%	70%	80%	90%	100%
Initial Consonants	1										
Final Consonants	2										
Initial Consonant Blends	3										
Final Consonant Blends	4										
Short Vowel Sounds	5										
Visual Discrimination of Vowel Sounds	6										
Auditory Syllabication	7										
Visual Syllabication	8										
Visual Memory of Known Demons	9										
Structural Analysis	10										
Structural Analysis of Compound Words	11										

SOURCE: Reading and Language Arts Center, Ferkauf Graduate School, Yeshiva University.

TEST–ITEM ANALYSIS

The fact is, of course, that a teacher or a staff could make up its own test items to sample various reading behaviors—why use a standardized test? The fact *also* is that most teachers do not want to make their own tests, that many teachers would not know what skills to tap in a test, and that some teachers would be unable to construct usable test items. In a few cases where teachers are able to design their own diagnostic tests, it is a waste of time to construct test items that already exist in inexpensive published tests. Since standardized group tests tap limited areas of reading, it is far more valuable for such talented teachers to use available standardized tests to sample certain skills and to construct other test items to tap skills not included in the standardized tests (written recall, flexibility of reading rate, reading in content areas, and so on).

The diagnostic form is used to record error patterns for each individual. For example, if five items on the test sample the youngster's ability to recall the sequence of events in a story, then we group these items as a reading behavior. If he misses three to five of these items we mark the behavior on the So-What Diagnosis form. In some cases a test will include only one or two items to sample a specific reading behavior. Whether or not a reading behavior is sampled by two items or ten, the statistical reliability of the accuracy of the score is highly questionable; this is the point in this program most often criticized by test specialists. However, test specialists are rarely classroom practitioners. They overlook the fact that the most a teacher can be is wrong when he *hypothesizes* that José is having trouble reading an index—a hypothesis based on only two test items.

The test-item analysis recorded on the So-What Diagnosis is not an indictment or a genotyping of José. It is, instead, a guide for the teacher to assign certain materials and activities to José because he *may* be having trouble in this specific area. What a delight for both José and the teacher to discover that test unreliability not reading deficiency is the cause of a low test score. Now José can work on some other deficiency. The point is that the diagnosis provides a guide to each individual's probable areas of deficiency and strength. And that is where learning begins.

Finally, the So-What Diagnosis gets its name from the third column in Figure 12–1. The purpose of the diagnosis is treatment, in this case learning. The So-What Diagnosis gets its name from the fact that no deficiency is recorded unless the names of appropriate materials and a note about the strategy for learning can be entered in the So-What column. A finding of deficiency in dictionary skills will be noted on the form only if the last column lists, for example, "*Macmillan Programmed Dictionary*/Worksheets 11–15: *Dictionary*—starts with alphabetizing drills." No more labels! No more numbers! If testing is relevant to teaching, then tests must help tell the teacher and the learner what he needs to learn.

A So-What Diagnosis helps the teacher pinpoint precisely what to teach his pupils. But it also puts the school on the spot. For with all the school's talk about individual differences, and with its groping for new administrative structures, such as ungrading, team teaching, and pupil grouping, these strategies, more often than not, *hide* individual differences. With the So-What Diagnosis the teacher is confronted with a variety of different needs *after* the grouping, *after* the ungrading, and *after* the teaching teams are formed. In other words, we cannot bury the differences in reading skill needs by administrative manipulations when the So-What Diagnosis for each pupil is on the teacher's desk, or, better yet, on the pupil's desk with a copy in his parents' hands. And this is true for high or low reading achievers, disadvantaged or not. Thus, the So-What Diagnosis forces the school to implement a different type of instructional program, at least in reading.

The Instructional Program

What reading skills to learn and the level at which to learn them will vary from individual to individual. A So-What Diagnosis tells us this. The pedagogical problem is how to operate a classroom that provides the skills and content each pupil needs at the level and rate he can best learn. One half of the solution to this problem is materials; the other half is teacher strategy.

MATERIALS

The teacher who wants to teach according to information provided by the So-What Diagnosis must have small amounts of a great variety of materials—theoretically one of everything that might be needed by a youngster—and must restructure these materials when necessary into self-directing learning materials. Self-directing materials have the following characteristics:

1. They require little or no direct teacher supervision in order for the pupil to use them.
2. They provide immediate feedback to the pupil concerning adequacy of his responses to stimuli.
3. They provide a systematic recording procedure for plotting progress and for spotting difficulties or impediments to progress.
4. They provide a means for the pupil to operate at his own rate of learning.
5. They provide opportunity for each pupil to operate individually or with small pupil learning teams or both.

"Aha! SRA Reading Labs!" exclaims the seasoned veteran of remedial reading. Yes, many of SRA's reading labs are based on these five principles. Much of the content of these labs is not as effective as the pedagogy intended and prescribed in the SRA Lab teacher manuals. But the lab's pedagogy is often effective enough to offset the weak content. That is why SRA kits are almost always found in self-directing reading centers. However, SRA kits barely scratch the surface of meeting individual reading needs. Compensatory programs should include practically every other available kit appropriate to the maturity levels of severely underachieving adolescent readers, for example, *The Reading Attainment Series* (Grolier), *The Webster Classroom Reading Clinic* (Webster/McGraw-Hill), *Skilpacers* and *Pacemakers* (Random House), *Developmental Reading Kits* (Addison-Wesley), *Study Skills Kits* and *Listening Skills Kits* (Educational Development Labs), *The Name of the Game* (New Dimensions), *Tactics* (Scott, Foresman). But all of these kits together barely meet the needs of retarded readers.

In addition to the kits, obtain two copies of every workbook available in the catalogs of every school publisher. Use paraprofessionals and/or Neighborhood Youth Corpsmen to restructure the workbooks on word attack and comprehension into self-directing, self-correcting materials cataloged by skill and level. The restructuring takes many forms, but the outcome is always material that provides a structured response sheet, a progress plotter, immediate feedback to the learner, and a method of storing and displaying the materials in such a way as to allow both teacher and pupil to put their hands on the exact content and level needed to meet a diagnosed need. In some instances the exercises may be torn out of their bindings and mounted on oak tag. Feedback sheets, response cards on which to record responses, and progress plotters are provided with each exercise. Each exercise is then filed according to skill and level. The result is a file of great quantities of readily available drill materials. Consider the amount and variety of materials available to a teacher when he has two copies each of fifteen different reading workbooks instead of thirty copies of the same one.

Reading labs and workbooks are certainly not sufficient for outfitting an adequate compensatory reading center. Phonic and vocabulary games may be obtained from Kenworthy, Bradley, Garrard Press, and other companies. If enough money is available, purchase one Controlled Reader Jr. (EDL), one Tachomatic 150 (Psychotechnics), one Tachomatic 500, one or two compact Graphlex SM 400 filmstrip projectors, and a Lafayette 2500 Tachistoscope (Lafayette Instruments) and some tachistoscopic attachments that allow any projector to be made into a tachistoscope or flash unit. The object is to have one of each machine from various companies so that a center has six or eight different controlled reading and tachistoscopic devices with accompanying filmstrips. The machines are motivators. They interest pupils and keep them reading even if it is an artificial reading situation. We find this motivation far more important than whatever debatable advantages may accrue from paced reading or from tachistoscopic training.[1]

---

[1] For a more complete list and review of the materials and equipment that can be used, see S. Alan Cohen, *Teach Them All to Read: Theory, Methods, and Materials for Teaching the Disadvantaged* (New York: Random House, 1969), Appendix A.

And what about books? For all their worth, kits, workbooks, and machines are still second best. They are merely ways of teaching people to read books. Yet books that "swing" are rarely found in significant quantities in classrooms at any grade. Is it any wonder then that so many adolescents are nonreaders in grade ten in spite of adequate reading achievement scores? For example, a recent National Council of Teachers of English survey showed that in 1967 the novel most often assigned in the American high school was still *Silas Marner*. Throughout the country the one glaring deficiency in materials, not only in regular classrooms but in reading centers, is trade books—literature. Both the small quantity of available books and the low quality of the books "allowed in" are the two major problems in providing adequate materials in reading centers for disadvantaged learners. Not just books in the school library but trade books in the content-area classroom and hundreds of exciting hardcover and paperback books about the real world must be in the reading centers.

Which books? Certainly not just *George Washington Carver* or *Booker T. Washington*. Adolescents in the black ghettos and in suburbia want to read *The Autobiography of Malcolm X* and *Manchild in the Promised Land*. But literature by and about blacks is not the whole story. What disadvantaged adolescents like to read is literature. And literature has very limited themes: interpersonal and intrapersonal strife and the damnation or resolution of the human predicament. There is very little else worth writing about. In such literature are the violence and passion, the sex and profanity that make beauty and nobility emerge or submerge in the human drama. These books cannot be withheld from the reading center because of community critics (many of whom are ghosts conjured up by fearful school administrators) who mask their prurience beneath dubious shrouds of purity. Literature always "tells it like it is," and the books we need in the schools are precisely these books that tell the truth. If we eliminate joy and pain, sex and violence, beauty and ugliness, passion and despair, revelation and ignorance, then all we have left is Dick, Sally, and Spot Grow Up. That certainly is not literature.

In our enthusiasm to tell it like it is, we should be careful to include not only *The Fire Next Time* in our urban reading centers but the Greek myths as well. In the Random House reading newspapers, *New York, New York*, the myths with all their sex, imagery, and violence were the most popular regular features among disadvantaged adolescent readers, preferred even above the popular, culturally familiar feature stories on urban subjects.

Hundreds of books on racks and in bins should be in the reading centers for disadvantaged learners—not on shelves that display the book spine and hide the colorful, enticing covers. The object is to sell these youngsters on literature, and the best way is to give them books that swing, colorfully displayed. There are some other "sale incentives." For example, award one free book for every three or five books read. Class trips may be taken to the paperback-book store to allow pupils to buy any books they choose, using ESEA (Elementary and

Secondary Education Act) project funds. Try some of the suggestions found in Fader and McNeil's book (1968) or in Cohen's book (1969) for getting reluctant readers to read.

How much does it all cost? Self-directing reading centers for disadvantaged adolescents have been set up for four to ten thousand dollars. Such centers can accommodate up to four teachers and serve about two hundred pupils per day. About 90 percent of the funds account for nonexpendable materials and equipment. The key is materials—a variety of self-directing materials. The old concept of Mark Hopkins on one end of a log and a boy on the other is impractical. Teachers and pupils need the tools to do the job. By designing and implementing the tools in a particular way, the effectiveness of the teaching and learning can be increased.

METHODS

In a self-directing classroom, the teacher's primary job is to provide the comfortable atmosphere that facilitates behavior change. When the organism perceives itself safe, it is more likely to try new behaviors. In contrast, under threat, the organism rigidifies and tends to resort to standard behaviors. One way the self-directing reading center gives the pupil a feeling of safety is by gearing all activities toward success. If a youngster fails to make an appropriate response to the materials with which he works, interpret this as a failure of the staff to provide the correct combination of content, sequence of instruction, and appropriate learning level for that individual. In this setting, pupils very quickly begin to perceive their occasional errors as diagnostic information rather than personal failure. At the same time allow the pupil in the reading center considerable freedom, which includes almost any reasonable behavior that neither breaks a law nor interferes with another person. For example, pupils may be allowed to come and go at will, to smoke, to eat, to sleep, to help others. Centers are usually set up under conditions that require each pupil to make a written request to enter the center. This is a commitment on his part, in return for which he must make visible gains in check-out tests in the various skills for which he is programmed. Meanwhile the teacher commits himself to minimize the amount of failure for each pupil by matching materials to pupil needs in a free and safe atmosphere for all learners.

The teacher schedules each pupil for three or four activities or pieces of material per class hour according to the So-What Diagnostic Profile. Each pupil has his own schedule. The only grouping that occurs results from two or more pupils being in the same part of the room at the same time working on similar materials. When a pupil has demonstrated his mastery of the skills, he is programmed for a new activity. Thus, the teacher is continually diagnosing and rescheduling pupils. The teacher is also providing on-the-spot first aid to those who cannot handle certain skills.

When teacher teams are available, the reading centers become even more effective. First, make skill specialists out of the team members. One teacher may specialize in teaching only code-busting to the illiterates such as Bobby who was described above. This teacher may work with Donald Smith's *Michigan Language Program* and back this up with other materials in word-attack skills, such as tachistoscopic training in sight words and phrases, drill in phonics and/or sight words. This specialist works in conjunction with a second specialist whose responsibility it is to run a center that specializes only in word-attack and vocabulary skills development for those who read better than Bobby does.

This second specialist is responsible for obtaining, modifying, and implementing only those materials and strategies needed to teach these skills, and he diagnoses and works with youngsters in this limited area only. Another specialist concentrates on comprehension skills. A fourth specialist concentrates on work-study skills. By specializing, each teacher becomes highly proficient in the area of his specialty. By meeting as a team at the beginning and end of each day, the four specialists can work out the optimal treatment for each youngster in each specialty. The teacher-pupil ratio and the class hours can fit the traditional school schedule, with each specialist operating a separate center for twenty or thirty pupils per class hour. Within the team, time allotments and pupil assignments are flexible.

If more ancillary personnel are available, the method can be even more effective. For example, paraprofessionals can aid teachers in each center by modifying materials on the spot. A specialist in English education may be utilized to conduct a separate "pay off" center. Here, small groups of pupils are taken out of a comprehension or work-study center. Each pupil selects a different book on the same theme, reads it, then joins others in discussion, dramatic readings, taped poetry sessions, personal problems sessions, and writing sessions. College undergraduates may be employed to lead these sessions. In some Job Corps camps such centers were modified so that vocabulary and word-attack skills were geared to the vocational vocabulary needed in the vocational training program at the camp. Another project is trying this same pedagogy in which points are given both for mastering learning modules and for appropriate classroom behavior. These points are converted to extrinsic rewards, in some cases, money. This is simply applied learning theory—"contingency management."

It is important to stipulate without reservation that adolescent underachievers, even those who are emotionally and socially maladjusted, can operate successfully in the self-directing classroom (Tannenbaum and Cohen, 1967). In two excellent studies, behavior problems were markedly reduced as achievement scores increased (Reinstein, 1967). Furthermore, three NDEA institutes at the Graduate School of Yeshiva University have demonstrated that teachers without previous professional training in reading can learn this pedagogy in about thirty hours of training.

Problems

The self-directing, diagnostic-prescriptive program described in this chapter has been implemented in many educational projects both in public schools and in nonschool poverty projects. Most adolescents and young adults participating were black or Puerto Rican urban school dropouts or "pre-dropouts." In a few research projects, rural disadvantaged whites and blacks responded well to the program. One reason the techniques seem to work is the adaptability of the pedagogy. At Roosevelt High School in a low-income area of the Bronx in New York City are a series of three separate skills centers, each specializing in one skill area. Yet the entire program is integrated into the high school English curriculum. Less than ten miles away in upper-middle-class Englewood Cliffs, New Jersey, a similar pedagogy is successfully integrated into a junior high school social studies and language arts curriculum for suburban high achievers. In this setting all the skills are studied in one center with one teacher. In another project four separate self-contained classrooms used the pedagogy in a special urban school for socially and emotionally disturbed boys. Recently, a group of adolescent delinquents spent a summer on parole, simultaneously reporting to their counselors and working in a reading center in a church on New York's West Side.

Yet, looking back on five years of projects using variations of this pedagogy, very few projects continued using the methodology after the original teachers left the scene. At first it seemed that only outstanding, creative, talented teachers could implement such a methodology. But several NDEA institutes have since demonstrated the ability to train "average" classroom teachers to implement the pedagogy. What we have discovered is that when teachers using the self-directing, diagnostic-prescriptive methodology leave for other types of jobs, the system, whether it be a public school system or a Job Corps camp, has not been amenable to maintaining and encouraging pedagogies that appear to be different from traditional teacher-directed, large- or small-group instruction. It appears too often that supervisory and administrative personnel, who represent responsibility for the permanence of program quality, are unable to maintain and develop instructional innovations. It seems that they really had little or no commitment to these programs in the first place. Perhaps successful innovative programs are too threatening to those who own and operate the present system.

A second problem involves the attitude and concern of educational radicals and revolutionists who concentrate on political change. They disagree with Havighurst (1968), who advocates changing the existing system. The revolutionists will not settle for change. They want complete abolition of that system. What will they replace it with? What guarantee have we that the replacement will be any more successful than the present system?

A third problem involves the low level of priority to which many educators, including radicals, relegate materials, both soft and hard ware. Whatever system survives, the Warners, Kohls, and Kozols will still not be in the classrooms. Instead, average teachers or laymen with average talents will continue to teach disadvantaged adolescents. But by controlling the materials they use and how they implement them—yes, even by introducing the computer and other hardware intelligently—we can directly influence the pedagogy. The problem is, How can we convince educators that the quality, number, and variety of materials they buy for their classrooms do make a major difference in the effectiveness of their teachers?

A fourth problem is the nonreading adolescent. The materials for young adults and high school and junior high school pupils who read *below* grade-level four on standardized tests are not good enough to teach them to read. Some breakthroughs have been made with a few programs recently published, but we are in no position at this time to make the type of statement that can be made about pupils with reading levels of at least grade five or six. For the latter, about a year's growth is possible every six weeks up to a grade eight or nine level as measured by standardized tests. Getting them up higher is a little more difficult and slow. But for the former group, we cannot make that claim. Large numbers of functionally illiterate adolescents cannot be brought up to high school reading levels with the present materials and strategies.

A fifth problem involves the lack of quality literature for adolescents reading at fourth- and fifth-grade levels. Macmillan's *Gateway Series*, Holt, Rinehart and Winston's *Impact*, Xerox's *The Way It Is*, and Addison-Wesley's *Voices of Man* are effective materials for those who read at or above a seventh-grade level. In spite of some publishers' claims to the contrary, these books will not work with pupils reading below a sixth-grade level, and much that they contain is too frustrating even for sixth-grade readers. Most teachers recognize that a pupil's comfortable reading level—one at which literature is read for content rather than skill building—is about two years below his reading level as measured by standardized tests. Motivation or no motivation, the severely retarded readers cannot read the material. Certainly we can read great literature to them and they can enjoy it and grow from it. But how can we give them relevant literature at their reading levels? Who can write it? And if someone could write it, who would buy it when publishers dare to print adult literature rewritten at a fourth-grade reading level? We have had evidence already that schools will not buy such literature no matter how hard they cry for it.

A sixth problem is teaching methodology. Not only critics outside professional education but the educationists themselves have sometimes denigrated pedagogy. In terms of methodologies designed *specifically* for the disadvantaged, the surface has barely been scratched.

Perhaps it is a little disappointing to look out at the harsh realities of the urban ghetto school and then look back at the pedagogy described in this chapter.

Nothing is new here—good literature that tells it like it is; diagnostic-prescriptive, personalized instruction. In light of the exciting and scholarly dissertations by linguists, sociologists, social anthropologists, and social psychologists, it appears that their accurate descriptions of their respective concerns within the universe are most relevant for designing programs of prevention. However, for programs to confront disadvantaged pupils in the schools now, an interdisciplinary effort is essential, with the learning psychologists providing particularly relevant principles: (1) immediate feedback as to the adequacy of the response; (2) stimuli presented at levels most likely to reach the individual; (3) very specific operational definitions of behavioral responses; (4) careful plotting of response patterns; (5) motivation drawn from reward; and (6) content that feeds the ego to make the instruction relevant to the learners.

These learning principles are not the unique property of blacks in Bedford Stuyvesant or Watts. They apply equally in Appalachia, San Antonio, Albuquerque, Scarsdale, San Diego, and Cicero.

13

Summary of Program Implications

Frank J. Guszak

THE approach of *Reading for the Disadvantaged* is interdisciplinary. The chapters in Parts I and II focus on the socioeconomic situation of the disadvantaged (Chapters 1–3), on factors influencing the ability and motivation of disadvantaged children to learn (Chapter 4), on learning theories (Chapter 5), and on language, language learning, and the language characteristics of specific groups (Chapters 6 and 7). The authors of the chapters in Part III review the implications of chapters in the first two parts for instructional programs at all levels, preschool through high school.

Nursery School and Kindergarten

Martin and Castaneda state that, although formal reading instruction is not normally begun until first grade, all preschoolers, linguistically different or not, should receive instruction in oral-language and conceptual skills, both of which are crucial to success in reading. Before first grade, equal consideration should be given to cognition and oral-language development. For disadvantaged children particularly, learning English as a second dialect or language goes hand in hand with cognitive development.

In preschool and kindergarten classes, beginning reading instruction takes place as children are taught labels for objects or play games with toys such as plastic alphabets. Other activities include those that foster in children a love of reading.

227

   Findings in sociology and psychology indicate the importance of (1) the child's acceptance of himself, his family, and school; (2) experiences that build extensive meanings; (3) an environment of literacy; and (4) the language modeling role of peers, parents, and the teacher. Middle-class children are aided greatly by the positive values of self, family, and school that they bring to school—values that disadvantaged children generally lack. One of the first tasks of teachers of the disadvantaged is providing an environment that fosters positive values. Acceptance, alone, of the child is not enough. Like any other child, a disadvantaged child responds to demanding learning encounters. Teachers must be sure that these encounters are appropriate; obviously, what is appropriate for most children is often not appropriate for a disadvantaged child.

   Possibly the greatest contribution that nursery and kindergarten programs can make is in the area of providing experiences that in the words of Hess (1964) affect "communication modes and cognitive structure" (pp. 172–73). If the preschool program can build an "extensive storehouse of meanings that can be handled orally" (p. 173), then the foundations of oral-language development required for beginning reading may be constructed.

   Children whose parents read to them or tell them stories generally delight in being read to and, in turn, desire to learn to read. Most disadvantaged children have had few, if any, such experiences and consequently have little inclination to read. Thus, priority should be assigned to experiences that encourage the desire to read.

   The role of nursery-school and kindergarten teachers as models of standard English is important. Teachers can provide the language modeling during language practice sessions and in the context of their work with conceptual development. "Meanings from concrete experience and their appropriate symbols in oral English should permeate the early school experience. Drill or practice in English to which children bring no meaning is not to be confused with learning language in the sense that is described here" (p. 174).

   Oral language change should go hand in hand with the development of concepts and inquiry skills. Disadvantaged children can be changed; they can be prepared for beginning reading so that for them, as for most children, the process is one of "decoding words and then speaking them and immediately perceiving their meaning" because "the meaning or image was acquired much earlier" (p. 175).

> Building the child's storehouse of meanings and developing his skills of inquiry are absolute necessities, for with the spoken words and meanings already acquired for the written symbols, learning to read becomes a problem of code breaking. It is important to remember that the code-breaking process of learning to read requires the seeking out and using of information, and that skills of information processing may be as vital to decoding as the parallel between the learner's oral speech and the printed word (p. 175).

At the nursery and kindergarten levels, disadvantaged pupils require a program planned and taught by "teachers who understand the needs of their pupils—both linguistic and cultural—and who view reading as a part of total language development on the principle that children involved in experiences planned for concept learning must work with the language necessary to handle the ideas" (p. 177).

Primary Level: Grades 1–3

When the linguistically different child arrives at the beginning of first grade, it is erroneously expected that he will soon learn to read. Unfortunately, rather than learning to read, many learn to identify school as an unpleasant place because they see themselves as unsuccessful participants. To perform successfully in school, a child must have a positive self-concept. A child's development of a positive self-concept depends largely on the school's acceptance of him, his family, his different social values, and particularly his language. The child should be encouraged to continue communicating in his own language when appropriate. The teacher's goal is to teach the child an "alternate pattern to express his needs at school" (p. 180).

Skills of listening and speaking require much initial attention. Before reading instruction in the standard language is begun, diagnostic techniques are used to determine the range and degree of language differences in the classroom. Children are encouraged to experiment with language following correct language models and carefully structured activities.

In the primary grades, just as at the preschool level, experiences that foster intellectual development are crucial. "Careful teachers of the disadvantaged take nothing for granted as new words and concepts are developed; instead, they spend considerable time relating known to unknown and developing precise meanings" (p. 181). Teachers help pupils build positive self-concepts not only by accepting their existing language but also by taking advantage of the "many rich possibilities for using children's life experiences to promote language growth" (p. 183).

Sensitivity to other needs that may interfere with a pupil's ability or desire to learn—health needs, financial needs, inadequate verbal or cognitive skills, and negative self-concept—is essential. Solutions to health and financial needs can often be found with local resources if teachers and school personnel are alert to them.

Most important, teachers at the primary level must continually diagnose the errors of their pupils "as the basis of the next day's diagnostic teaching techniques" (p. 188). Subsequent instruction then provides "an individualized sequential task for the child that is related to his present needs for learning" (p. 189).

York and Ebert conclude by noting that "the key words for teachers of disadvantaged children are *respect* and *expectation*" (p. 190).

> No other task is more important, especially in the primary years, than that of giving a child the feeling that he is important and that he can achieve success! Much of this feeling of worth and achievement can be accomplished, moreover, by simply giving the child the opportunity to develop the language with which to express his wonder, curiosity, discovery, and feelings (p. 190).

Intermediate Level: Grades 4–6

Like York and Ebert, Harmer is concerned primarily with (1) the acquisition of skill in standard American English and (2) the development and maintenance of a positive self-concept. Harmer makes three general recommendations to teachers of the disadvantaged: (1) continued instruction in prerequisites to reading, such as oral language, vocabulary, concept development, and so on; (2) direct attention to cognitive development; and (3) abolition of the practice of "covering" a textbook within a fixed period of time.

Harmer believes that children who speak nonstandard dialects of English need not produce standard oral American English in order to begin reading instruction profitably in the primary grades, even if the reading materials are in standard American English. Children who come to school speaking another language obviously must have oral command of English before beginning reading in that language. Initially, instruction for relationships and generalizations should be *deductive*, "since the children are still acquiring the standard language in which the rules being taught will apply" (p. 194).

Positive self-concepts may be provided through learning situations in which pupils experience real success and which show them that they are accepted, regarded as important individuals. In addition, intermediate-grade teachers must be keenly sensitive to the artificial pacing imposed on disadvantaged children by inappropriate skill expectations. Harmer also recommends that reading instruction for disadvantaged children emphasize the visual-kinesthetic approach. "From the standpoint of sheer maintenance of attention or involvement of the children, visual-kinesthetic methods are recommended and are readily implemented through the use of appropriate films, filmstrips, and audio-visual devices that require manipulation by the pupil" (p. 197).

The self-reinforcement value of electronic aids also makes them most desirable. In addition, these aids provide valuable post facto means for judging pupil performances teachers are unable to observe firsthand.

Like teachers at the primary level, teachers of intermediate grades are oriented to diagnostic, problem-solving instruction. They must carefully assess the reading competencies and deficiencies of their pupils, determine specific skill needs, and then design a specific teaching program to suit the needs of individual pupils or small pupil groups.

Junior High School Level: Grades 7–9

After noting the paucity of research and programs in the area of teaching reading to disadvantaged junior high school pupils, Kinneavy and Rutherford (1) indicate areas of needed research; (2) suggest general implications for instruction; and (3) describe what they consider to be a most useful plan for meeting the special needs of these pupils.

Most of the research pertinent to disadvantaged learners concerns preschool and primary-grade children rather than junior high school pupils. However, inferences can be drawn from many of these studies. Deutsch (1964) discovered a marked auditory deficiency in younger disadvantaged children. The auditory-discrimination factor, however, fails to correlate highly with reading abilities by the fifth grade, which suggests that the necessary auditory-discrimination skill may not be a prime factor in the junior high school. It should be pointed out, though, that teachers must have positive evidence for this conclusion.

A second study, by Katz (1967), suggests that "deficiencies in perceptual skills, such as discrimination and attention, may be major contributors to reading disability in the earlier school grades; whereas deficiencies in cognitive abilities, such as problem-solving, may be more significant factors in the middle elementary grades" (p. 200). Many causes can be suggested for deficiencies in cognitive abilities, but one obvious possibility is the neglect of cognitive supports in the primary programs because of a preoccupation with the sounds of letters and words. Before any interpretations can be made that relate to junior high school pupils, there must be definitive studies of cognitive deficiencies among pupils in grades seven through nine.

Although a number of compensatory-education programs at the junior high school level have been successful, few have been evaluated objectively. Most such programs were heavily supported by additional staff and resources not typically available.

Kinneavy and Rutherford make the following points about disadvantaged junior high school pupils and the reading program.

1. Opportunities for use of oral language and for improvement continue to be important (p. 202).
2. Closely related to this need is the need for vocabulary enrichment (p. 202).
3. Many so-called errors in oral reading result from mispronounciation rather than faulty recognition, and this is basically a language problem, not a reading problem (p. 203).
4. Disadvantaged pupils are frequently less flexible in the learning process than the majority of pupils. They perform better when they can continue

with a task for a period of time instead of switching from one task to another (p. 203).

5. It should be noted that their reasoning processes are typically inductive rather than deductive, and they have difficulty developing abstract concepts and making generalizations (p. 203).

6. The motivational level of these pupils and their aspirations for academic and vocational achievement are relatively low (p. 203).

The motivational factor may well be the most crucial factor in teaching reading to disadvantaged junior-high-schoolers. Because many disadvantaged pupils do not consider reading highly relevant, the task of teachers is to make it so by tailoring a curriculum that permits the pursuit of relevant concerns through reading.

Kinneavy and Rutherford believe the aims of discourse rather than the skills of discourse are the most important concerns of the junior high school reading program. The following aims were discussed: information, persuasion, entertainment, and expression. In order to prepare a relevant reading program, teachers should enter the subculture of their pupils to

> find out what kinds of information teenagers actually are interested in acquiring, or what kinds of problems they are attempting to solve, or what issues they are being persuaded of, or what kinds of discourse actually entertain them, or what personal or social aspirations they are really attempting to express (p. 207).

Suggested as sources of potentially relevant information are the sports page of the daily newspaper, hobby magazines, and business letters.

The second important aim of discourse is persuasion. It has been suggested that the disadvantaged are well aware of their exploitation by others through the persuasive use of language. Materials written at an appropriate reading level for disadvantaged junior-high-schoolers and containing examples of persuasion relevant to them hardly exist at all. Teachers must turn to the media of the subculture, where examples abound on billboards, in transcripts of radio and television ads, in newspaper and magazine ads, and so on.

In discussing the most common aim of discourse in reading and English classes, entertainment, Kinneavy and Rutherford offer interesting comments about what a literature program should and should not be:

> Reading a story or a poem for delight is one of the great benefits of an education. And "delight" is precisely the point. Any literature program that forgets that literature is primarily intended for pleasure has prostituted literature. The study of plot, theme, characterization, and setting, of rhyme and rhythm, and of other aspects of language aims ultimately to heighten the delight we receive from literature. The delight may be from a great epic or tragedy, or it may be from a simple pun or limerick (p. 209).

The simpler forms of literature are especially pertinent. Selections from relevant folk and pop literature are the most promising examples of literary entertainment. Several lists of such readings (e.g., Dodds, 1968; Ornstein, 1967) have been compiled.

Expression is the final aim of discourse. Expressive discourse is concerned with expression of an individual's or a group's aspirations and feelings. Although most expressive discourse is oral, many written examples are available. Exposing subcultural groups to the expressive aspirations of individuals or groups from their own subcultures as early as possible is of great importance. At the junior high school level the program emphasis moves from skills diagnosis in a supportive environment to include the provision of reading tasks that pupils perceive as relevant.

Senior High School Level: Grades 10–12

Cohen believes that the usual social, economic, psychological, and linguistic explanations for the poor school performance of disadvantaged pupils often are alibis for poor teaching. In seeking implications for programs that will succeed, Cohen places heavy emphasis on the basics of learning psychology.

Noting that certain groups of ghetto children survive as far as high school despite their disadvantagedness, Cohen divides such survivors into the following categories:

1. The first group of survivors is composed of the 10 percent who are high achievers. They will outlast the typical high school curriculum, which is at best mediocre . . . (p. 212).
2. A second group is functionally literate. They read from grade six to grade eight levels when they enter high school. They conform. They come to school on time; they avoid serious confrontations with the system; and they learn to tolerate the endless busy work, the drab texts, and the annual salutes to George Washington Carver and Martin Luther King (p. 212).
3. A third group rarely reaches grade ten—the nonreaders. Yet, some of them avoid the principal or guidance department for nine years and arrive one sunny September in grade ten. They languish in the back row or run errands reliably for the teacher or assistant principal (pp. 212–13).

Cohen devotes the chapter to a description of what he believes to be the best kind of reading program for pupils in the second and third groups. Successful reading instruction for underachieving high school pupils rests on the following determinations:

1. how to *intensify* the instructional sequence so that the content or skill that needs to be learned and the level and rate at which it can be learned are adjusted to each individual (p. 213).

2. how to use material and curriculum goals that are relevant to the individual (p. 213).

The first determination is essentially that facing the diagnostic, problem-solving teacher who was described earlier in the chapters on the primary and intermediate grades. The second is the prominent concern of Kinneavy and Rutherford in the chapter on junior high school.

The high school diagnostic teacher is not a seeker of causes, as is the medical diagnostician, but rather one who describes exactly the specific behaviors an individual can and cannot perform. The diagnostic teacher then charts the appropriate course of action according to (1) the materials needed and (2) the learning strategies to be employed.

A great portion of Chapter 12 is devoted to the description of instruments to diagnose specific reading skills and to observations of word recognition problems common to certain groups of retarded readers. Emphasized in the discussion is the idea that normative behaviors are not relevant; instead, individual skill needs requiring attention should be the major focus.

The result of diagnosis, then, is a profile of each pupil's skill needs that includes specific references to the materials and learning techniques to be utilized. Such a diagnosis is appropriately called the So-What Diagnosis because no deficiency is recorded unless the names of appropriate materials and a note about the strategy for learning is written into the critical So-What column.

Once diagnosis is accomplished by the So-What technique, the instructional program is divided into two major areas of concern: materials and methods. Of course, materials and methods cannot be completely separated; there is much implicit method or strategy in the ways in which materials are prepared and used.

To implement the program implied by the So-What Diagnosis, the teacher must have small amounts of a great variety of materials so that any pupil's skill needs can be met. But possession of such materials is not enough; equally important is the need to restructure these materials into self-directing learning materials. This is one of the most important elements of this methodology—individualized instruction. A description of the characteristics of self-directing learning materials follows:

1. They require little or no direct teacher supervision in order for the pupil to use them.
2. They provide immediate feedback to the pupil concerning adequacy of his response to stimuli.
3. They provide a systematic recording procedure for plotting progress and for spotting difficulties or impediments to progress.
4. They provide a means for the pupil to operate at his own rate of learning.
5. They provide opportunity for each pupil to operate individually or with small pupil learning teams or both (p. 219).

Among the materials recommended are kits; workbooks; phonic and vocabulary games; hardware, such as filmstrip projectors and tachistoscopes; and lots of books that "swing," such as *The Autobiography of Malcolm X* and *Manchild in the Promised Land.* Especially pertinent is literature that disadvantaged adolescents like to read—literature that details interpersonal and intrapersonal strife.

In this individualized learning environment, the teacher is a facilitating agent who must provide the comfortable atmosphere that facilitates behavior change; gear all activities toward success; view incorrect responses not as pupil failures but staff failures in administering to the pupils' needs; allow the pupil considerable freedom in the reading center insofar as it does not break a law or interfere with others; program each pupil for three or four activities or pieces of material per class hour according to his skill needs; and provide on-the-spot first aid to the pupil encountering difficulties with certain skills.

Reflecting upon problems that hinder the reading development of the disadvantaged adolescent, Cohen indicates that programs such as his tend to wither and die when the key people operating them move on. The traditional conceptualizations of teacher-directed large- and small-group classrooms are cited as the prime factors in such declines. Eventually, such conceptualizations overcome individualized programs.

Other problems center around materials: educators are not seeking out the available quality materials, both software and hardware, that can make a vital difference. There is, however, a lack of appropriate reading materials for adolescents reading at or below the fifth-grade level.

Cohen concludes by suggesting that the dissertations of linguists, sociologists, social anthropologists, and social psychologists are most relevant for designing programs of prevention. However, for the job at hand in high schools today, the most pertinent need seen is the intelligent application of basic learning principles.

Suggestions for Further Reading and a Brief Review of Research in Progress

Joe L. Frost

BOOKS, PARTS OF BOOKS, AND PAMPHLETS

Amsden, Constance. *A Reading Program for Mexican-American Children. First Interim Report.* Los Angeles: California State College, 1966.

Bloom, Benjamin S., Allison Davis, and Robert D. Hess. *Compensatory Education for Cultural Deprivation.* New York: Holt, Rinehart and Winston, 1965.

Brophy, William A., and Sophie D. Aberle. *The Indian: America's Unfinished Business.* Norman: University of Oklahoma Press, 1966.

Cheyney, Arnold B. *Teaching Culturally Disadvantaged in the Elementary School.* Columbus, Ohio: Charles E. Merrill, 1967.

Cohen, S. Alan. *Teach Them All to Read: Theory, Methods and Materials for Teaching the Disadvantaged.* New York: Random House, 1969.

Corbin, Richard, and Muriel Crosby. *Language Programs for the Disadvantaged.* Champaign, Ill.: National Council of Teachers of English, 1965.

Cowles, Milly. *Perspectives in the Education of Disadvantaged Children.* Scranton, Pa.: International Textbook Company, 1967.

Croft, Kenneth. *Reading and Word Study: For Students of English as a Second Language.* Englewood Cliffs, N. J.: Prentice-Hall, 1960.

Deutsch, Martin, and others. *The Disadvantaged Child: Studies of the School Environment and the Learning Process.* New York: Basic Books, 1967.

Estes, Dwain M., and David W. Darling. "Improving Educational Opportunities of the Mexican-American." *Proceedings* of the Texas Conference for the Mexican-American. Austin: Texas Education Agency, 1967.

Evertts, Eldonna L. *Dimensions of Dialect.* Champaign, Ill.: National Council of Teachers of English, 1967.

237

Fagan, Edward R., ed. *English and the Disadvantaged.* Scranton, Pa.: International Textbook Company, 1967.

Forbes, Jack D. *Mexican Americans, A Handbook for Educators.* Berkeley, Calif.: Far West Laboratory for Educational Research and Development, 1967.

Frost, Joe L. "Developing Literacy in Disadvantaged Children." In Joe L. Frost, ed., *Issues and Innovations in the Teaching of Reading.* Glenview, Ill.: Scott, Foresman, 1967, pp. 263–75.

———— "The Teacher and the Culture of Poverty." In Joe L. Frost and Thomas Rowland, *The Elementary School: Principles and Problems.* Boston: Houghton Mifflin, 1969, pp. 35–81.

———— and Glenn R. Hawkes, eds. *The Disadvantaged Child: Issues and Innovations.* 2nd ed. Boston: Houghton Mifflin, 1970.

———— and Thomas Rowland. "Cognitive Development and Literacy in Disadvantaged Children: A Structure-Process Approach." In Joe L. Frost, ed., *Early Childhood Education Rediscovered.* New York: Holt, Rinehart and Winston, 1968, pp. 374–401.

Gordon, Edmund W., and Doxey A. Wilkerson. *Compensatory Education for the Disadvantaged, Programs and Practices: Preschool through College.* New York: College Entrance Examination Board, 1966.

Gottleib, David. *Understanding Children of Poverty.* Chicago: Science Research Associates, 1968.

Hentoff, Nat. *Our Children Are Dying.* New York: Viking Press, 1966.

Herndon, James. *The Way It Spozed To Be.* New York: Simon and Schuster, 1968.

Hess, Robert D., and Roberta Meyer Bear, eds. *Early Education: Current Theory, Research, and Action.* Chicago: Aldine Publishing, 1966.

Hickerson, Nathaniel. *Education for Alienation.* Englewood Cliffs, N. J.: Prentice-Hall, 1966.

Keach, Everett T., and others. *Education and Social Crisis: Perspectives on Teaching Disadvantaged Youth.* New York: John Wiley & Sons, 1967.

Kohl, Herbert. *36 Children.* New York: The New American Library, 1967.

Kontos, Peter G., and James J. Murphy. *Teaching Urban Youth—A Source Book for Urban Education.* New York: John Wiley & Sons, 1967.

Kozol, Jonathan. *Death at an Early Age.* Boston: Houghton Mifflin, 1967.

Loretan, Joseph O., and Shelley Umans. *Teaching the Disadvantaged.* New York: Bureau of Publications, Teachers College, Columbia University, 1966.

Mackintosh, Helen K., Lillian Gore, and Gertrude M. Lewis. *Educating Disadvantaged Children Under Six.* Washington, D. C.: United States Department of Health, Education and Welfare, Office of Education, 1965.

Manuel, Herschel T. *Spanish Speaking Children of the Southwest.* Austin: University of Texas Press, 1965.

Miller, Elizabeth W., ed. *The Negro in America: A Bibliography.* Cambridge, Mass.: Harvard University Press, 1969.

Miller, Harry L. *Education for the Disadvantaged.* New York: The Free Press, 1967.

Passow, A. Harry, Miriam L. Goldberg, and Abraham J. Tannenbaum, eds. *Education of the Disadvantaged.* New York: Holt, Rinehart and Winston, 1967.

Pope, Lillie. *Guidelines to Teaching Remedial Reading to the Disadvantaged.* Brooklyn: Book-Lab, 1967.

Rees, Helen E. *Deprivation and Compensatory Education: A Consideration.* Boston: Houghton Mifflin, 1968.

Rosenthal, Robert, and Lenore Jacobson. *Pygmalion in the Classroom.* New York: Holt, Rinehart and Winston, 1968.

Smith, Nila Blanton, and Ruth G. Strickland. *Some Approaches to Reading.* Washington, D. C.: Association for Childhood Education International, 1969.

Strickland, Ruth G. "The Contribution of Structured Linguistics to the Teaching of Reading Composition and Grammar in the Elementary School." *Bulletin of the School of Education,* Indiana University, Bloomington, Vol. 40 (January, 1964).

Strom, Robert D. *Teaching in the Slum School.* Columbus, Ohio: Charles E. Merrill, 1965.

Taba, Hilda, and Deborah Elkins. *Teaching Strategies for the Culturally Disadvantaged.* Chicago: Rand McNally, 1966.

Trubowitz, Sidney. *Handbook for Teaching in the Ghetto School.* Chicago: Quadrangle Books, 1968.

Webster, Staten W. *Understanding the Educational Problems of the Disadvantaged Learner.* San Francisco: Chandler Publishing, 1966.

ARTICLES

"Appalachia's Satellite Network." *Reading Newsreport,* Vol. 1 (June, 1967), pp. 46–48.

Arnold, Richard D. "Teaching English as a Second Language." *The Reading Teacher,* Vol. 21 (April, 1968), pp. 634–39.

Atzet, Jan. "A Study of Phonetic Symbolism Among Native Navajo Speakers." *Journal of Personality and Social Psychology,* Vol. 1 (May, 1965), pp. 524–28.

Bailey, Beryl Loftman. "Some Aspects of the Impact of Linguistics on Language Teaching in Disadvantaged Communities." *Elementary English,* Vol. 45 (May, 1968), pp. 570–78, 626.

Baratz, Joan C. "Linguistic and Cultural Factors in Teaching Reading to Ghetto Children." *Elementary English,* Vol. 46 (February, 1969), pp. 199–203.

Benson, J. T. "Teaching Reading to the Culturally Different Child: Language Experience Approach." *Conference on Reading, University of Pittsburgh Report,* Vol. 22 (1966), pp. 140–51.

Bereiter, C., and S. Engelmann. "Teaching Disadvantaged Children the Language of Instruction." *Canadian Education and Research Digest,* Vol. 8 (October, 1967), pp. 126–36.

Blatt, B., and F. Garfunkel. "Educating Intelligence: Determinants of School Behavior of Disadvantaged Children." *Exceptional Child,* Vol. 33 (May, 1967), pp. 601–08.

Blatt, Gloria T. "The Mexican American in Children's Literature." *Elementary English,* Vol. 45 (April, 1968), pp. 446–51.

Bloom, Sophia. "Israeli Reading Methods for Their Culturally Disadvantaged." *The Elementary School Journal,* Vol. 66 (March, 1966), pp. 300–10.

Boyer, Mildred. "Poverty and the Mother Tongue." *Educational Forum,* Vol. 29 (March, 1965), pp. 290–96.

Cazden, Courtney B. "Subcultural Differences in Child Language: An Inter-Disciplinary Review." *Merrill-Palmer Quarterly,* Vol. 12 (July, 1966), pp. 185–219.

Cheyney, Arnold B. "Curricula Methods Used by Outstanding Teachers of Culturally Disadvantaged Elementary School Children." *The Journal of Negro Education*, Vol. 35 (Spring, 1966), pp. 174–77.

Ching, Doris C. "Reading, Language Development, and the Bilingual Child." *Elementary English*, Vol. 46 (May, 1969), pp. 622–28.

Christian, Chester. "The Acculturation of the Bilingual Child." *Modern Language Journal*, Vol. 49 (March, 1965), pp. 160–64.

Cohen, D. H. "Effects of Literature on Vocabulary and Reading Achievement." *Elementary English*, Vol. 45 (February, 1968), pp. 209–13.

Cohen, S. Alan. "Some Conclusions about Teaching Reading to Disadvantaged Children." *The Reading Teacher*, Vol. 20 (February, 1967), pp. 433–35.

Cook, Mary Jane, and Margaret Sharp. "Problems of Navajo Speakers in Learning English." *Language Learning*, Vol. 16, Nos. 1 and 2 (1966), pp. 21–30.

Cramer, Ward, and Suzanne Dorsey. "A Summer Developmental Program for Rural Students." *The Reading Teacher*, Vol. 22 (May, 1969), pp. 710–14.

"Crash Program in Spanish and Mexican-American Culture." *School and Society*, Vol. 97 (February, 1969), pp. 87–88.

Criscuolo, N. P. "Enrichment and Acceleration in Reading." *The Elementary School Journal*, Vol. 68 (December, 1967), pp. 142–46.

Crosby, Muriel. "Reading and Literacy in the Education of the Disadvantaged." *The Reading Teacher*, Vol. 19 (October, 1965), pp. 18–21.

Davis, A. "Teaching Language and Reading to Disadvantaged Negro Children." *Elementary English*, Vol. 42 (November, 1965), pp. 791–97.

Ecroyd, Donald H. "Negro Children and Language Arts." *The Reading Teacher*, Vol. 21 (April, 1968), pp. 624–29.

Emans, Robert. "What Do Children in Inner Cities Like to Read?" *The Elementary School Journal*, Vol. 69 (December, 1968), pp. 118–22.

Feitelson, Dina. "Teaching Reading to Culturally Disadvantaged Children." *The Reading Teacher*, Vol. 22 (October, 1968), pp. 55–61.

Fishman, Joshua. "Bilingualism, Intelligence and Language Learning." *Modern Language Journal*, Vol. 49 (April, 1965), pp. 227–36.

———— "The Status and Prospects of Bilingualism in the United States." *Modern Language Journal*, Vol. 49 (March, 1965), pp. 143–55.

Froelich, Martha, Florence Blitzer, and Judith Greenberg. "Success for Disadvantaged Children." *The Reading Teacher*, Vol. 21 (October, 1967), pp. 24–33.

Gaarder, Bruce. "Teaching the Bilingual Child: Research, Development and Policy." *Modern Language Journal*, Vol. 49 (March, 1965), pp. 165–74.

Garza, Nick E. "Teaching English as a Second Language: Some Innovations." In Joe L. Frost, ed., *Issues and Innovations in the Teaching of Reading*. Glenview, Ill.: Scott, Foresman, 1967, pp. 275–79.

Gomberg, Adeline W. "The Lighthouse Day Camp Reading Experiment with Disadvantaged Children." *The Reading Teacher*, Vol. 19 (January, 1966), pp. 263–66.

Goolsby, Thomas, Jr. "Listening Achievement in Head Start." *The Reading Teacher*, Vol. 21 (April, 1968), pp. 658–61.

Granite, Harvey R. "Language Beacons for the Disadvantaged." *The Elementary School Journal*, Vol. 66 (May, 1966), pp. 420–25.

Gray, S. W. "Before First Grade: The Imprint of the Low-Income Home." *Claremont Reading Conference Yearbook*, Vol. 31 (1967), pp. 141–55.

"Guidelines for Testing Minority Group Children." *Journal of Social Issues*, Vol. 20 (April, 1964).

Hakes, David. "Psychological Aspects of Bilingualism." *Modern Language Journal*, Vol. 49 (April, 1965), pp. 220–26.

Hernandez, L. F. "Teaching English to the Culturally Disadvantaged Mexican-American Student." *English Journal*, Vol. 57 (January, 1968), pp. 87–92.

Hunt, J. McVicker. "Has Compensatory Education Failed: Has It Been Attempted?" *Harvard Educational Review*, Vol. 39 (Spring, 1969), pp. 278–300.

Kaplan, Robert. "Cultural Thought Patterns in Intercultural Education." *Language Learning*, Vol. 16, Nos. 1 and 2 (1966), pp. 1–20.

Keener, Beverly H. "Individualized Reading and the Disadvantaged." *The Reading Teacher*, Vol. 20 (February, 1967), pp. 410–12.

Kennedy, V. P., and R. E. Roush. "Reading and Teaching the Poverty Child." *Texas Outlook*, Vol. 51 (June, 1967), pp. 18–19.

Kincaid, Gerald. "A Title I Short Course for Reading Teachers." *The Reading Teacher*, Vol. 20 (January, 1967), pp. 307–12.

Krail, J. B. "Audio-Lingual Approach and the Retarded Reader." *Journal of Reading*, Vol. 11 (November, 1967), pp. 93–104.

Krippner, Stanley. "Materials and Methods in Reading." *Education*, Vol. 85 (April, 1965), pp. 467–73.

Lloyd, Helene M. "What's Ahead in Reading for the Disadvantaged?" *The Reading Teacher*, Vol. 18 (March, 1965), pp. 471–76.

Loban, Walter. "Teaching Children Who Speak Social Class Dialects." *Elementary English*, Vol. 45 (May, 1968), pp. 592–99, 618.

Lopez, P. "Regional Program for Migrant Education." *Childhood Education*, Vol. 45 (September, 1968), pp. 22–27.

Love, Joseph. "La Raza: Mexican-American in Rebellion." *Trans-Action*, Vol. 6 (February, 1969), pp. 35–41.

Madison, Agnes. "Growth in Perception of Reading, Writing, and Spelling for the Educationally Disadvantaged." *The Reading Teacher*, Vol. 22 (March, 1969), pp. 513–16.

Manuel, Herschel T. "Recruiting and Training Teachers for Spanish-Speaking Children in the Southwest." *School and Society*, Vol. 96 (March 30, 1968), pp. 211–14.

McConnell, F., and others. "Language Development and the Culturally Disadvantaged Child." *Exceptional Child*, Vol. 35 (April, 1969), pp. 597–606.

McDavid, Raven I., Jr. "Variations in Standard American English." *Elementary English*, Vol. 45 (May, 1968), pp. 561–64, 608.

"Mexican American Children Discover Themselves in the Reading Process." *Claremont Reading Conference Yearbook*, Vol. 31 (1967), pp. 107–20.

Morrison, Coleman, and Albert J. Harris. "Effect of Kindergarten on the Reading of Disadvantaged Children." *The Reading Teacher*, Vol. 22 (October, 1968), pp. 4–10.

Napoli, Joseph. "Environmental Factors and Reading Ability." *The Reading Teacher*, Vol. 21 (March, 1968), pp. 552–57.

242 Suggestions for Further Reading

Olsen, James. "The Verbal Ability of the Culturally Different." *Educational Forum*, Vol. 29 (March, 1965), pp. 280–84.

Philion, William L., and Charles Galloway. "Indian Children and the Reading Program." *Journal of Reading*, Vol. 12 (April, 1969), pp. 553–60.

Ramsey, Wallace. "Reading in Appalachia." *The Reading Teacher*, Vol. 21 (October, 1967), pp. 57–63.

Ruddell, Robert B. "Oral Language and Development of Other Language Skills." *Elementary English*, Vol. 43 (May, 1966), pp. 489–98.

Schoephoerster, Hugh, and others. "The Teaching of Prereading Skills in Kindergarten." *The Reading Teacher*, Vol. 19 (February, 1966), pp. 352–57.

Skinner, V. P. "Why Many Appalachian Children are Problem Readers: We Create the Problems." *Journal of Reading*, Vol. 11 (November, 1967), pp. 130–32.

Spiegler, Charles G. "A Cure for Allergy to Reading." *Education Digest*, Vol. 29 (April, 1964), pp. 35–38.

Stauffer, Russel G. "Certain Convictions About Reading Instruction." *Elementary English*, Vol. 46 (January, 1969), pp. 85–89.

Strang, Ruth. "Teaching Reading to the Culturally Disadvantaged in Secondary Schools." *Journal of Reading*, Vol. 10 (May, 1967), pp. 527–35.

Stull, E. G. "Reading Materials for the Disadvantaged: from Yaki to Tlingit to Kotzebue." *The Reading Teacher*, Vol. 17 (April, 1964), pp. 522–27.

Wakefield, Mary L., and N. J. Silvaroli. "A Study of the Language Patterns of Low Socio-Economic Groups." *The Reading Teacher*, Vol. 22 (April, 1969), pp. 622–23.

Weaver, S. J., and A. Weaver. "Psycholinguistic Abilities of Culturally Deprived Negro Children." *American Journal of Mental Deficiency*, Vol. 72 (September, 1967), pp. 190–97.

Whipple, Gertrude. "Multi-Cultural Primers for Today's Children." *Education Digest*, Vol. 29 (February, 1964), pp. 26–29.

Wilt, Miriam. "Talk, Talk, Talk." *The Reading Teacher*, Vol. 21 (April, 1968), pp. 611–17.

Wynn, S. J. "Beginning Reading Program for the Deprived Child." *The Reading Teacher*, Vol. 21 (October, 1967), pp. 40–47.

RESEARCH REPORTS

Anderson, Lorena. "Reading in Appalachia." *The Reading Teacher*, Vol. 20 (January, 1967), pp. 303–06.

Andersson, Theodore. "A New Focus on the Bilingual Child." *Modern Language Journal*, Vol. 49 (March, 1965), pp. 156–59.

Arnold, Richard D. "Retention in Reading of Disadvantaged Mexican-American Children During the Summer Months." Paper presented at the International Reading Association Convention, Boston, April, 1968. In *1968 IRA Proceedings*.

Berninghausen, David, and Richard Faunce. "An Exploratory Study of Juvenile Delinquency and the Reading of Sensational Books." *Journal of Experimental Education*, Vol. 33 (Winter, 1964), pp. 161–68.

Bernstein, B. "Language and Social Class." *British Journal of Sociology*, Vol. 11 (1960), pp. 271–76.

Blom, Gaston, Richard Waite, and Sara Zimet. "Ethnic Integration and Urbanization of the First Grade Reading Textbook." *Psychology in the Schools*, Vol. 4 (April, 1967), pp. 176–81.

Bollenbacher, Joan. "Study of the Effect of Mobility on Reading Achievement." *The Reading Teacher*, Vol. 15 (March, 1962), pp. 356–60.

Botha, Elize, and Anne Close. "Achievement Motivation and Speed of Perception in Relation to Reading Skill." *Perceptual and Motor Skills*, Vol. 19 (August, 1964), p. 74.

Brazziel, William T., and Mary Terrel. "An Experiment in the Development of Readiness in a Culturally Disadvantaged Group of First Grade Children." *The Journal of Negro Education*, Vol. 31 (Winter, 1962), pp. 4–7.

Caplan, Stanley, and Ronald A. Ruble. "A Study of Culturally Imposed Factors on School Achievement in a Metropolitan Area." *The Journal of Educational Research*, Vol. 58 (September, 1964), pp. 16–21.

Carlton, Lessie, and Robert Moore. "The Effects of Self-Directive Dramatization on Reading Achievement and Self-Concept of Culturally Disadvantaged Children." *The Reading Teacher*, Vol. 20 (November, 1966), pp. 125–30.

Cooper, Bernice. "An Analysis of the Reading Achievement of White and Negro Pupils in Certain Public Schools of Georgia." *The School Review*, Vol. 27 (Winter, 1964), pp. 462–71.

Cox, F. N. "Test Anxiety and Achievement Behavior Systems Related to Examination Performance in Children." *Child Development*, Vol. 35 (Summer, 1965), pp. 382–88.

Criscuolo, Nicholas. "How Effective are Basal Readers with Culturally Disadvantaged Children?" *Elementary English*, Vol. 45 (March, 1968), pp. 364–65.

Deutsch, Martin. "The Role of Social Class in Language Development and Cognition." *American Journal of Orthopsychiatry*, Vol. 35 (January, 1965), pp. 78–88.

Dolan, G. Keith. "Counseling as an Aid for Delayed Readers." *Journal of Reading*, Vol. 8 (November, 1964), pp. 129–35.

Downie, N. M. "Comparison Between Children Who Have Moved From School With Those Who Have Been in Continuous Residence on Various Factors of Adjustment." *Journal of Educational Psychology*, Vol. 44 (January, 1953), pp. 50–52.

Ellingsworth, Huber, and Paul Deutschmann. "Book Readership by a Sub-Elite Latin American Group." *Journal of Communication*, Vol. 14 (December, 1964), pp. 238–44.

Ervin, Susan. "Grammar and Classification." Paper read at American Psychological Association, New York, September, 1957.

——— and W. R. Miller. "Language Development," *Child Psychology*. Sixty-second Yearbook of National Society for the Study of Education, Part I, N. B. Henry, ed. Chicago: University of Chicago Press, 1963, pp. 108–43.

Fillmer, Henry, and Helen Kahn. "Race, Socio-Economic Level, Housing, and Reading Readiness." *The Reading Teacher*, Vol. 21 (November, 1967), pp. 153–57.

Ford, Nick Aaron. "Improving Reading and Writing Skills of Disadvantaged College Freshmen." *College Composition and Communication*, Vol. 18 (May, 1967), p. 4.

Foster, Marion, and Donald Black. "A Comparison of Reading Achievement of Christchurch, New Zealand, and Edmonton, Alberta, Public School Students of the Same Age and Number of Years of Schooling." *Alberta Journal of Educational Research* Vol. 11 (March, 1965), pp. 21–31.

Frazier, A. "A Program for Poorly Languaged Children." *Ohio State University Talent Development Project Bulletin*, No. 8, 1963.

Frost, Joe L. "Effects of an Enrichment Program on the School Achievement of Rural Welfare Recipient Children." Paper presented at the National Conference, American Educational Research Association, Chicago, February, 1968. Office of Education Contract No. 3–6–068107–0670.

——— and Geneva Pilgrim. "Effects of a Diagnostic Reading Program on the Achievement of Drop-Out Youth." Unpublished research, University of Texas at Austin, 1969.

Gordon, Edmund W. "Characteristics of Socially Disadvantaged Children." *Review of Educational Research*, Vol. 35 (December, 1965), pp. 377–88.

Greenberg, Judith, and others. "Attitudes of Children from a Deprived Environment Toward Achievement Related Concepts." *The Journal of Educational Research*, Vol. 59 (October, 1965), pp. 57–62.

Grotberg, Edith. "Learning Disabilities and Remediation in Disadvantaged Children." *Review of Educational Research*, Vol. 35 (December, 1965), pp. 413–25.

Hanson, Earl, and Alan Robinson. "Reading Readiness and Achievement of Primary Grade Children of Different Socio-Economic Strata." *The Reading Teacher*, Vol. 21 (October, 1967), pp. 52–56.

Harris, Albert J., and Blanche Serwar. "Comparing Reading Approaches in First Grade Teaching with Disadvantaged Children." *The Reading Teacher*, Vol. 19 (May, 1966), pp. 631–35, 642.

——— and Lawrence Gold. "Comparing Reading Approaches in First Grade Teaching with Disadvantaged Children—Extended into Second Grade." *The Reading Teacher*, Vol. 20 (May, 1967), pp. 698–703.

Harris, T., W. Otto, and T. Barrett. "Summary and Review of Investigations Relating to Reading July 1, 1966 to June 30, 1967." *The Journal of Educational Research*, Vol. 61 (February, 1968), pp. 243–64.

Helper, Malcolm, and Sol Garfield. "Use of the Semantic Differential to Study Acculturation in American Indian Adolescents." *Journal of Personality and Social Psychology*, Vol. 2 (December, 1965), pp. 817–22.

Horn, Thomas D. "Three Methods of Developing Reading Readiness in Spanish-Speaking Children in First Grade." *The Reading Teacher*, Vol. 20 (October, 1966), pp. 38–42.

Hyman, Irwin, and Deborah Kliman. "First Grade Readiness of Children Who Have Had Summer Head Start Programs." *Training School Bulletin*, Vol. 43 (February, 1967), pp. 163–67.

Justman, Joseph. "Academic Aptitude and Reading Test Scores of Disadvantaged Children Showing Varying Degrees of Mobility." *Journal of Educational Measurement*, Vol. 2 (December, 1965), pp. 151–55.

Karp, Joan, and Irving Sigel. "Psychoeducational Appraisal of Disadvantaged Children." *Review of Educational Research*, Vol. 35 (December, 1965), pp. 401–12.

Katz, Phyllis, and Martin Deutsch. "Modality of Stimulus Presentation in Serial Learning for Retarded and Normal Readers." *Perceptual and Motor Skills*, Vol. 19 (October, 1964), pp. 627–33.

Kennedy, W. A., V. Van Deriet, and J. C. White, Jr. "A Normative Sample of Intelligence and Achievement of Negro Elementary School Children in the Southeastern U. S." *Monographs of the Society for Research in Child Development*, 1963.

Lloyd, Bruce. "The Effects of Programmed Perceptual Training on the Reading Achievement and Mental Maturity of Selected First Grade Pupils: A Pilot Study." *Journal of Reading Specialist*, Vol. 6 (December, 1966), pp. 49–55.

Marclay, H., and E. Ware. "Cross-Cultural Use of the Semantic Differential." *Behavioral Science*, Vol. 6 (July, 1961), pp. 185–90.

McCanne, R. "Approaches to First Grade English Reading Instruction for Children from Spanish-Speaking Homes." *The Reading Teacher*, Vol. 19 (May, 1966), pp. 670–75.

McGinnies, Elliott. "A Cross-Cultural Comparison of Printed Communications Versus Spoken Communication in Persuasion." *Journal of Psychology*, Vol. 60 (May, 1965), pp. 1–8.

Neville, Donald. "The Relationship Between Reading and Intelligence Test Scores." *The Reading Teacher*, Vol. 17 (January, 1965), pp. 257–61.

Noél, Doris. "Comparative Study of the Relationship Between the Quality of the Child's Language Usage and the Quality and Types of Language Used in the Home." *The Journal of Educational Research*, Vol. 47 (November,1953), pp. 161–67.

Otto, W. "Inhibitory Potential Related to the Reading Achievement of Negro Children." *Psychology in the Schools*, Vol. 3 (April, 1966), pp. 161–63.

———— "Sibling Patterns of Good and Poor Readers." *Psychology in the Schools*, Vol. 2 (January, 1965), pp. 53–57.

Parker, Edwin, and William Paisley. "Predicting Library Circulation from Community Characteristics." *Public Opinion Quarterly*, Vol. 24 (Spring, 1965), pp. 39–53.

Perrodin, A. F., and Walter Snipes. "The Relationship of Mobility to Achievement in Reading, Arithmetic and Language in Selected Georgia Elementary Schools." *The Journal of Educational Research*, Vol. 39 (March, 1966), pp. 315–19.

Raph, Jane. "Language Development in Socially Disadvantaged Children." *Review of Educational Research*, Vol. 35 (December, 1965), pp. 389–400.

Robinson, Alan. "Reliability of Measure Related to Reading Success of Average, Disadvantaged and Advantaged Kindergarten Children." *The Reading Teacher*, Vol. 15 (December, 1966), pp. 203–09.

Roebeck, Mildred. "Effects of Prolonged Reading Disability: A Preliminary Study." *Perceptual and Motor Skills*, Vol. 19 (August, 1964), pp. 7–12.

Rosen, E. "A Cross-Cultural Study of Semantic Profiles and Attitude Differences: Italy." *Journal of Social Psychology*, Vol. 49 (May, 1959), pp. 137–44.

Rowland, Monroe, and Patricia Hill. "Race, Illustrations and Interest in Materials for Reading and Creative Writing." *The Journal of Negro Education*, Vol. 34 (Winter, 1965), pp. 84–87.

Santostefano, Sebastiano, Louis Rutledge, and David Randall. "Cognitive Styles and Reading Disability." *Psychology in the Schools*, Vol. 2 (January, 1965), pp. 57–62.

Seelye, H. Ned. "Field Notes on Cross-Cultural Testing." *Language Learning*, Vol. 16, Nos. 1 and 2 (1966), pp. 77–86.

Snipes, Walter. "The Effect of Moving on Reading Achievement." *The Reading Teacher*, Vol. 20 (December, 1966), pp. 242–46.

Soares, Anthony T., and Louise M. Soares. "Self-Perceptions of Culturally Disadvantaged Children." *American Educational Research Journal*, Vol. 6 (January, 1969), pp. 31–43.

Spencer, Doris U. "Individualized vs. Basal Reading Program in Rural Communities." *The Reading Teacher*, Vol. 19 (May, 1966), pp. 595–600.

———— "Individualized vs. Basal Reading Program in Rural Communities—Grades One and Two." *The Reading Teacher*, Vol. 21 (October, 1967), pp. 11–17.

Staats, Arthur, and William Butterfield. "Treatment of Nonreading in a Culturally Deprived Juvenile Delinquent: An Application of Reinforcement Principles." *Child Development*, Vol. 36 (December, 1965), pp. 925–42.

Stemmler, Anne. "An Experimental Approach to the Teaching of Oral Language and Reading." *Harvard Educational Review*, Vol. 36 (Winter, 1966), pp. 42–59.

Wilkerson, Doxey A. "Programs and Practices in Compensatory Education for Disadvantaged Children." *Review of Educational Research*, Vol. 35 (December, 1965), pp. 426–40.

Worley, Stinson, and William Story. "Socio-Economic Status and Language Facility of Beginning First Graders." *The Reading Teacher*, Vol. 20 (February, 1967), pp. 400–03.

Yamamoto, Kaoru. "Socio-Economic Status of Children and Acquisition of Grammar." *The Journal of Educational Research*, Vol. 60 (October, 1966), pp. 71–74.

Yoes, Deck, Jr. "Reading Programs for Mexican-American Children of Texas." *The Reading Teacher*, Vol. 20 (January, 1967), pp. 313–18.

SOURCES OF INFORMATION
AND SELECTED EXAMPLES
OF RESEARCH IN PROGRESS

Center for Urban Education, New York City. Program to improve literacy in urban schools.

Davis, A. L. "Dialect Research and the Needs of the Schools." *Elementary English*, Vol. 45 (May, 1968), pp. 558–60, 608.

Educational Resource Information Center for Disadvantaged Children and Youth. Yeshiva University, New York, N. Y.

Educational Resource Information Center for Reading. Indiana University, Bloomington, Ind.

Educational Resource Information Center for the Teaching of English. National Council of Teachers of English, Champaign, Ill.

Northwest Regional Development Laboratory, Portland, Ore. Program to improve education for the culturally different.

Southwest Educational Development Laboratory, Austin, Tex. Development and assessment of materials and techniques for a bidialectic and bilingual language program.

Southwest Regional Development Laboratory, Los Angeles, Calif. Development and assessment of instructional materials and methods K–4, to teach young children to read, write, speak, and understand.

Southwestern Cooperative Educational Laboratory, Albuquerque, N. Mex. Program to develop materials and methods for teaching primary grades language arts to Mexican-Americans and American Indians.

References and Index
to Authors of Works Cited

The numbers in **bold face** following references give the text pages on which the work is cited. Citations in the text are made by author and date of publication.

INTRODUCTION

*Arnold, Richard D. *1965–66 (Year Two) Findings, San Antonio Language Research Project.* Austin: University of Texas, 1968.
———— "Reliability of Test Scores for the Young Bilingual Disadvantaged." *The Reading Teacher*, Vol. 22 (January, 1969), pp. 341–45.
———— "Retention in Reading of Disadvantaged Mexican-American Children During the Summer Months." Paper presented at the International Reading Association Convention, Boston, April, 1968. In *1968 IRA Proceedings.*
———— "Social Studies for the Culturally and Linguistically Different Learner." Elementary Education Supplement of *Social Education* (January, 1969).
———— "Teaching English as a Second Language." *The Reading Teacher*, Vol. 21 (April, 1968), pp. 634–39.
*Fowler, Elaine D. *An Evaluation of Brengleman-Manning Linguistic Capacity Index as a Predictor of Reading Achievement of Spanish-Speaking First Grade Students.* Austin: University of Texas, 1969.
Horn, Thomas D. "Listening-Speaking Problems of Disadvantaged Children: A Role in the Reading and Language Arts Program." In Frank P. Greene and Robert A. Palmatier, eds., *Reading: The Third Level.* Syracuse, N. Y.: Division of Summer Sessions, Syracuse University, 1968, pp. 13–20.

---

* The Introduction is based primarily on these materials, which may be obtained by writing to the Learning Disabilities Center, The University of Texas at Austin, 604 West 24th Street, Austin, Tex. 78705.

247

248 *italic* *References and Index to Authors*

——— *A Study of the Effects of Intensive Oral-Aural English Language Instruction, Oral-Aural Spanish Language Instruction and Non-Oral-Aural Instruction on Reading Readiness in Grade One*. Austin: University of Texas, 1966.

——— "Three Methods of Developing Reading Readiness in Spanish-Speaking Children in First Grade." *The Reading Teacher*, Vol. 20 (October, 1966), pp. 38–42.

*Jameson, Gloria Ruth. *The Development of a Phonemic Analysis for an Oral English Proficiency Test for Spanish-Speaking School Beginners*. Austin: University of Texas, 1967.

*Knight, Lester N. *1966–67 (Year Three) Findings: A Comparison of the Effectiveness of Intensive Oral-Aural English Instruction, Intensive Oral-Aural Spanish Instruction, and Non-Oral-Aural Instruction on the Oral Language and Reading Achievement of Spanish-Speaking Second and Third Graders*. Austin: University of Texas, 1969.

*McDowell, Neil A. *A Study of the Academic Capabilities and Achievements of Three Ethnic Groups: Anglo, Negro and Spanish Surname, in San Antonio, Texas*. Austin: University of Texas, 1966.

*MacMillan, Robert W. *A Study of the Effect of Socioeconomic Factors on the School Achievement of Spanish-Speaking School Beginners*. Austin: University of Texas, 1966.

Milius, Peter. "Billion-a-Year Plan Termed Failure in Education of the Poor." *Austin American* (January 7, 1969), p. 9.

*Ott, Elizabeth H. *A Study of Levels of Fluency and Proficiency in Oral English of Spanish-Speaking School Beginners*. Austin: University of Texas, 1967.

*Pauck, Frederick G. *An Evaluation of the Self-Test as a Predictor of Reading Achievement of Spanish-Speaking First Grade Children*. Austin: University of Texas, 1968.

*Peña, Albar A. *A Comparative Study of Selected Syntactical Structures of the Oral Language Status in Spanish and English of Disadvantaged First Grade Spanish-Speaking Children*. Austin: University of Texas, 1967.

Stemmler, Anne. "An Experimental Approach to the Teaching of Oral Language and Reading." *Harvard Educational Review*, Vol. 36 (Winter, 1966), pp. 42–59.

*Swanson, Mary E. *1967–68 (Year Four) Findings: A Comparative Study of the Effects of Oral-Aural Teaching Techniques on Pupils' Gain in Reading. Language and Work Study Skills in Grades Three and Four*. Austin: University of Texas, 1969.

*Taylor, Thomasine H. *1968–69 (Year Five) Findings: A Comparative Study of the Effects of Oral-Aural Language Training on Gains in English Language for Fourth and Fifth Grade Disadvantaged Mexican-American Children*. Austin: University of Texas, 1969.

CHAPTER 1

Bernstein, B. "Social Class and Linguistic Development: A Theory of Social Learning." In A. H. Halsey, J. Floud, and C. A. Anderson, eds., *Economy, Education, and Society*. New York: The Free Press, 1961. **15**

Bird, Alan R. *Poverty in Rural Areas in the United States*. Washington, D. C.: United States Department of Agriculture, Agricultural Economics Report No. 63 (November, 1965). **20**

Deutsch, Martin. "The Disadvantaged Child and the Learning Process." In A. Harry Passow, ed., *Education in Depressed Areas*. New York: Teachers College Press, Columbia University, 1963, pp. 163–79. **15**

Hess, Robert D. "Educability and Rehabilitation: The Future of the Welfare Class." Paper presented at the Thirtieth Groves Conference on Marriage and the Family. Mimeographed. Committee on Human Development, University of Chicago, 1964. Used by permission of the author. **16, 17**

Orshansky, Mollie. "Counting the Poor: Another Look at the Poverty Profile." *Social Security Bulletin*, Vol. 28 (January, 1965). **20**

United States Bureau of the Census. *Family Income, 1959.* Washington, D. C.: Government Printing Office, 1960. **20**

CHAPTER 2

Ford, Thomas R., ed. *The Southern Appalachian Region.* Lexington: University of Kentucky Press, 1962. **24n**

Gans, Herbert J. *The Urban Villagers.* New York: The Free Press, 1962. **26**

Hodges, Harold M., Jr. *Social Stratification: Class in America.* Cambridge, Mass.: Schenkman Publishing Co., 1964. **28, 28n**

Kelley, Earl C. "The Fully Functioning Self." In *Perceiving, Behaving, Becoming: A New Focus on Education.* Washington, D. C.: National Education Association, Association for Supervision and Curriculum Development, 1962, pp. 12–20. **46**

Kerner Commission Report, March, 1968. (Final report: *United States National Advisory Commission on Civil Disorders.* Washington, D. C.: Government Printing Office, 1968.) **36**

Nelson, Hart M. "A Review of the Literature Pertaining to Appalachia, Stressing Attitudes to Social Change and Religious and Educational Orientations." Paper presented to the Boards of Christian Education of the United Presbyterian Church in the U. S. A. and the Presbyterian Church in the U. S., May, 1967. **24n**

President's National Advisory Commission on Rural Poverty. *Rural Poverty in the United States.* Washington, D. C.: Government Printing Office, 1968. **22n**

Ramsey, Ralph J. *Forms and Scope of Poverty in Kentucky.* Lexington, Ky.: Extension Service, Resource Development Series 10, 1968. **21n**

Reifel, Ben. "Cultural Factors in Social Adjustment." *Indian Education*, No. 298 (April 15, 1957). **42**

Spang, Alonzo. "Counseling the Indian." *Journal of American Indian Education*, Vol. 5 (October, 1965). **46**

Taylor, Carl C., and others. *Rural Life in the United States.* New York: Alfred A. Knopf, 1949. **24n**

Thomas, Robert, see Wax and Thomas (1961).

Underhill, Ruth. *Here Come the Navajo.* Indian Life and Customs, No. 8. Lawrence, Kans.: Hashell Institute Print Shop, January, 1953. **44**

United States Bureau of the Census. "Extent of Poverty in the United States: 1959 to 1966." *Current Population Reports*, Series P-20, No. 54. Washington, D. C.: Government Printing Office, 1968. **21**

United States Department of Labor. *The Negro Family.* Washington, D. C.: Government Printing Office, March, 1965. **32**

Warner, Lloyd. *Democracy in Jonesville.* New York: Harper & Row, 1949. **28, 29**

Washburn, Wilcomb E. "A Moral History of Indian-White Relations: Needs and Opportunities for Study." *Ethnohistory*, Vol. 4 (Winter, 1957), pp. 47–61. **42**

250 *References and Index to Authors*

Wauneka, Annie D. "Helping People to Understand." *The American Journal of Nursing*, Vol. 62 (July, 1962), pp. 88–90. **45**

Wax, Rosalie, and Robert Thomas. "American Indians and White People." *Phylon*, Vol. 22 (Winter, 1961), p. 306. **45**

Weller, Jack E. *Yesterday's People.* Lexington: University of Kentucky Press, 1965. **24n**

Zintz, Miles V. "Problems of Classroom Adjustment of Indian Children in Public Elementary Schools in the Southwest." *Science Education*, Vol. 46 (April, 1962), pp. 261–69. **44**

―――― *Education Across Cultures.* Dubuque, Iowa: William C. Brown, 1963. **44**

CHAPTER 3

Browning, Harley, and S. Dale McLemore. *A Statistical Profile of the Spanish Surname Population of Texas.* Austin: Bureau of Business Research, University of Texas, 1964. **55, 59**

Burmer, John H. *Spanish-Speaking Groups.* Durham, N. C.: Duke University Press, 1954. **58**

Davis, James A., see Nicholas and Davis (1964).

Eells, Kenneth, and others. *Intelligence and Cultural Differences.* Chicago: University of Chicago Press, 1951. **61**

Ferguson, George A. *Statistical Analysis in Psychology and Education.* New York: McGraw-Hill, 1957. **63**

Folger, John K., and Charles B. Ram. *Education of the American Population.* Washington, D. C.: United States Department of Commerce, 1969. **56**

Holtzman, Wayne H., see Moore and Holtzman (1965).

Huyck, Earl E., see Page and Huyck (1964).

Jacobson, Lenore, see Rosenthal and Jacobson (1968).

Laswell, Thomas E. *Class and Stratum.* Boston: Houghton Mifflin, 1965. **59, 60**

McLemore, S. Dale, see Browning and McLemore (1964).

MacMillan, Robert W. "A Study of the Effect of Socioeconomic Factors on the School Achievement of Spanish-Speaking School Beginners." Unpublished Ph.D. dissertation, University of Texas at Austin, 1966. **58, 60, 69, 70, 71**

Madsen, William B. *The Mexican-American of the Southwest.* New York: Holt, Rinehart and Winston, 1964. **69**

Manuel, Herschel T. *Spanish-Speaking Children of the Southwest.* Austin: University of Texas Press, 1965. **51, 55, 69, 71**

Moore, Bernice M., and Wayne H. Holtzman. *Tomorrow's Parents.* Austin: University of Texas Press, 1965. **59, 69**

Morris, Willa. *Occupational Information in the Elementary School.* Chicago: Science Research Associates, 1964. **59**

Murray, Sister Mary John. *A Socio-Cultural Study of 118 Mexican-American Families Living in a Low-Rent Public Housing Project in San Antonio.* Washington, D. C.: Catholic University of America Press, 1954. **69**

Nicholas, Robert C., and James A. Davis. "Characteristics of Students of High Academic Aptitude." *The Personnel and Guidance Journal*, Vol. 42 (April, 1964), pp. 794–800. **60**

Page, William J., and Earl E. Huyck. *Appalachia.* Washington, D. C.: Department of Health, Education and Welfare, 1964. **55**

Ram, Charles B., see Folger and Ram (1969).

Rosenthal, Robert, and Lenore Jacobson. *Pygmalion in the Classroom.* New York: Holt, Rinehart and Winston, 1968. **71**

Saunders, Lyle. *Cultural Differences and Medical Care.* New York: Russell Sage Foundation, 1954. **69, 71**

Sitomer, Curtis J. *Christian Science Monitor,* Vol. 57 (November 5, 1965). **50, 55, 59**

Tuck, Ruth D. *Not with the Fist.* New York: Harcourt, Brace & World, 1946. **55, 71**

United States Bureau of the Census. *Census of the Population.* Washington, D. C.: Government Printing Office, 1960a. **55, 60**

—— *Census of Population, Classified Index of Occupations and Industries.* Washington, D. C.: Government Printing Office, 1960b. **55**

—— *General Social and Economic Characteristics.* Washington, D. C.: Government Printing Office, 1960c. **52, 54, 63, 67**

—— *Income of All Persons.* Washington, D. C.: Government Printing Office, 1960d. **56**

—— *Nonwhite Population by Race.* Washington, D. C.: Government Printing Office, 1960e. **52, 53, 57, 63, 64, 67**

—— *Persons of Spanish Surname.* Washington, D. C.: Government Printing Office, 1960f. **51, 52, 54, 55, 63, 64**

—— *Social Characteristics.* Washington, D. C.: Government Printing Office, 1960g. **55**

—— *Subject Reports, School Enrollment,* Series PC(2)-5A. Washington, D. C.: Government Printing Office, 1960h. **68**

—— *United States Summary, Detailed Characteristics.* Washington, D. C.: Government Printing Office, 1960i. **54**

—— *United States Summary, General Social and Economic Conditions.* Washington, D. C.: Government Printing Office, 1960j. **55, 65**

United States Commission on Civil Rights. *Civil Rights Digest,* Vol. 1 (Fall, 1968), pp. 42–43. **52, 55**

United States Department of Commerce. *Current Population Reports: Population Estimates.* Series P-25, No. 385 (February 14, 1968), Table 1. **50**

United States Department of Labor. *The Negroes in the United States.* Bulletin No. 1511 (June, 1966). **51, 61**

—— *Recent Trends in Social and Economic Conditions of Negroes in the United States.* Series P-23, No. 26. BLS Report No. 347 (July, 1968). **53, 59**

United States Senate. Report No. 554 (August 30, 1967). **65**

Witmer, Helen L. "Children and Poverty." *Children,* Vol. 11 (November–December, 1964), pp. 207–13. **49**

Woods, Sister Frances Jerome. *Cultural Values of American Ethnic Groups.* New York: Harper & Row, 1956. **71**

CHAPTER 4

Amster, Harriett. "Effect of Instructional Set and Variety of Instances on Children's Learning." *Journal of Educational Psychology,* Vol. 57 (1966), pp. 74–85. **94**

Antonitis, Joseph J., Roger B. Frey, and Alan Baron. "Group Operant Behavior: Effects of Tape-Recorded Verbal Reinforcers on the Bar-Pressing Behavior of Preschool Children in a Real-Life Situation." *Journal of Genetic Psychology*, Vol. 105 (1964), pp. 311–31. **94**

Baron, Alan, see Antonitis, Frey, and Baron (1964).

Bee, Helen L., see Maccoby and Bee (1965).

Bereiter, C. "Fluency Abilities in Pre-School Children." *Journal of Genetic Psychology*, Vol. 98 (1961), pp. 47–48. **95**

Bernstein, B. "Social Class and Linguistic Development: A Theory of Social Learning." In A. H. Halsey, Jean Floud, and C. A. Anderson, eds., *Education, Economy, and Society*. New York: The Free Press, 1961. **94**

Black, Millard H., and others. *Visual Experiences for Creative Growth*. Columbus, Ohio: Charles E. Merrill, 1968. **88**

Bloom, Benjamin S., ed. *Taxonomy of Educational Objectives: Handbook I, Cognitive Domain*. New York: David McKay, 1956. **82**

Braine, M. "Piaget on Reasoning: A Methodological Critique and Alternative Proposals." *Monographs of the Society for Research in Child Development*, Vol. 27 (1962), pp. 41–60. **95**

Clark, K. B. *Prejudice and Your Child*. Boston: Beacon Press, 1963. **90**

Conner, Orval Max. "The Effects of Neuro-Muscular Activity on Achievement and Intelligence of Kindergarten Children." *Dissertation Abstracts*, Vol. 26 (1966), p. 4493. **93**

Corah, Norman L., Sally A. Jones, and Barbara B. Miller. "The Relation of Verbal Intelligence and Color-Form Discriminative Ability to Children's Color-Matching and Form-Matching Behavior." *Journal of Psychology*, Vol. 62 (1966), pp. 221–28. **90**

Deutsch, Martin. "Early Social Environment: Its Influence on School Adaptation." *The School Dropout*. Washington, D. C.: National Education Association, 1964, pp. 163–80. **94**

Douglass, Malcolm P. "Laterality and Knowledge of Direction." *The Elementary School Journal*, Vol. 66 (1965), pp. 68–74. **90**

Dowley, Edith, see Sears and Dowley (1963).

Emmerich, Walter. "Stability and Change in Early Personality Development." *Young Children*, Vol. 21 (March, 1966), pp. 233–43. **92**

Erikson, E. H. "The Problem of Ego Identity." *Journal of the American Psycho-Analysis Association*, Vol. 4 (1956), pp. 56–121. **92**

Estvan, Frank J. "Studies in Social Perception: Objectivity." *The Journal of Educational Research*, Vol. 59 (March, 1966), pp. 320–26. **92**

Fisher, Seymour. "The Body Image as Source of Selective Cognitive Sets." *Journal of Personality*, Vol. 33 (1965), pp. 536–52. **91**

Frank, L. K. "Fundamental Needs of the Child." *Mental Hygiene*, Vol. 22 (1958), pp. 353–79. **92, 95**

Frey, Roger B., see Antonitis, Frey, and Baron (1964).

Gellert, Elizabeth. "The Effect of Changes in Group Composition on the Behavior of Young Children." *British Journal of Social and Clinical Psychology*, Vol. 1 (1962), pp. 168–91. **93**

Hanley, Charles, and Dominic J. Zerbollo. "Developmental Changes in Five Illusions Measured by the Up-and-Down Method." *Child Development*, Vol. 36 (1965), pp. 437–52. **91**

Havighurst, Robert J. *Human Development and Education*. London: Longmans, Green, 1953. **92, 94, 95**

Hendrickson, L., and Siegmar Muehl. "The Effect of Attention and Motor Response Pertaining on Learning to Discriminate B and D in Kindergarten Children." *Journal of Educational Psychology*, Vol. 53 (1962), pp. 236–41. **90**

Herr, Selma E. *Campus Outlines: Diagnostic and Corrective Procedures in Teaching Reading*. Columbia, Mo.: Lucas Brothers, 1955. **83**

James, Barbara E. "Tactile Discrimination in Young Children." *Dissertation Abstracts*, Vol. 26 (1966), p. 4797. **91**

Jones, Sally A., see Corah, Jones, and Miller (1966).

Kephart, N. C. *The Slow Learner in the Classroom*. Columbus, Ohio: Charles E. Merrill, 1960. **90, 92**

Larder, Diane L. "Effect of Aggressive Story Content on Nonverbal Play Behavior." *Psychological Reports*, Vol. 98 (1962), pp. 95–111. **95**

Lehtinen, L. E., see Strauss and Lehtinen (1947).

Maccoby, Eleanor E., and Helen L. Bee. "Some Speculations Concerning the Lag Between Perceiving and Performing." *Child Development*, Vol. 36 (June, 1965), pp. 367–77. **93**

Martin, W. E. "An Armchair Assessment of Nursery Education." *Journal of Nursery Education*, Vol. 16 (1960–61), pp. 90–96. **93**

Miller, Barbara B., see Corah, Jones, and Miller (1966).

Moffitt, Alan R., see Ryan and Moffitt (1966).

Montague, D. O. "Arithmetic Concepts of Kindergarten Children in Contrasting Socio-Economic Areas." *The Elementary School Journal*, Vol. 64 (1964), pp. 393–97. **94**

Muehl, Siegmar. "Relation Between Word-Recognition Errors and Hand-Eye Preference in Preschool Children." *Journal of Educational Psychology*, Vol. 54 (1963), pp. 316–21. **90**

Muehl, Siegmar, see also Hendrickson and Muehl (1962).

Russell, D. H. *Children's Thinking*. Waltham, Mass.: Blaisdell, 1956. **94, 95**

Ryan, Thomas J., and Alan R. Moffitt. "Response Speed as a Function of Age, Incentive Value, and Reinforcement Schedules." *Child Development*, Vol. 37 (March, 1966), pp. 103–13. **92**

Sears, Pauline S., and Edith Dowley. *Research on Teaching in Nursery School, Handbook of Research on Teaching*. Chicago: Rand McNally, 1963. **88**

Simon, Maria D. "Body Configuration and School Readiness." *Child Development*, Vol. 30 (1959), pp. 493–512. **91**

Stevenson, Harold W., and Nancy G. Stevenson. "Social Interaction in an Inter-Racial Nursery School." *Genetic Psychology Monographs*, Vol. 61 (February, 1960), pp. 37–75. **93**

Stevenson, Nancy G., see Stevenson and Stevenson (1960).

Strauss, A. A., and L. E. Lehtinen. *Psychopathology and Education of the Brain-Injured Child*. New York: Grune & Stratton, 1947. **91**

Vernon, M. D. "The Development of Perception in Children." *The Journal of Educational Research*, Vol. 3 (1960), pp. 2–11. **90**

Zerbollo, Dominic J., see Hanley and Zerbollo (1965).

Zunich, Michael. "Development of Responsibility Perceptions of Lower and Middle Class Children." *The Journal of Educational Research*, Vol. 56 (1963), pp. 497–99. **92**

CHAPTER 5

Ausubel, David P. "Adults vs. Children in Second-Language Learning: Psychological Considerations." *Modern Language Journal*, Vol. 48 (1964), pp. 421–25. **113**

—— *The Psychology of Meaningful Verbal Learning*. New York: Grune & Stratton, 1963. **110, 111**

Bandura, Albert, and Richard H. Walters. *Social Learning and Personality Development*. New York: Holt, Rinehart and Winston, 1963. **104**

Brooks, Nelson. *Language and Language Learning*. 2nd ed. New York: Harcourt, Brace & World, 1964. **101, 102**

Davis, Gary. "A Note on Two Basic Forms of Concepts and Concept Learning." *Journal of Psychology*, Vol. 62 (1966), pp. 249–54. Used by permission of the author and The Journal Press. **106, 107, 108, 109**

Ferster, Charles B., and Burrhus F. Skinner. *Schedules of Reinforcement*. New York: Appleton, 1957. **107**

Goodwin, William, see Klausmeier and Goodwin (1966).

Klausmeier, Herbert J., and William Goodwin. *Learning and Human Abilities*. 2nd ed. New York: Harper & Row, 1966. **100**

Krasner, Leonard. "Studies of the Conditioning of Verbal Behavior." In Sol Saporta, ed., *Psycholinguistics: A Book of Readings*. New York: Holt, Rinehart and Winston, 1961. **102**

Lambert, Wallace E. "Psychological Approaches to the Study of Language. Part I: On Learning, Thinking and Human Abilities." *Modern Language Journal*, Vol. 47 (February, 1963a), pp. 51–62. **105**

—— "Psychological Approaches to the Study of Language. Part II: On Second Language Learning and Bilingualism." *Modern Language Journal*, Vol. 47 (March, 1963b), pp. 114–21. **105**

Politzer, Robert L., and Louis Weiss. "Developmental Aspects of Auditory Discrimination, Echo Response, and Recall." *Modern Language Journal*, Vol. 53 (1969), pp. 75–85. **105, 114**

Rivers, Wilga. *The Psychologist and the Foreign Language Teacher*. Chicago: University of Chicago Press, 1964. **99, 104**

Skinner, Burrhus F., see Ferster and Skinner (1957).

Southwest Educational Development Laboratory. *Oral Language Development: Bilingual Education Program, Language Through Experiences in Social Understandings, Grade 1*. Austin, Tex., 1968. **109**

—— *Oral Language Development. Science 1*. Austin, Tex., 1968. **109**

Staats, Arthur, and Carolyn K. Staats. *Complex Human Behavior*. New York: Holt, Rinehart and Winston, 1964. **100, 101, 102, 104**

Staats, Carolyn K., see Staats and Staats (1964).

Walters, Richard H., see Bandura and Walters (1963).

Weiss, Louis, see Politzer and Weiss (1969).

CHAPTER 6

Abercrombie, David. "The Social Basis of Language." *English Language Teaching*, Vol. 3 (1948), pp. 1–11. **121**

Bach, Emmon, and Robert T. Harms, eds. *Universals in Linguistic Theory*. New York: Holt, Rinehart and Winston, 1968. **119**

Bailey, Beryl Loftman. "Toward a New Perspective in Negro English Dialectology." *American Speech*, Vol. 40 (1965). **117**
Beale, Calvin L., see Bertrand and Beale (1965).
Bertrand, Alvin L., and Calvin L. Beale. *The French and Non-French in Rural Louisiana: Study of the Relevance of Ethnic Factors to Rural Development*. Baton Rouge: Louisiana Agricultural Experiment Station Bulletin No. 606 (1965). **128**
Brengelman, Fred. "Contrasted Grammatical Structures in English and Spanish." Unpublished paper, Fresno State College, 1964. **126**
Calfee, Robert, and Richard L. Venezky. "Optimal Techniques for Teaching Reading to Culturally Deprived Children." A research program submitted to the Institute for Research on Poverty, University of Wisconsin, 1968. **132**
Carroll, John B. "Language Development in Children." In Sol Saporta, ed., *Psycholinguistics: A Book of Readings*. New York: Holt, Rinehart and Winston, 1961. **117**
Conwell, Marilyn J., and Alphonse Juilland. *Louisiana French Grammar I*. The Hague: Mouton & Co., 1963. **128**
Cook, Mary Jane, and Margaret Sharp. "Problems of Navajo Speakers in Learning English." *Language Learning*, Vol. 16, Nos. 1 and 2 (1966), pp. 21–30. **124, 130**
District of Columbia Urban Language Study Project Description. Washington, D. C.: Center for Applied Linguistics, 1965. **124**
Entwisle, Doris R. *Developmental Sociolinguistics: Inner City Children*. Baltimore, Md.: Johns Hopkins Press, 1967. **125**
Foreman, Grant. *Sequoyah*. Norman: University of Oklahoma Press, 1938. **122**
Gleason, H. A., Jr. *An Introduction to Descriptive Linguistics*. New York: Holt, Rinehart and Winston, 1961. **117, 118**
Goodman, Kenneth S. "Dialect Barriers to Reading Comprehension." In Eldonna L. Evertts, ed., *Dimensions of Dialect*. Champaign, Ill.: National Council of Teachers of English, 1967, pp. 39–46. **122**
Greenberg, Joseph H., ed. *Universals of Language*. Cambridge, Mass.: The M.I.T. Press, 1963. **119**
Haile, Fr. Berard. *A Manual of Navaho Grammar*. St. Michaels, Ariz.: 1926. **120**
Harms, Robert T., see Bach and Harms (1968).
Hill, Archibald. *Introduction to Linguistic Structures*. New York: Harcourt, Brace & World, 1958, pp. 68–88. **118**
――― "The Typology of Writing Systems." In William M. Austin, ed., *Papers in Linguistics in Honor of Leon Dostert*. New York: Humanities Press, 1967, pp. 92–99. **121**
Hoijer, Harry. "The Apachean Verb." *International Journal of American Linguistics*, Vol. 11 (1945), pp. 121–30, 193–203. **120**
――― "The Apachean Verb." *International Journal of American Linguistics*, Vol. 12 (1946), pp. 51–59. **120**
――― "The Apachean Verb." *International Journal of American Linguistics*, Vol. 14 (1948), pp. 247–59. **120**
――― "The Apachean Verb." *International Journal of American Linguistics*, Vol. 15 (1949), pp. 12–22. **120**
Juilland, Alphonse, see Conwell and Juilland (1963).
Labov, William. "Contraction, Deletion, and Inherent Variability of the English Copula." Paper presented to the Linguistic Society of America, Chicago, December, 1967. **125**

—— "Stages in the Acquisition of Standard English." In Roger W. Shuy, ed., *Social Dialects and Language Learning*. Champaign, Ill.: National Council of Teachers of English, 1964. **123, 133**

Lado, Robert. *Linguistics Across Cultures*. Ann Arbor: University of Michigan Press, 1957. **121**

Lambert, Wallace E. "Psychological Approaches to the Study of Language. Part I: On Learning, Thinking and Human Abilities." *Modern Language Journal*, Vol. 47 (February, 1963), pp. 51–62. **121**

Lenneberg, Eric H. *Biological Foundations of Language*. New York: John Wiley & Sons, 1967. **118**

Loflin, Marvin D. *A Note on the Deep Structure of Nonstandard English in Washington, D. C.* Washington, D. C.: Center for Applied Linguistics, n.d. **124**

McDavid, Raven I., Jr. "A Checklist of Significant Features for Discriminating Social Dialects." In Eldonna L. Evertts, ed., *Dimensions of Dialect*. Champaign, Ill.: National Council of Teachers of English, 1967. **123**

Menyuk, Paula. *Sentences Children Use*. Cambridge, Mass.: The M.I.T. Press, 1969. **117, 119**

Ohannessian, Sirarpi. *Conference on Navajo Orthography*. Washington, D. C.: Center for Applied Linguistics, June, 1969. **131**

Pederson, Kee A. "Non-Standard Negro Speech in Chicago." *Non-Standard Speech and the Teaching of English*. Washington, D. C.: Center for Applied Linguistics, 1964, pp. 16–23. **124**

Rosenzweig, Mark K. "Comparisons Among Word-Association Responses in English, French, German, and Italian." *American Journal of Psychology*, Vol. 74 (1961), pp. 347–60. **121**

Sapir, Edward. *Language*. New York: Harcourt, Brace & World, 1921. **120**

Sharp, Margaret, see Cook and Sharp (1966).

Smith, Riley B. "Interrelatedness of Certain Deviant Grammatical Structures in Negro Non-Standard Dialects." Paper presented to the American Dialect Society, New York, December, 1968. **117**

Stewart, William A. "Foreign Language Teaching Methods in Quasi-Foreign Language Situations." *Non-Standard Speech and the Teaching of English*. Washington, D. C.: Center for Applied Linguistics, 1964a. **117, 124**

—— "Urban Negro Speech: Sociolinguistic Factors Affecting English Teaching." *Social Dialects and Language Learning*. Washington, D. C.: Center for Applied Linguistics, 1964b. **123, 124**

United States Bureau of the Census. *Eighteenth Census of the United States*. Washington, D. C.: Government Printing Office, 1960. **127**

Venezky, Richard L. "English Orthography: Its Graphical Structure and Its Relation to Sound." *Reading Research Quarterly*, Vol. 2 (1967), pp. 75–105. **122**

Venezky, Richard L., see also Calfee and Venezky (1968).

Young, Robert W. "A Sketch of the Navaho Language." *The Navaho Yearbook*. Window Rock, Ariz.: Navaho Agency, 1961. **130**

CHAPTER 7

Beadle, J. H. *The Underdeveloped West; or, Five Years in the Territories*. Philadelphia: The National Publishing Company, 1873. **163**

Haugen, Einor. *Bilingualism in the Americas: A Bibliography and Research Guide.* University, Ala.: American Dialect Society, 1956. **159**

Hickerson, Nathaniel. *Education for Alienation.* Englewood Cliffs, N. J.: Prentice-Hall, 1966. **157**

Hoijer, Harry. "Cultural Implications of Some Navajo Linguistic Categories." *Language*, Vol. 27 (1951). **163n**

—— and others. *Linguistic Structures of Native America.* Viking Fund Publications in Anthropology, No. 6. New York: Viking Fund, 1946. **165**

Horn, Thomas D. "A Study of the Effects of Intensive Oral-Aural English Language Instruction, Oral-Aural Spanish Language Instruction, and Non-Oral-Aural Language Instruction on Reading Readiness and Power, Grade 1." Austin: University of Texas, College of Education (supported during 1964–65 by the Cooperative Research Branch, Office of Education, United States Department of Health, Education, and Welfare), 1964–68. **160**

Labov, William. "Contraction, Deletion, and Inherent Variability of the English Copula." *Language*, Vol. 44 (1969), pp. 718–22. **153n**

—— "A Note on the Relation of Reading Failure to Peer Group Status." *Teachers College Record*, Vol. 70 (1969), pp. 395–405. **140n**

—— "Some Sources of Reading Problems for Negro Speakers of Nonstandard English." In A. Frazier, ed., *New Directions in Elementary English.* Champaign, Ill.: National Council of Teachers of English, 1967, pp. 140–67. **140n, 154n**

—— and others. *A Study of the Non-Standard English of Negro and Puerto Rican Speakers in New York City*, Final Report on Cooperative Research Project 3288. Washington, D. C.: Center for Applied Linguistics, 1968. **140n**

Peña, Albar A. *A Comparative Study of Selected Syntactical Structures of the Oral Language Status in Spanish and English of Disadvantaged First Grade Spanish-Speaking Children.* Austin: University of Texas, 1967. **158**

Psycholinguistics, Supplement to *International Journal of American Linguistics*, Vol. 20 (October, 1954). **163n**

Riessman, Frank. *The Culturally Deprived Child.* New York: Harper & Row, 1962. **158, 160**

Sapir, Edward. "Language and Environment." Reprinted in *Selected Writings of Edward Sapir.* Ed. by D. J. Mandelbaum. Berkeley: University of California Press, 1949. **163n**

United States Bureau of Indian Affairs. *Teaching Indian Pupils to Speak English.* Washington, D. C.: Government Printing Office, 1904. **166**

Whorf, Benjamin Lee. "An American Indian Model of the Universe." *International Journal of American Linguistics*, Vol. 16 (1950). **163n**

—— *Language, Thought, and Reality.* Ed. by John B. Carroll. Cambridge, Mass.: The M.I.T. Press, 1956. **163n**

CHAPTER 8

Gardner, Riley W. "A Psychologist Looks at Montessori." In Joe L. Frost, ed., *Early Childhood Education Rediscovered.* New York: Holt, Rinehart and Winston, 1968, pp. 78–90. **170**

Hess, Robert D. "Educability and Rehabilitation: The Future of the Welfare Class." Paper presented at the Thirtieth Groves Conference on Marriage and the Family.

Mimeographed. Committee on Human Development, University of Chicago, 1964. Used by permission of the author. **173**

Jensen, Arthur R. "Learning in the Preschool Years." In Willard W. Hartup and Nancy L. Smothergill, eds., *The Young Child: Reviews of Research*. Washington, D. C.: National Association for Young Children, 1967, pp. 125–35. **170**

Luria, A. R., and F. I. Yudovich. *Speech and the Development of Mental Processes in the Child*. Ed. by Joan Simpton. London: Staples Press, 1968. **171**

Vygotsky, L. S. *Thought and Language*. Cambridge, Mass.: The M.I.T. Press, 1962. **171**

Yudovich, F. I., see Luria and Yudovich (1968).

CHAPTER 9

Arnold, Richard D. "Retention in Reading of Disadvantaged Mexican-American Children During the Summer Months." Paper presented at the International Reading Association Convention, Boston, April, 1968a. In *1968 IRA Proceedings*. **183**

——— "Teaching English as a Second Language." *The Reading Teacher*, Vol. 21 (April, 1968b), pp. 634–39. **187**

Bruner, Jerome. *The Process of Education*. Cambridge, Mass.: Harvard University Press, 1960. **182**

Ching, Doris C. "Methods for the Bilingual Child." *Elementary English*, Vol. 42 (January, 1965), pp. 22–27. **181**

Edman, Marion. "Literature for Children Without." *Library Quarterly*, Vol. 37 (January, 1967), pp. 32–45. **181**

Jackson, Phillip W. "The Way Teaching Is." *The Way Teaching Is*, report of the Seminar on Teaching, Association for Curriculum Development, Center for Study of Instruction of the National Education Association, 1967, pp. 7–28. **188**

Jacobs, Leland B. "Teaching Children More About Words and Their Ways." *Elementary English*, Vol. 41 (January, 1964), pp. 30–34. **188**

Kane, Peter E. "Role Playing for Educational Use." *Speech Teacher*, Vol. 13 (November, 1964), pp. 320–23. **181**

Kohl, Herbert. *Teaching the "Unteachable."* New York: A New York Review Book, 1967. **183**

Loban, Walter. "Oral Language Proficiency Affects Reading and Writing." *Instructor*, Vol. 75 (March, 1966). **186**

Manning, John. "Assessing Pupil Growth in Language." In Paul C. Burns and Leo M. Schell, eds., *Elementary School Language Arts: Selected Readings*. Chicago: Rand McNally, 1969, pp. 471–74. **181**

Peyton, Jim. *Nonpromotion*. Bulletin of the Bureau of School Service, College of Education, University of Kentucky, Lexington, Vol. 40 (March, 1968). **189**

Riessman, Frank. *The Culturally Deprived Child*. New York: Harper & Row, 1962. **183**

Ruddell, Robert B. "Oral Language and Development of Other Language Skills." *Elementary English*, Vol. 43 (May, 1966), pp. 489–98. **181**

Smith, Dora V. "Developmental Language Patterns of Children." In Paul C. Burns and Leo M. Schell, eds., *Elementary School Language Arts: Selected Readings*. Chicago: Rand McNally, 1969, pp. 65–75. **182**

Soares, Anthony T., and Louise M. Soares. "Self-Perceptions of Culturally Disadvantaged Children." *American Educational Research Journal*, Vol. 6 (January, 1969), pp. 31–43. **183**

Soares, Louise M., see Soares and Soares (1969).

Strickland, Ruth G. "Implications of Research in Linguistics for Elementary Teaching." *Elementary English*, Vol. 40 (February, 1963), pp. 168–71. **181**

———— *The Language Arts in the Elementary School*. Boston: Heath, 1957. **180**

CHAPTER 10

Baratz, Joan C. *Linguistic and Cultural Factors in Teaching Reading to Ghetto Children.* Washington, D. C.: Center for Applied Linguistics, 1968. Mimeograph. **193, 195**

Bereiter, C., and S. Engelmann. *Teaching Disadvantaged Children.* Englewood Cliffs, N. J.: Prentice-Hall, 1966. **192**

Engelmann, S., see Bereiter and Engelmann (1966).

Flint, Richard W. "Your Attitudes Are Showing." *Weekly Reader 2, Teachers Edition*, Vol. 38 (September 18, 1968), p. 1. **195**

Furst, Norma, and Marciene S. Mattleman. "Classroom Climate." *National Education Association Journal*, Vol. 57 (April, 1968), pp. 22–24. **195**

Mattleman, Marciene S., see Furst and Mattleman (1968).

CHAPTER 11

Bloom, Benjamin S., Allison Davis, and Robert D. Hess. *Compensatory Education for Cultural Deprivation.* New York: Holt, Rinehart and Winston, 1965. **203**

Brazziel, William T., and Margaret Gordon. "Replications of Some Aspects of the Higher Horizons Program in a Southern Junior High School." *The Journal of Negro Education*, Vol. 32 (Spring, 1963), pp. 107–13. **201**

Corbett, Edward P. J. *Classical Rhetoric for the Modern Student.* New York: Oxford University Press, 1965. **209n**

Corbin, Richard, and Muriel Crosby. *Language Programs for the Disadvantaged.* Champaign, Ill.: National Council of Teachers of English, 1965. **203**

Crosby, Muriel, see Corbin and Crosby (1965).

Davis, Allison, see Bloom, Davis, and Hess (1965).

Deutsch, Cynthia P. "Auditory Discrimination and Learning: Social Factors." *Merrill-Palmer Quarterly of Behavior and Development*, Vol. 10 (July, 1964), pp. 277–96. **200, 206**

Deutsch, Martin. "The Disadvantaged Child and the Learning Process." In A. Harry Passow, ed., *Education in Depressed Areas.* New York: Teachers College Press, Columbia University, 1963, pp. 163–79. **202**

Deutsch, Martin, see also Katz and Deutsch (1963).

Dodds, Barbara. *Negro Literature for High School Students.* Champaign, Ill.: National Council of Teachers of English, 1968. **209**

Figurel, J. Allen. "Limitations in the Vocabulary of Disadvantaged Children: A Cause of Poor Reading." In J. Allen Figurel, ed., *Improvement of Reading Through Classroom Practice.* Conference Proceedings of the International Reading Association, Vol. 9. Newark, Del.: IRA, 1964, pp. 164–65. **203**

Gordon, Edmund W., and Doxey A. Wilkerson. *Compensatory Education for the Disadvantaged, Programs and Practices: Preschool Through College*. New York: College Entrance Examination Board, 1966. **204**

Gordon, Margaret, see Brazziel and Gordon (1963).

Hess, Robert D., see Bloom, Davis, and Hess (1965).

Katz, Phyllis. "Verbal Discrimination Performance of Disadvantaged Children: Stimulus and Subject Variables." *Child Development*, Vol. 38 (March, 1967), pp. 233–42. **200**

——— and Martin Deutsch. "Relation of Auditory-Visual Shifting to Reading Achievement." *Perceptual and Motor Skills*, Vol. 17 (October, 1963), pp. 327–32. **200**

Kinneavy, James L. *A Theory of Discourse*. Englewood Cliffs, N. J.: Prentice-Hall, forthcoming. **206n**

Ornstein, Allen C. "101 Books for Teaching the Disadvantaged." *Journal of Reading*, Vol. 10 (May, 1967), pp. 546–51. **208n, 209**

Raph, Jane. "Language Development in Socially Disadvantaged Children." *Review of Educational Research*, Vol. 35 (December, 1965), pp. 389–400. **200**

Riessman, Frank. *The Culturally Deprived Child*. New York: Harper & Row, 1962. **203**

Saine, Lynette. "Evaluating the Needs of the Culturally Disadvantaged Reader in Grades Nine Through Fourteen." In Alan Robinson, ed., *Meeting Individual Differences in Reading*. Supplementary Educational Monographs, Vol. 26 (December, 1964), pp. 128–33. **202**

Smiley, Marjorie B. *A Family Is a Way of Feeling*. New York: Macmillan, 1967, 1968. **210n**

Stout, Doris. "Evaluating the Needs of the Culturally Disadvantaged Reader in Grades Four Through Eight." In Alan Robinson, ed., *Meeting Individual Differences in Reading*. Supplementary Educational Monographs, Vol. 26 (December, 1964), pp. 124–28. **202**

Strang, Ruth. "Teaching Reading to the Culturally Disadvantaged in Secondary Schools." *Journal of Reading*, Vol. 10 (May, 1967), pp. 527–35. **202**

Turner, Richard H. *The Turner-Livingston Reading Series*. Chicago: Follett Publishing, 1964. **208n**

Wilkerson, Doxey A. "Programs and Practices in Compensatory Education for Disadvantaged Children." *Review of Educational Research*, Vol. 35 (December, 1965), pp. 426–40. **201**

Wilkerson, Doxey A., see also Gordon and Wilkerson (1966).

Wrightstone, J. Wayne. "Demonstration Guidance Project in New York City." *Harvard Educational Review*, Vol. 30 (Summer, 1960), pp. 247–51. **201**

CHAPTER 12

Clark, Willis W., see Tiegs and Clark (1963).

Cloward, Robert, see Cohen and Cloward (1965).

Cohen, S. Alan. "Some Learning Disabilities of Socially Disadvantaged Puerto Rican and Negro Children." *Academic Therapy Quarterly*, Vol. 11 (Fall, 1966), pp. 37–41. **214**

—— "Diagnosis and Etiology or Operation Overthink." *Proceedings: 1967 International Convocation on Children and Young Adults with Learning Disabilities*, Pittsburgh, Home for Crippled Children, 1967, pp. 135–42. **213**

—— *Research and Teaching Reading to Disadvantaged Learners: Implications for Further Research and Practice*. Symposium, International Reading Association Convention, Boston, 1968a. **212, 214**

—— "Socially Disadvantaged Americans: Slow Learners." *The Slow Learning Child* (University of Queensland, Australia), Vol. 14 (March, 1968b), pp. 153–60. **214**

—— *Teach Them All to Read: Theory, Methods, and Materials for Teaching the Disadvantaged*. New York: Random House, 1969. **220n, 222**

—— and Robert Cloward. *Diagnostic Test of Word Attack Skills*—Experimental ed. New York: Reading and Language Arts Center, Graduate School, Yeshiva University, 1965. **214**

Cohen, S. Alan, see also Tannenbaum and Cohen (1967).

Coleman, James S. *Equality of Educational Opportunity*. Washington, D. C.: Government Printing Office, 1966. **211**

Fader, Daniel N., and Elton B. McNeil. *Hooked on Books: Program and Proof*. New York: Berkley Publishing, 1968. **222**

Havighurst, Robert J. "Requirement for a Valid 'New Criticism.' " *Phi Delta Kappan*, Vol. 40 (September, 1968), pp. 20–26. **224**

McNeil, Elton B., see Fader and McNeil (1968).

Mueser, Anne Marie. "Teaching the Bilingual to Read: Problems Encountered in the Content Areas." Paper presented to the International Reading Association Convention, Kansas City, Mo., 1969. **212, 214**

Reinstein, Steven. "A Study of the Effects of Skills Centers." Unpublished Master's thesis, City College of New York, 1967. **223**

Tannenbaum, Abraham J., and S. Alan Cohen. *Development and Demonstration of a Self-Instructional Program for Emotionally Disturbed Boys*. Washington, D. C.: United States Office of Education, OE 1–6–062528–2092, 1967. **223**

Tiegs, Ernest W., and Willis W. Clark. *California Reading Test*. Monterey: California Test Bureau, 1963. **216**

Index

Intermediate grades, reading in, 191–98
IQ, 5, 60–61, 112–13

Job Corps camps, 223
Junior high school, reading in, 199–210

Kerner Commission report, 36–37
Kindergarten, reading in, 169–77

Language
  culture and, 119–21, 162–63
  discourse and, 206–10
  functions of, 99–100, 114
  meaning and, 107, 123–24
  of middle-class families, 15–18
  new concepts and, 106
  oral, 5–7, 86, 176, 180–82, 203
  pattern changes in, 179–82
  psychology of, 99–100
  reading as development of, 169–71, 192
  symbolic nature of, 99, 102, 106, 122
  of working-class families, 15–18
  see also Black speech; Dialects; Language
    characteristics; Linguistics; Standard
    American English
Language characteristics
  of blacks, 124–25, 139–55
  of Cajuns, 128–29
  of Navajos, 129–31, 163–64
  of nonstandard dialect speakers, 123–24
  of Spanish-speakers, 126–27, 158–60
  of whites, 135–39
Language instruction
  curriculum, 4–5
  goals of, 3, 6–7, 38–39, 105–06
  grouping pupils for, 133
  modeling in, 104, 111, 173, 181
  orthography and, 121–22
  phonology and, 118
  semantics and, 119–21
  symbol-sound relations in, 122
  syntax and, 119
  in vernacular of child, 133
  vocabulary in, 117
  see also Language learning; Reading in-
    struction
Language learning
  age and, 105–06, 174
  cognitive structure and, 113–14
  concept formation and, 111
  cultural and linguistic differences in, 99–
    114, 163–64
  of infants, 204
  physiological motor skills and, 111
  pronunciation in, 107, 111
  reinforcing in, 102–04
  setting and, 105–06
  see also Concept learning; Learning

Learning
  abstraction, 106
  through conditioning, 100–04
  defined, 100–01
  laws of, 100–01
  reinforcing in, 102–04, 107
  skill categories in, 100
  theories of, 101–14
  see also Concept learning; Language learn-
    ing
Life experiences, language and, 120, 183, 193
Linguistically different child, 3, 11, 99–114,
    163–64
  cognitive structure of, 112–13
  sociology of, 174–75
Linguistic method, defined, 116
Linguistics
  language instruction and, 117–22
  methodology and, 131–32
  opinions in, about language teaching, 132–
    34
  reading instruction and, 115–16
  in TESOL programs, 116–17
Listening, as language skill, 180, 191, 193
Low achiever
  profile of, 76–78
  treatments for, 80–83
  see also Poor reader

Meaning, language and, 107, 123–24
Metropolitan Achievement Test, 141–42
Metropolitan Readiness Test, 60
Mexican-Americans
  attitude toward education among, 69–70
  dialect of, 159
  educational levels of, 58, 61–64
  income levels of, 50, 53–55, 58
  occupational status of, 58–60, 71
  population growth of, 51
  segregation of, 70–71
  see also Spanish-speakers
Modeling, language learning and, 104, 111,
    173, 181
Mother-child communication, 16–17, 33–34
Motivation, learning and, 102–04, 194–95
Moynihan report, 32
Muscle coordination, reading skills and, 92

NAACP, 23, 49–50
National Merit Scholarships, and parent's oc-
    cupation, 60
Navajo (language), 129–31, 163–64
Nonstandard English, 35–36, 123–25, 136–39,
    144–55
Nursery school, reading in, 169–77

Occupations, economic status and, 58–61